FRINGE BENEFITS:

Wages or Social Obligation?

An Analysis with Historical

Perspectives from Paid Vacations

By DONNA ALLEN

Formerly Extension Teacher
New York State School of Industrial
and Labor Relations

CORNELL UNIVERSITY

Ithaca, New York

1964

PRINTED IN THE UNITED STATES OF AMERICA BY

W. F. HUMPHREY PRESS INC., GENEVA, NEW YORK

To

Dana, Indra, Martha, and Mark

Contents

Part I

THE NATURE OF FRINGE BENEFITS

Chapter 1. *The Problem: Are Fringe Benefits Wages?* 3

The Confusion 5

Some Definitions of "Wages" 8

The Task Ahead 21

Chapter 2. *The Case for Fringe Benefits as Non-Wages* 25

Social Obligations Privately Imposed on Industry 27

Non-Wages to Provide Social Benefit 29

Non-Wages to Increase Work-Force Productivity 37

Part II

PAID VACATIONS: NON-WAGES TO INCREASE PRODUCTIVITY: THE MANAGEMENT PHASE, 1910–1940

Chapter 3. *Employers Experiment with Paid Vacations, 1910–1935* 47

Factors Explaining Early Coverage 48

Psychological Gap 51

World War I 53

The 1920's 55

Temporary Plans of the 1920's 60

Early Depression Years, 1930–1935 64

No Union or Employee Demand for Vacations 67

√ Vacation Pay Not Wages 71

Summary 73

Chapter 4. *Vacation Coverage Surges to 50 Percent, 1935–1940* 75

√ Dual Value Vacation Plans 77

Productivity Increase Is Main Value 79

Union Disinterest in Vacations 83

Contractual Plans Originated with Management 85

✓ New View of Vacations................................. 88

Summary.. 94

Part III

PAID VACATIONS IN TRANSITION: THE WAR PERIOD,
1941–1945

Chapter 5. *The War Labor Board Adopts Employer View of Vacations*.. 99

Employers Favor Wartime Vacations....................... 100

Union Vacation Demands Begin........................... 101

WLB: Vacation Pay Is Not Wages......................... 103

WLB Adopts Employer Rationale.......................... 106

WLB Permits Pay in Lieu of Vacation..................... 108

WLB Adopts "Standard Plan"............................ 112

Employers Protest Extension to Seasonal Workers.............. 117

WLB Grants to "Regular" Seasonal Workers.................. 118

"Irregular" Seasonal Workers Get Plans..................... 120

Summary.. 125

Chapter 6. *The War Labor Board Shifts Its Rationale*.............. 128

Vacation Pay Granted at Military Leave as Bonus............. 131

Vacation Pay Granted at Layoffs as Severance Pay............ 132

WLB Shifts to Earned-Right Rationale...................... 136

Full Earned-Right Logic Not Applied....................... 142

Wages Concept Not Accepted............................. 145

Summary.. 151

Part IV

PAID VACATIONS: NON-WAGES TO PROVIDE SOCIAL
BENEFIT: THE POSTWAR YEARS, 1946–1960

Chapter 7. *The Earned-Right Theory and Practice*................. 155

Vacations as Employee Social Benefit....................... 156

Employer Obligation to Rest Employees..................... 157

Vacations Not Earned Rights in Most Plans................. 158

Clauses Limiting Eligibility................................ 161

Postwar Arbitration Cases................................ 164

Arbitrators Discard Employers' Eligibility Requirements........ 168

Vacations Due Because Earned by Service................... 173

Employers Sent to Bargaining Table....................... 179

FRINGE BENEFITS:

Wages or Social Obligation?

CORNELL STUDIES IN INDUSTRIAL
AND LABOR RELATIONS: *VOLUME XIII*

Cornell Studies in Industrial and Labor Relations are research monographs developed by faculty and staff of the New York State School of Industrial and Labor Relations.

IN THIS SERIES

I *Wartime Manpower Mobilization: A Study of World War II Experience in the Buffalo-Niagara Area,* by Leonard P. Adams. 184 pp. 50c.

II *AFL Attitudes toward Production: 1900–1932,* by Jean Trepp McKelvey. 160 pp. $1.00.

III *Sources of Wage Information: Employer Associations,* by N. Arnold Tolles and Robert L. Raimon. 368 pp. $1.00.

IV *The Labor Injunction in New York City, 1935–1950,* by Jacob Seidenberg. 192 pp. $1.00.

V *Nonferrous Metals Industry Unionism, 1932–1954: A Story of Leadership Controversy,* by Vernon H. Jensen. 344 pp. $1.25.

VI *The Industrial Mobility of Labor as a Probability Process,* by Isadore Blumen, Marvin Kogan, and Philip J. McCarthy. 176 pp. $3.00.

VII *Empire in Wood: A History of the Carpenters' Union,* by Robert A. Christie. 376 pp. $2.25.

VIII *Workers and Industrial Change: A Case Study of Labor Mobility,* by Leonard P. Adams and Robert L. Aronson. 224 pp. $3.00.

IX *Hawthorne Revisited:* MANAGEMENT AND THE WORKER, *Its Critics, and Developments in Human Relations in Industry,* by Henry A. Landsberger. 132 pp. $1.75.

X *Conflict Within the AFL: A Study of Craft Versus Industrial Unionism, 1901–1938,* by James O. Morris. 336 pp. $5.00.

XI *Union Democracy: Practice and Ideal—An Analysis of Four Large Local Unions,* by Alice H. Cook. 256 pp. $4.75.

XII *Procedures and Policies of the New York State Labor Relations Board,* by Kurt L. Hanslowe. 224 pp. $4.00.

XIII *Fringe Benefits: Wages or Social Obligation?* by Donna Allen. 288 pp. $4.75.

PUBLISHED BY
THE NEW YORK STATE SCHOOL OF
INDUSTRIAL AND LABOR RELATIONS

A Contract College of the State University · Cornell University, Ithaca, New York

CONTENTS

Arbitrators' Awards Inconsistent with Theory................ 182
Few Arbitrators See Limited Vacation Right................. 184
Summary... 186

Chapter 8.   *The Deferred Wage Fallacy*....................... 188

Arbitrators Describe Vacations as Deferred Wages............ 191
"Legal" Justification..................................... 192
The Deferred Wage Theory Spreads......................... 194
Evidence of the Parties' Intent............................ 196
Arbitrators' Reasoning................................... 199
The Basic Fallacy....................................... 203
Arbitrators Discard Rest Purpose......................... 204
Conflicts with Practice................................... 208
Summary... 216

Part V

UNDERSTANDING FRINGE BENEFITS

Chapter 9.   *The Practical Effects of the Wage Concept*.............. 221

The "Wages" Test of Eligibility............................ 222
Fringe Benefits Held to be "Wages"........................ 225
Fringe Benefit "Wages" Not Allocable to Past Service......... 227
Fringe Benefit "Wages" Allocated to a Period of No Service..... 229
"Wages" Test Defeats Fringe Benefit Purpose................ 232
Involuntary Vacations Defeat Purpose...................... 235
SUB Not "Wages" but a Social Benefit...................... 241
SUB Reasoning Applies Equally to Other Fringe Benefits....... 245
The Wage Purpose as Pay for Service...................... 248

Chapter 10.   *The Dynamics of Fringe Benefit Development*............ 251

Unions Seek Equality of Social and Wage Obligations.......... 253
Employer-Instituted Fringe Benefits as Social Obligations....... 259
Some Implications—Public and Private..................... 263

Index... 269

PART I

The Nature of Fringe Benefits

→ CHAPTER 1 ←

The Problem: Are Fringe Benefits Wages?

THIS country has been witnessing a social revolution of significant proportions. In the modest name of "fringe benefits," a whole system of social benefits has been developing in private industry, reported in the press in bits and pieces and known more by its extent than by its nature and significance.

The fact that this system is developing largely through private collective bargaining is significant; never before in industrial society has a system of such scope even been approached outside of government auspices. While Galbraith and others are urging that we put more of our income into "social overhead," now that we are so productivity-prosperous, the extent to which we are, in fact, already doing exactly that has gone largely unremarked. Yet it is a remarkable phenomenon.

Many of the social benefits which unions and other liberal groups have failed to win in the form of legislation have been quietly but continually adopted privately by unions and employers in collective bargaining agreements. And employers, even in the absence of unions, have been adopting many of these benefits voluntarily. For example, despite the failure of state unemployment insurance laws to come close to benefit standards proposed by both the Eisenhower and Kennedy Administrations, this income gap has been closed for almost two million workers by private supplementary unemployment benefit plans. Private pension plans to supplement Social Security benefits now cover an estimated twenty-

3

two million workers. And, whereas Congress has rejected national health insurance, private health and welfare plans now cover over a hundred million workers and their dependents.[1]

Other types of social benefits have arisen privately in this country even when there has been no attempt to gain them in welfare legislation. A most important example is paid vacations, which in the United States have never been proposed seriously as a legal requirement, the form in which they have been won in almost all other countries.

Given continued high productivity, there may be no end to the list of social benefits to receive private attention. Certainly new ones are still being added each year as old ones are improved. It would be rash to predict the limits to this development. Many broad-scale programs have been and are still being devised to ease technological displacement. It is not impossible to conceive of private aid to local housing (without the stigma and the strings of "company" houses) and aid to education beyond the scholarship programs already under way, as, for instance, by matching tuition grants.

New ways are also being found to extend old perimeters. Companies have already felt the economic sting of proposals to raise pension benefits for those already retired as well as those who will retire in the future. In recent negotiations in the can industry, a signal benefit was won for senior workers when employer-paid health and welfare benefits were extended to retirees and their dependents, in full, just as if they were still working.

Thus, the movement makes progress in areas where the general public has not yet recognized the "social responsibility" of an affluent society.

In less than twenty years, the fringe benefit movement has quietly transformed our concepts of the employer-employee relationship by its imposition of new, *social* obligations upon those who hire the service of others. But if this is a social revolution privately imposing a new kind of obligation upon employers, the fact is the best kept secret of modern times. Both parties and all

[1]Alfred M. Skolnik, "Growth of Employee-Benefit Plans 1954–1961," *Social Security Bulletin*, vol. 26, April 1963, p. 5.

third parties take turns seeing who can deny it with the most convincing arguments.

The Confusion

Had this movement for fringe benefits been taking place through legislation, there would be little question of its social nature. But these benefits come to workers as income from private employers. What, then, is the nature of this income? Is it a part of the pay for their service? Is it "wages," or is it something to be called "non-wages"?

Those who use the term "non-wages" imply that there is a distinction between various forms of employee income payments. But when one looks for a basis for making such a distinction, he finds that no one is sure what either "wages" or "non-wages" is. Not the worker nor his employer, nor the economist, nor even the government agencies and other third parties who make decisions based upon the nature of this income can provide a consistent and unwavering distinction.

If you ask the worker himself what his non-wage benefits are, he will respond by enumerating various fringe benefits he receives at his work place. But then if you ask him what his weekly "wages" are, he will give you a figure which includes payments stemming from many of the "non-wage" benefits, such as pay for a holiday that fell during the week.

If you ask the economist, you find the same type of confusion. Although much has been written about wages and their function in the economy, there is very little in the literature about non-wage benefits and what these payments represent. The economist tends to lump all payments to labor together as "wages." Some economists do speak of the growth of "non-wage" payments in reporting on various wage studies; but, after this use of the expression, they proceed to compare average weekly "wages" which include many fringe payments: holiday and vacation pay, call-in pay, premiums of one kind or another. What does "non-wage" mean to them?

Sometimes "wages" refers to the employer's labor cost, at other times to the employee's income, though the two are not the same figure since the employer counts as labor costs certain items that are not income to the employee. It is not uncommon to find the labor economist using the word "wages" in one and the same study to mean labor cost, employee income, basic wage rates per hour, or wage rates plus some fringe benefit payments. Economists are aware of the problem, and some have called for enlightenment on this question, as, for example, "Clearly the many facets of non-wage compensation need to be explored and integrated with wage theory and economic analysis."[2] But there have been too few responses.

Employers also have questions about these payments. The U. S. Chamber of Commerce, in its 1957 study of fringe costs, noted:

Differences of opinion regarding what constitutes fringe benefits and how they should be computed indicate the need for a generally accepted definition of fringe benefits, and for a uniform method of comparing fringe benefits with employee compensation.[3]

The legislators, too, who write and revise the many laws using the word "wages" evidence the general lack of a clear meaning for the term.[4]

The problem is one both of understanding the nature of these payments and then of having useful definitions for the terms "wage" and "non-wage" that reflect that understanding.

Does it matter?

It matters very much because important decisions affecting workers' income and welfare and employers' costs and taxes hang upon the question of what "wages" are and whether fringe benefits are "wages" or something else. Interpretations of the word "wages" determine eligibility to unemployment compensation benefits for millions of workers on layoff, or how much former workers of a

---

[2]Richard Lester, *As Unions Mature* (Princeton: Princeton University Press, 1958), p. 137.

[3]U. S. Chamber of Commerce, *Fringe Benefits 1957* (Washington: Chamber of Commerce of the U.S.A., 1958), p. 25.

[4]For example, see U. S. Congress, House, Committee on Education and Labor, *Report on H.R. 10946, Amendments to the Davis-Bacon Act*, 87th Cong., 2nd sess., pp. 4, 5. The amendment reported on proposed to include fringe benefits in the act's definition of "wages." The committee called fringe benefits "much needed welfare programs" that are "bargained for, in lieu of wages,..." and therefore should be "included as wages...." A few sentences later, the report says, "they now represent a very significant portion of wages..." and then comments that the "worker receives his 'real' wages not only in the pay envelope after necessary deductions, but also in the form of these fringe benefits...."

bankrupt firm will receive, or what prevailing wage will be paid for work on government contracts. For the employer the difference means higher or lower labor costs and taxes. Third parties in industrial relations—arbitrators and administrators of state and federal labor laws, as well as the courts called upon to uphold or reverse their decisions—need to know which payments are wages, which if any are non-wages, and why.

The word "wages" is defined or used in the Bankruptcy Act, the Labor-Management Relations Act, the Social Security Act, state unemployment insurance laws, and the Fair Labor Standards Act. The Bureau of Internal Revenue lives and breathes the word "wages." It is found also in the Davis-Bacon Act, the Walsh-Healey Public Contracts Act, and other laws both state and federal. As presently interpreted, however, the definitions of "wages" in these laws are in conflict with each other, sometimes even within a single state and under a single law.

Most administrators of these laws have found that some distinction must be made between payments within the classification of income. But with so much variation in definition and interpretation, how do they tell non-wages from wages? Is there no solid, unwavering definition of "wages" which one can point to as a guide in all decisions whether they involve eligibility to unemployment compensation, payment to employees in bankruptcy cases, taxation as income or deduction as labor costs, arbitrability of disputes over certain fringes, and so on? Or, perhaps much more important, is there no such guide to aid legislators in writing or revising the laws that deal with the various aspects and effects of workers' income? At present they are forced to use terminology which has no firm meaning and which is, therefore, not only susceptible to misconstruction but may confuse those to whom the law applies. Worse, political pressure readily becomes the deciding factor as to whether a payment is to be considered "wages" or not on the basis of the effect of ruling one way or another.

At this point, inquiry and analysis are sorely needed by both the theorist and the practitioner. First, however, let us take a brief look at some of the definitions that are currently held and at the criteria each one suggests for calling some fringe payments "wages"

7

and others "non-wages." This will provide the best starting point for finding a firm rationale by which to make a useful distinction. In Chapter 2, such a rationale will be proposed.

Some Definitions of "Wages"

Wages: Pay for Service. Prior to the fringe benefit movement, "wages" had a simple, clearly understood and agreed-upon definition: pay for the worker's actual service. In those days, employee income from an employer was essentially of two kinds: first, wage payments stemming from the hourly wage rate and other payments similarly based upon production; and, second, employer gratuities not in payment for the actual productive service. Legal definitions written in that day reflected this understanding. For example, typical of the state unemployment compensation laws, written in the mid-1930's, is this definition of "wages":

...all remuneration *for personal services,* including commissions, bonuses, and the cash value of all remuneration in any medium other than cash....[5]

With the addition of fringe benefit payments, appearing for the most part in union agreements and for that reason not considered gratuities, the question arose: Are these payments a form of remuneration "for personal service"? Or are some of them wages and not others? And if so, by what criterion are non-wages to be distinguished from wages?

The fringe benefit movement burst quite suddenly upon the scene about ten years after the above definition of "wages" was written, when the government's wartime economic policy permitted many fringe benefits in lieu of increases in the hourly rate of pay. After the war, fringe benefits proliferated at such a rate that few had the time or occasion to ponder their underlying significance. We have been too busy measuring their cost, coverage, and the extent of their benefit provisions to give thought and study to their nature. What inquiry there was necessarily concentrated on their effect on workers' income and employers' costs since

[5]Commerce Clearing House, *Topical Law Reports, Unemployment Insurance Reporter* (hereafter referred to as CCH, *op. cit.*), vol. 3, Delaware, P 4068, italics added.

these matters were obviously important to the parties involved. But even this inquiry into the economic effects of fringe benefits was strictly a private venture, since in all cases government administrators were bound by a legal definition or use of the word "wages" and had to give their opinions in these terms.

As cases involving fringe benefit payments came to those who were administering the various state and federal laws, *ad hoc* decisions had to be made at once without the benefit of any broad study of what the fringes were all about. Their decisions, when rationalized in the accompanying opinions, contributed great confusion to the "wage" definition and even greater confusion to the effort to understand the nature of fringe benefits. One needs only to sample these administrators' and court rulings to see the variety of contradiction and conflict—though all were carefully kept within the legal and agreed-upon definition of "wages" as payment "for personal service."

Wages: All Income. The most inclusive definition holds that all income from an employer is "wages" in payment for a worker's service by whatever name or in whatever form the payment comes to him. Often cited in support of this view is the *Nierotko* case in which the U. S. Supreme Court, while ruling that "back pay" awarded by the NLRB constituted "wages" under the Social Security Act, held that the "service" for which compensation was paid need not be only work actually done but included the entire employer-employee relationship.[6] To give another example, the Texas Supreme Court held all income to be "wages" in payment "for personal services," including even unemployment compensation benefits provided by law.[7] Under this broad definition, any fringe benefit could be held to be "wages," according to the Texas Attorney General, as "one of the inducements by which the employee agreed to perform services and labor for the employer."[8]

The Michigan Supreme Court stated in 1951 that pay for a holiday not worked was "wages" under the unemployment com-

[6]Social Security Board v. Nierotko, 327 U.S. 358 (1946).
[7]Friedman v. American Surety Co. of New York, *et al.*, 137 Texas 149, 151 S.W. 2d 570 (1941).
[8]Texas Attorney General Opinion, No. WW-13. Jan. 30, 1957. CCH, *op. cit.*, vol. 9, Texas, P 8201.

pensation law as "compensation for the duties *and relations the employees assumed incident to their employment.*"[9] Yet, although this language would appear to cover all fringe payments as "wages" when defined thus broadly, the Michigan Supreme Court in other cases did not express so broad a view, allowing some fringes a classification as not "wages."[10] And the Michigan unemployment compensation law itself states that ". . . payments in the form of termination, separation or dismissal allowances, and bonuses, shall not be deemed wages. . . ."[11]

The broad definition of "wages" as all income was found by most administrators of both federal and state laws to be too restricting. Although the rationales given for various limitations ranged, as we shall see, from the legalistically technical to the lofty, it was politically necessary or desirable to rule certain fringe benefits to be "wages" but others not to be, depending upon the effect the determination would have. Thus, under the unemployment compensation laws, terminal vacation payments were usually held to be "wages" in order to disqualify laid-off workers in receipt of such pay from unemployment benefits,[12] while supplementary unemployment benefits (SUB) were often ruled not to be "wages" in order to qualify workers. For example, when Vermont ruled on SUB, it took note of the *Nierotko* case mentioned above, but then denied that "wages" meant pay for service stemming from the entire employer-employee relationship. Pointing out that holding SUB to be "wages" would disqualify workers for unemployment compensation, Vermont said:

. . . only by the most restrictive interpretation could the added benefits be called "remuneration for service" and we do not propose to resort

[9]General Motors Corporation v. Michigan Unemployment Compensation Commission. Michigan Supreme Court. Oct. 1, 1951. Bureau of National Affairs, *Labor Relations Reference Manual* (hereafter referred to as *LRRM*) (Washington: BNA, 1935 to date), vol. 28, p. 89, italics added. Throughout this chapter, examples are meant only to illustrate a view held at some time and not to indicate any definitive or necessarily current view, although in some cases a reversal, a reinterpretation, or a subsequent change in the law may be noted.

[10]For example, see Mooney v. Unemployment Compensation Commission, 336 Mich. 344, 58 N.W. 2d 94 (1953).

[11]CCH, *op. cit.*, vol. 5, Michigan, P 4103.

[12]See Chapter 9 which discusses this situation in more detail.

10

to that type of interpretation to defeat a plan which has obvious social-economic benefits. . . .[13]

The U. S. Supreme Court also gave a less restricting definition of "wages" than in its *Nierotko* decision in reference to another law, the federal Bankruptcy Act. Under that law, the holding of a fringe benefit payment to be "wages" would give it priority in payment to workers over the debts owed other creditors of a bankrupt firm. The majority found, in the *Embassy Restaurant* case in 1959, that employer contributions to a welfare fund were not "wages" due the workers under the act, explaining that since workmen's compensation debts had been given a different status in the legislative history of that act,

It is therefore evident that not all types of obligations due employees from their employers are regarded by Congress as being within the concept of wages, even though having some relation to employment.[14]

On the other hand, the definition held by the Court minority of Black, Douglas, and Warren, that "wages" should include all payments to employees except gifts, would have brought about the distribution of the welfare fund moneys among the former workers of the bankrupt Embassy Restaurant.[15]

In 1962, legislation was introduced and supported by liberals in Congress to broaden the definition of "wages" as used in the Davis-Bacon Act to include fringe benefit payments. The main effect of this change would be to increase the "prevailing wage" and the overtime rate to be paid by employers with government contracts in the construction industry. Employers with union agreements favored the proposal as a protection to their competitive position, while non-union contractors and conservatives in Congress opposed it on the grounds that it would raise labor costs. No one on either side, nor the legislators, to judge by the testimony given and by the House Education and Labor Committee Report on the bill, seemed to care much whether fringe benefits really were "wages," even if they had had a definition of

[13]Vermont Attorney General Opinion, No. 224. June 4, 1957. CCH, *op. cit.*, vol. 9, Vermont, P 8090.

[14]U.S. v. Embassy Restaurant, Inc. U. S. Supreme Court. March 9, 1959. *LRRM*, vol. 43, p. 2632.

[15]*Ibid.*, p. 2634.

"wages" by which to judge. During three days of hearings, they concentrated instead upon the economic effects of including fringe benefits in the definition of "wages."[16]

Also reflecting political interest in effects, state legislators have been revising their unemployment insurance laws during the past ten or so years by adding to, or excluding from, the definition of "wages" one or another of the fringe benefits, usually without rationale or explanation. Some states excluded what other states included. These amendments to a state's law made more difficult the job of the administrators and courts who had to follow legislative intent and yet were still bound by the legal definition of "wages" as pay for personal service. As fringe benefits not mentioned in the law came before them for interpretation, they had to give some rationale for their decisions. Running through these many decisions is a general reliance upon certain characteristics to distinguish that part of income, excluding the fringes, that all agreed was "wages"—characteristics such as the attachment of it to particular service and the fact that it was legally due a worker. Do these characteristics, or any other reasoning used to explain a decision, yield a rationale for distinguishing between wages and non-wages that can be applied uniformly to all fringe benefits?

Wages: Payments Attached to Service. The necessity of relating a payment to the personal service an employee renders has been felt and expressed by almost all who seek to make a distinction between wage and non-wage income payments to employees. Not only does the definition of "wages" appear to require it, but attachment to service is clearly a characteristic of the hourly rate of pay which is based directly on such service and which, all agree, is "wages." However, very few fringe benefits relate to service in any such way. Most of them, in fact, relate to no work, as in the case of vacations, pay for holidays not worked, pensions, severance pay, and SUB, as some states have acknowledged.[17]

[16]U. S. Congress, House, Special Subcommittee on Labor of the Committee on Education and Labor, *Hearings on H.R. 9656, to Amend the Davis-Bacon Act to Include Fringe Benefits,* 87th Cong., 2nd sess., p. 27 and throughout subsequent pages.

[17]See, for example, Wisconsin Industrial Commissioners' Statement. June 1, 1956. *LRRM,* vol. 38, p. 96.

As later chapters will show, it was quickly discovered that a payment could be called "wages" simply by attaching it to previous service; it then became "deferred wages" in payment for that past service. This device renders the criterion useless. Examination of the interpretations of state unemployment insurance laws reveals that every fringe benefit that can affect unemployment benefits has been held to be "wages" in at least one state and not "wages" in another, on the grounds that it either does or does not attach to service. For example, pensions have been called "wages" in Maine as payment for past services,[18] but not "wages" in Pennsylvania because no services are rendered during the period covered by the pension.[19] The Minnesota Supreme Court also noted that no service is rendered the employer after termination of employment in ruling that severance pay was not "wages."[20] Texas, on the other hand, has held severance pay to be "wages" for past personal services.[21]

Reliance upon this definition of "wages" as a criterion for distinguishing between wages and non-wages has often become a mask for the real criterion used, which may be a prejudgment based upon some desired effect the ruling may have, varying according to political pressures. To this extent, it has provided a rationalization instead of a rationale. A later chapter discusses this point in more detail.

Wages: Payments Legally Due. There is no question that hourly wages in payment of personal services performed for an employer

[18]This was the ruling of the Maine Employment Security Commission, until overruled by the Maine Supreme Judicial Court, in Dubois v. Maine Employment Security Commission. April 25, 1955. CCH, *op. cit.*, vol. 5, Maine, P 8119.

[19]Keystone Mining Co. v. Board of Review, 167 Pa. Super. Ct. 256, 75 A. 2d 3 (1950). Revision in the law in 1959 changed the treatment of pension payments but did so without mentioning the term "wages." CCH, *op. cit.*, vol. 8, Pennsylvania, P 4104. It is of interest to note also that the current Pennsylvania law defines "wages" as "all remuneration...paid by an employer to an individual with respect to his employment except that the term 'wages' shall not include...," *ibid.*, P 4028. This provides a broad definition with specific exceptions and does not attach "wages" to personal services as the definitions in most state unemployment insurance laws do.

[20]Ackerson and Hendrichs v. Western Union Telegraph Co. Minnesota Supreme Court. June 1, 1951. *LRRM*, vol. 28, p. 88.

[21]Western Union Telegraph Co. v. Texas Employment Commission, *et al.*, 243 S.W. 2d 217 (1951).

are legally due workers under both federal and state laws. Some then take this characteristic as a definition of "wages" and hold that where a fringe payment can be shown to be legally due, it, too, can be called "wages."

The U. S. Supreme Court has thrown doubt on the value of this criterion, however, by holding that the Miller Act, which provides that

...every person who has furnished labor...and who has not been paid in full...shall have the right to sue on [a] payment bond...for the sum or sums justly due him,[22]

"does not limit recovery on the statutory bond to 'wages.'"[23] The Supreme Court found that contributions to a welfare fund were "justly due" under the act, even though it also found them not to be "wages."[24]

Many third parties assume that the provision of a fringe benefit payment in a labor agreement makes the payment legally due and proves it to be "wages."[25] Courts have often enforced payment of one or another fringe benefit provided by collective agreement on the grounds that it is, therefore, "wages" and legally due.[26] Some unemployment compensation laws specify as "wages" "dismissal payments legally required," and the courts, interpreting such laws, have held that collectively bargained severance payments are "wages," as one court said, "since the allowance...is an obligation which the employer is legally bound to pay under the terms of the union contract."[27] A few other laws make their meaning

[22]49 Stat. 794, 40 U.S.C. § 270 (b) (a) (1952).

[23]U.S. v. Embassy Restaurant, Inc., p. 2633.

[24]*Ibid.*

[25]Chapter 8 discusses this point more fully in reference to paid vacations. As will be seen in that discussion, there has been a persistent feeling that anything that can be called "wages" can be declared legally due with a clear conscience. For example, terminal vacation pay not expressly provided in the contract is commonly awarded by arbitrators in the guise of "wages" or "deferred wages" or some acceptable cognate.

[26]Textile Workers Union of America, *et al.* v. Paris Fabric Mills, Inc. New Jersey Superior Court, Appellate Division. Oct. 30, 1952. *LRRM,* vol. 31, p. 2167. There have also been cases where fringe benefits provided voluntarily by the employer have been held to be legally due, but the practice is not uniform throughout the states. Generally, it has been held that there must be a contract creating the rights, but sometimes a unilateral plan is held to be a contract. Commerce Clearing House, *Pension Plan Guide,* vol. 1, "Employee Rights," P 7800.

[27]Industrial Commissioner of Colorado v. Sirokman, *et al.* Colorado Supreme

clear, as, for instance, the Oklahoma law which excludes from its definition of "wages" "dismissal payments. . .which the employing unit is not legally required to make by law *or contract.*"[28]

But this definition of "wages" as a criterion for distinguishing wages from non-wages is not uniformly applied, either. By such a criterion, of course, all fringes in firms not having a union contract would be "non-wages." Yet, neither state unemployment insurance laws nor the administrative agencies consistently consider, and many do not consider at all, whether fringe benefits stem from a collectively bargained contract or whether they are provided voluntarily by the employer. Some state laws, as noted above, make a distinction between contractual and non-contractual provision of a fringe benefit, while others expressly state that no distinction is to be made. The Pennsylvania law, until 1961, did both: vacation pay was "wages" ". . .whether or not legally required to be paid" and dismissal payments were "wages" only if they were "legally required to be paid."[29] Nevertheless, the Pennsylvania Superior Court had held in 1949 that voluntary dismissal payments were also "wages."[30]

Thus, the test of whether a payment is legally due provides no firm criterion to indicate whether fringe benefit payments are wages or non-wages.

Court. Jan. 28, 1957. CCH, *op. cit.*, vol. 2, Colorado, P 8129. The Colorado law excluded from its "wages" definition "dismissal payments which the employer is not legally required to make," *ibid.*, P 4015. In Pennsylvania, a dismissal payment made to employees not under a contract but by company custom was held not legally required. Referee Decision No. 618-A7-53, June 19, 1953. CCH, *op. cit.*, vol. 8, Pennsylvania, P 1995.

[28]CCH, *op. cit.*, vol. 8, Oklahoma, P 4071, italics added.

[29]*Ibid.*, Pennsylvania, P 4025. The Bureau of Employment Security notes in this connection: "In many States all dismissal payments are included as wages for contribution purposes after December 31, 1951, as they are under the Federal Unemployment Tax Act. Other States continue to define wages in accordance with the Federal Unemployment Tax Act prior to the 1950 amendments so as to exclude from wages, dismissal payments which the employer is not legally required to make. To the extent that dismissal payments are included in taxable wages for contribution purposes, claimants receiving such payments are not unemployed, or not totally unemployed, for the weeks concerned." U.S. Department of Labor, Bureau of Employment Security, *Comparison of State Unemployment Insurance Laws as of January 1, 1962*, BES No. U-141 (Washington: G.P.O., 1962), pp. 110–112. In general, the last sentence applies to other fringe benefits as well.

[30]Fazio v. Board of Review, 164 Pa. Super. Ct. 9, 63 A. 2d 489 (1949).

Wages: Payments That Are "Vested." A variation on the "legally due" definition of "wages" is occasionally given as a criterion for distinguishing non-wages and is given in almost every state in their unemployment compensation rulings that SUB is not wages. This definition holds, as one state said, that benefits payable to individuals "from a Trust Fund in which they have no vested interest cannot be considered as 'wages'...."[31] Another state in explaining its SUB trust funds explained that:

The employees have no vested interest in the assets of the Fund. Some or all of the employees may never receive benefits from it. The plan affords them the possibility of receiving benefits in the future, in varying amounts and for varying periods. It can hardly be said that such benefits are "compensation for personal services."[32]

Nevertheless, although this could also be said of other fringe benefit trust funds, not all have been held not to be to "wages," as some states have acknowledged.[33]

By this criterion it is the conditional or contingent nature of a fringe benefit that determines whether the fringe is pay for service and, therefore, "wages." One state said of SUB:

Under the plan, an individual's right to receive a "benefit" provided for in the plan is contingent upon many factors; whereas, ordinarily, an individual's right to receive remuneration for services performed is absolute.[34]

By this reasoning almost all fringe benefits would be non-wages. Perhaps the most notable characteristic of fringe benefits is that they are "contingent upon many factors." This is particularly true of pensions, vacation pay, and even holiday pay, which is commonly paid on the condition that the day before and the day after the holiday will be worked—even though of all fringes these have been called "wages" the most often. Several courts have noted that an employee has no vested right to severance pay, and that

[31]Alabama Department of Industrial Relations, Director's Ruling. July 12, 1956. CCH, *op. cit.*, vol. 1A, Alabama, P 5501.

[32]New Jersey Attorney General Formal Opinion, No. 39–1955. Nov. 10, 1955. *LRRM*, vol. 36, p. 223.

[33]See, for example, Industrial Commissioner of New York. Opinion dated Oct. 7, 1955. *LRRM*, vol. 36, p. 225.

[34]Oklahoma Attorney General Opinion. June 28, 1956. CCH, *op. cit.*, vol. 8, Oklahoma, P 8084.

it, therefore, can not be "wages," if the worker is not eligible for it when he quits or is discharged for cause.[35] The same should be true of the payment of accrued vacation pay at such employment termination; yet these payments are usually held to be "wages."[36] But not all states consider the non-vested or conditional nature of fringe benefits to be significant. Utah's unemployment compensation law excludes the following from its definition of "wages": pensions, sickness or accident disability payments, and medical and hospitalization expense connected with such disability, whether or not paid through a trust fund.[37]

The same confusion is apparent elsewhere than in the administration of unemployment insurance laws. In testimony on the proposed amendment to the Davis-Bacon Act mentioned earlier, the Secretary of Labor commented that because of the act's

requirement that wages be paid "unconditionally" the Department of Labor has not interpreted the term as including fringe benefits, unless the employees have a vested right in them. Only those fringe benefits unconditionally paid, such as vacation allowances, have been considered wages.[38]

Vacations are presently included, he said, "because they are vested in the particular worker."[39] Yet many, if not most, of them in the construction industry are provided through trust funds.

The Secretary apparently did not feel that the conditional or non-vested nature of fringe payments ought to be a distinguishing criterion. Fringe benefits should be defined as "wages" in the Davis-Bacon Act, he said, because fringe benefits are "a form of compensation" and an "important part of the wage structure, regardless of the form which these benefits take."[40] Rather than holding fringe benefits in trust funds to be non-wages, this proposed amendment would, in fact, count them as "wages" *only*

[35]For example, see Globe Democrat Publishing Co. v. Industrial Commission, *et al.* St. Louis Court of Appeals. May 7, 1957. *LRRM,* vol. 40, p. 142. See also Ackerson and Hendrichs, *op. cit.,* pp. 88–89.

[36]See Chapter 7 which discusses the extent of this practice.

[37]CCH, *op. cit.,* vol. 9, Utah, P 4090. In another provision of the law, added in 1959, benefits are to be reduced by 50 percent for those receiving a pension from the employer. *Ibid.,* P 4004.

[38]*Hearings on H.R. 9656, to Amend the Davis-Bacon Act to Include Fringe Benefits,* p. 13.

[39]*Ibid.,* p. 35.   [40]*Ibid.,* p. 13.

17

where they are paid through a trust fund.[41] The Secretary even cited their conditional nature, saying that pensions "may be vested or non-vested but they are not like benefits that are payable in particular terms of money at the time." Pension trust funds, he said, are generally "only payable in the future."[42] By this logic, the contingent nature of fringe benefits is important, but once the conditions are met, the fringes would be unconditionally due and would then be "wages."[43]

Obviously, consideration of whether a fringe benefit is non-vested, whether it is paid through a trust fund, or whether it is a conditional or contingent payment has yielded no reliable criterion to distinguish non-wages from wages.

Non-Wages: Payments for Purposes Other Than for Service. Despite the commonly used definitions discussed above, as well as many others of a more limited application,[44] no firm criterion applicable to all fringes and for all laws is yet in evidence. Wages as pay "for personal services" remains the only firm and agreed-upon definition; yet its characteristics, as applied, have not been helpful in determining what fringe benefits are—unless no fringe benefits are "wages" to pay for service and all have some other purpose. This idea that all fringe benefits might be "non-wages" has never been suggested, however, although its opposite, that all fringes are "wages," has occasionally been proposed, as discussed above.

Nevertheless, the use of a definition that limits "wages" to payment for service, while allowing for a "non-wages" category for income that is not in payment for service, has at least been

---

[41]*Ibid.*, p. 1.

[42]*Ibid.*, p. 35.

[43]Idaho's SUB Opinion commented: "...no one is certain of ever receiving benefits from the fund and the benefits which any employee may receive are not necessarily related to the services rendered by him. Of course, on qualifying for benefits under the Plan, the expectancy of the employee is replaced by a vested right." Idaho Attorney General Legal Opinion. August 16, 1957. *Supplementation of Unemployment Benefits, Federal and State Rulings, Statutes and Cases in Full Text,* 2nd ed. (hereafter referred to as *SUB*) (Washington: Industrial Union Department, AFL-CIO, 1957), p. 62.

[44]Montana, for example, suggested that SUB is not wages because, among other reasons, SUB is a form of insurance whereas wages are remuneration for services. Official Interpretation No. 85, Adopted by the Montana Unemployment Compensation Commission. June 28, 1957. CCH, *op. cit.,* vol. 6, Montana, P 8137.

hinted. A New Jersey court, finding that sickness disability benefits were not "wages" under that state's unemployment insurance law, stated:

...the act places the status of wages only on those monies which represent remuneration for service rendered and which are paid *for* employment rather than *because* of employment.[45]

What are monies paid "because of" employment? The wording seems to suggest a category of payments occasioned by the existence of the employment relationship which are not payment "for" the actual service rendered during it but which are paid for some other reason or purpose. Gratuities may be such payments, but it is not generally considered that sickness benefits are gratuities. Nor is SUB so considered.

Missouri implied that SUB was a payment made "because of" employment. It cited the New Jersey court's language as providing a definition of "wages" applicable to SUB. It said:

Under the authority of this case, only the consideration paid *for* employment and not *because* of employment, constitutes wages. Applying such a definition to the term "wages" with reference to "remuneration," the receipt of benefits under the plan would not constitute wages since the benefits would not be paid *for* employment.[46]

As noted earlier, Vermont rejected the broad definition of all income as "wages" in payment for service in order to find that SUB, though income, was not pay for service because it had a different purpose, namely, the same purpose as the unemployment compensation law.

But use of a payment's purpose as a criterion for distinguishing between income payments appears to be another case of rationalization after the fact. In rejecting the *Nierotko* definition as too inflexible, Vermont seemed concerned principally about the effect of its ruling, noting that the *Nierotko* decision was aimed at making benefits (social security credits) available to the employee, and, if the same definition of wages were used in the SUB case, benefits (unemployment compensation) would be denied.[47] Yet

---

[45]Bartholf v. Board of Review, 36 N.J. Super. 359, 115 A. 2d 624 (1955), italics in original.

[46]Missouri Attorney General Opinion. June 21, 1956. *SUB*, p. 119, italics in original.

[47]Vermont Attorney General Opinion.

19

Vermont, like almost all other states, laid great stress on the coincidence of purpose between SUB and unemployment compensation, adding, "and legal niceties are not appropriate to defeat this worthwhile end."[48]

In any case, the "purpose" criterion was not applied uniformly to the various fringe benefits, even where it was used. For example, the California Unemployment Insurance Appeals Board, without inquiring into the purpose for which the other payments had been negotiated, said in its decision on SUB:

The declared purpose of the Chrysler Corporation plan is to *supplement* state unemployment insurance benefits to specified levels and not to replace or duplicate them, which is the nature of vacation pay and severance and in-lieu-of-notice payments.[49]

In Missouri, which had cited the "for" and "because of" distinction as a definition determining that SUB is not "wages" because it is not "for" employment, the law itself prevented the application of this criterion to all fringe benefits by containing a clause stating: "Vacation pay and holiday pay shall be considered as wages. . . ."[50]

Despite these limitations upon the use of a criterion based upon whether a payment was "for" employment or had some other purpose or reason for being paid, the "purpose" criterion was sometimes used with real clarity. The Minnesota Supreme Court, holding that severance pay was not "wages," noted a different purpose than pay for service. The purpose of a severance payment, it said, was:

Partial compensation for loss of seniority rights; loss of possible pension rights; compensation for retraining or acquiring new skills; and many others could be mentioned.[51]

Others who used the "purpose" criterion were less clear. In one case, for instance, a payment made to an employee to meet a guaranteed annual wage in the absence of sufficient work during the year was held to be "wages" because, the court said, "It served

[48]*Ibid.*

[49]California Unemployment Insurance Appeals Board, Benefit Decision No. 6540. Oct. 18, 1957. *LRRM*, vol. 40, p. 18, italics in original.

[50]CCH, *op. cit.*, vol. 6, Missouri, P 4034.

[51]Ackerson and Hendrichs.

the same purpose as 'wages' to the recipient in that it helped him to meet the expenses of living. . . ."[52] The fact that this is true of all other fringe benefits did not bother the court.

Sometimes consideration of the purpose of a fringe benefit payment seemed only to add confusion. A Pennsylvania court considered pensions with reference to the purpose of unemployment compensation benefits. But it held that "since the pensioner performs no services during the period covered by the pension payments," a pension is not "wages" in payment for personal services. What, then, is the purpose of pensions? "The purpose of a pension plan," this court said, "is 'to pay additional compensation for services rendered in the past. . . .'"[53]

The Task Ahead

The use of myriad definitions of "wages," with the variability in the application of each on a law-by-law, fringe-by-fringe, and case-by-case basis, has added nothing but confusion to the question of what the term "wages" means and whether fringe benefit payments are "wages" or "non-wages." Worse, these conflicting definitions and interpretations have obscured almost hopelessly the real nature of these new "fringe" income payments.

Efforts by the parties to state the nature and purpose of the fringe benefits they negotiated have been to no avail. Not only have the parties often disagreed in their statements on the purposes of various fringe benefits in arguments before administrative agencies, courts, and other third parties, but even when they did agree, the administrators and others often dismissed the assertions. Note was taken by some states of the fact that the parties had stated in certain SUB plans: "Neither the Company's contributions nor any Benefit paid under the Plan shall be considered a part of any employee's wages for any purpose."[54] But then the state authorities might add "which, of course, is not conclusive"[55] or observe

[52]Tweton, *et al.* v. Oregon State Unemployment Compensation Commission. Oregon Circuit Court, Multnomah County. May 10, 1955. *LRRM*, vol. 36, p. 227.
[53]Keystone Mining Co.
[54]Massachusetts Attorney General Opinion. August 1, 1955. CCH, *op. cit.*, vol. 5, Massachusetts, P 8188.
[55]Oklahoma Attorney General Opinion.

that, after all, the parties could say anything they wished in the plan but that the agency had to go beyond these statements and, as one state said, consider certain other evidence "which may not be casually disposed of."[56] But in reference to most fringe benefits, rarely did a third party examine the nature of the payments themselves.

In any event, none of these third parties was called upon to make a judgment on *all* fringe benefit payments. Nor were they prepared to. Nor, probably, did they wish to. The flexibility of having no firm definitions and no firm criteria may have distinct advantages for those in public positions and for those whose livelihood depends in part or whole upon the acceptability of their decisions. In fact, great flexibility is necessary when the guidelines are faulty, to allow maneuvering room for the conscientious and insightful third parties.

This survey of the confusion that exists on this question leads inexorably to the conclusion that some degree of precision must be introduced into the terms "wages" and "non-wages" to avoid a situation where what is favorable today may be unfavorable tomorrow—the inevitable result of deciding these questions on the basis of a given ruling's effect, or on subjective judgments as to how justice may be done, or on the basis of technicalities far from the intent of the parties or from the interest of the general public. This is not to say that complete standardization of terminology and interpretation can, or should, ever be attained. In a field as dynamic as industrial relations, rigidity is as much to be avoided as happenstance. Yet it would seem that the real danger is that, for want of any firm criteria, decisions as to the nature of wage and non-wage payments will continue to be almost completely fortuitous or will be decided by political pressures.

The basic fault lies not so much with those who are called upon to make these *ad hoc* decisions relative to one fringe at a time as with the lack of a broad consideration of all fringes, based upon an understanding of what the fringe benefit movement really represents. The laws can better say what they mean, but before they can do so, legislators must know something of the nature of

[56]California Unemployment Insurance Appeals Board, *op. cit.*, p. 17.

22

the various income payments they are to deal with. All of the laws need to be updated to take realistic cognizance of the fringe benefit age and not rely on terminology that no longer has adequate definition. Legal definitions will of necessity be slow in evolving. But if some analytical approach can be developed, a beginning can be made toward a rationale which may eventually enable the legislators to speak in terms all can understand and to accomplish more effectively what they intend should be public policy.

Starting with the agreement that "wages" are certainly the hourly rate of pay and such other payments as are clearly based on production, Chapter 2 proposes a rationale which takes the intent of the parties as the proper beginning point and considers the purpose for the addition of each new "fringe" in the spectrum of employee income payments.

In Chapters 3 through 8, this rationale is tested and illustrated in reference to the actual development of the first, and now the most widely adopted, fringe benefit to arise privately, the one upon which the current theories of fringe benefits as "wages" were based and from which they then spread to other fringe benefit payments. No understanding of the fringe benefit movement and what fringe payments are is possible without a study of paid vacations not only because it was here that the whole "wage" controversy began but because the story of vacations, by virtue of its long development through every stage a fringe benefit can pass through, supplies the standard by which all fringes may be judged.

In the final two chapters we return again to the fringe benefit movement as a whole to make further analysis from the vantage point of this standard and to reapply the criterion Chapter 2 proposes to the problems facing both theorist and practitioner that we have just been discussing. In particular, the last chapter deals in more general terms with the significance of the fringe benefit movement itself and with the dynamics of fringe benefit development.

Our goal throughout is to find some order in the chaos and to achieve some of the understanding that is so badly needed. If we indeed have a social revolution occurring in private industry, we must not haphazardly force it into some statutory definition of "wages" set up before the fringe benefit movement was even dreamed of nor, as is now being done, deny that the fringe benefit movement has any social significance by simply calling these payments part of income or part of wages for actual service which just happen to be taken, for some unexplained reason, in these unusual forms. Rather let us inquire directly into the social purpose and the social nature of these fringes by considering what was intended by the parties who created the troublesome fringe benefits in the first place.

CHAPTER 2

The Case for Fringe Benefits as Non-Wages

ALTHOUGH more widely provided than most people realize, fringe benefits before World War II were rare among union demands and where they did appear on the bargaining agenda had a low priority. Fringe benefits for the most part were thought of as employer gratuities, appreciated, perhaps, but not the answer to workers' more pressing need for a higher money wage for the essentials of life, food, rent, and clothing. Following the lean years of the long depression, workers' emphasis during World War II was still on increasing their money income, but just as their bargaining power was strengthened by wartime full employment, their goal was blocked.

The government's wartime economic policy of limiting wage increases diverted union demands toward every non-wage benefit so far imagined. The War Labor Board then permitted many of these benefits, on the "fringe" of wages, as it said, on the grounds that since they were not wage rate increases but were social in nature, they were not inflationary and could be permitted. The WLB was careful to point out these characteristics of fringe benefits, since the distinction justified its wartime policy of permitting them during the wage freeze. Some of the payments, the Board noted, simply provided time off and did not add income to the worker's total for the year, as in the case of paid vacations and paid holidays where such time had not previously been taken off without pay. Such benefits did represent an additional cost to the employer, but the WLB explained that this possible inflationary effect was more than offset by the social effects which would result in additional employee productivity. Sick leave plans, holidays, and vacations were to restore or to rest an employee for greater productivity in the succeeding work period.[1]

If the fringe benefit movement was thus initiated by the unions perhaps as much by default as by choice, its initiation was at least announced on the grounds of the social effects of fringe benefits and because they were *not* a wage increase. But the wartime prosperity was an essential ingredient; it was felt in terms of an abundant supply of good paying jobs with lots of overtime. Many workers were quite content to receive an extra week of paid vacation or a sick leave plan in lieu of higher wages, even though it still might not have been the worker's choice if he had been given a choice. And fringe benefits newly tasted were whetting an appetite for more.

After the war, it was the continuation of prosperity and full employment that determined that the fringe benefit movement was here to stay and was no temporary wartime wage substitute. The postwar period of prosperity was sufficiently long and sufficiently great to support not only a higher economic standard of living but also a higher standard of social welfare. Workers began to turn in a positive way toward securing a greater measure of social benefit and security.

Political activity by unions for social legislation during and immediately after the war was notable, but so was the attack upon them for it. As one after another of their efforts failed—from Social Security improvements to national health insurance—private bargaining for fringe benefits—from pensions to health and welfare funds—increased.

Realistically, there probably was no political alternative to the private approach, given the considerable economic power of some unions and the limited political power of the labor movement as a whole. The very prosperity that makes social gains as well as money gains possible is, perhaps ironically, the same period in which legislative gains in the social field become least possible

[1] See Chapter 5 for fuller discussion of wartime wage and fringe benefit policy.

and tax increases to support them virtually impossible. Tax moves at such a time are in the direction of reducing business taxes and of making the tax structure less, not more, progressive. The cry at these times is for a reduction in social spending in the name of economy and budget balancing.

As the experience of the immediate postwar years bears out, the leveling of taxes on the "excess profits" resulting from increased productivity is politically the most unlikely event of all. Those who would be subject to such taxes are often the ones who stand the firmest against increasing the social costs of government and are the most vocal in calling for budget balancing. Yet, this is the same money which has been financing the private fringe benefit movement in its major impact. There is an economic logic to the situation where the prosperity that makes social legislation impossible has made the private developments possible.

Unable to get political support for social legislation, the unions sought their social gains in the only way open to them. The money which the long period of increasing productivity was making available for such gains did not lie in the tax revenue columns of the federal budget but in the profit columns of the companies the unions dealt with. The social benefits were negotiated into private contracts.[2]

Social Obligations Privately Imposed on Industry

In these private contracts, workers fixed upon the very industries which most persistently opposed social legislation the same kind of obligation to provide social benefits that public measures would have fixed upon those industries.[3] The differences were differences only in extent, as a few comparisons will illustrate.

[2]This is not to say that these organized employers did not have some good reasons of their own for yielding to the private demands in preference to legislated social gains, as will be discussed later. Using their profits from the increasing productivity for their own employees was, of course, more advantageous to them than paying it in taxes for social benefits that would go to workers in other industries, particularly to those in low-productivity industries or even to the unemployed, with perhaps very few of their own relatively high-paid workers receiving any of the benefits directly.

[3]Of course, not all of the fringe benefits privately negotiated would have received public attention in any case. The comparison here is only with those which might have been legislated.

The Supreme Court decision that pensions were negotiable gave the stamp of approval to the unions' concept of employer responsibility for keeping former employees financially secure in their old age. It had already been recognized in the social security legislation, but on a shared basis for workers as a group and industry as a whole. The private pension plans imposed this same social obligation on individual employers for their individual workers and not always on a shared basis—the move for non-contributory pension plans places the obligation entirely upon the employer.

In the case of health and welfare plans, the privately negotiated benefits have established an industry social obligation, not yet imposed publicly, to pay part of the costs of the illnesses of its individual workers. Workmen's compensation had previously fixed industry's responsibility for protecting its employees only from the economic hazard of job-connected injuries or illnesses.

Supplementary unemployment benefits extend an industry obligation already publicly recognized, but the new plans for health care for retired employees impose a social responsibility upon industry which, even on a shared basis, Congress is still considering whether to make public policy.

Social in origin and in concept, the fringe benefit movement was advanced in the postwar period by conscious choice of employees and their unions. With wage controls gone after the war, there was no question that workers were seeking fringe benefits by choice. By the fourth yearly round of postwar bargaining in 1949, the fringe benefit movement was in full swing. This time, unlike during the war period, it was the workers themselves who were limiting the wage increases and asking more fringe benefits. With money available for both, the workers made clear they did not want to take it all in wage rate increases; they repeatedly rejected employer offers of an equal amount in wage increases where such offers were tendered. The preference for social benefits was strong enough to cause long strikes, such as the 103-day UAW-Chrysler strike for pensions, and legal actions pressed to the highest courts, as in the case of the Steelworkers for pensions.

Underlying these decisions to divide the available money be-

28

tween wages and social benefits was the growing belief that the employer had two obligations attendant upon his use of workers' services: the first was to compensate workers adequately for the actual service they rendered, at the rate of so much per hour; and then, beyond this, to assume certain obligations of a social nature essentially unrelated to production but existing because of the employment relationship. Those who hired the labor of others took on certain social responsibilities pertaining to the needs of the man in his life off the job and in the society of which he was a part.[4]

The social nature of fringe benefits becomes most apparent upon close examination of them.

Non-Wages to Provide Social Benefit

In examining these fringe benefit payments, our criterion is the purpose for the payment. To learn what the parties intended in negotiating them, we take first those payments which have been the result of employee or union demands. Later we shall consider labor cost items which the employer voluntarily incurs. These include some of the same payments which have resulted from union demands, and we shall then inquire into the employer's reasons for making these same payments.

So that our "purpose" criterion may make a useful and reliable distinction between wages and non-wages, we compare the various fringe benefit payments with what all agree to be "wages": all payments made for the purpose of compensating a worker for his actual personal service, including not only the hourly rate of pay but piecework payments, incentive earnings, production bonuses,

[4]As derived from Webster's "cooperative relationships [of an individual] with one's fellows" and "pertaining to human relationships in general," the word "social" is used broadly here to comprehend man's needs as they are determined by and in association with his fellows: family, friends, and community—by standards which they set up together. It is like the use of the word "social" in such terms as "social security," where the benefit is seen accruing to individuals as part of society, and hence to the benefit of society as a whole. However, in the case of each fringe called a social benefit, the sense in which it is "social" will be noted.

The social needs are sometimes seen as having been created by industry (as for unemployment benefits or annual rest periods), but in other cases the employer is simply being asked to *take* a responsibility for the social needs, even though he has had no part at all in creating them (as in the case of paid time off to give jury service or enjoy national holidays).

commissions, and other payments in money or kind, based directly or indirectly upon production or productive service, which the employer intended and the employee understood to be payment for that service. In order to fulfill their purpose, these payments are of necessity directly related to productive service.

As we apply this standard, we find that all other payments and costs are non-wages (with a minor exception that will be noted), having a different purpose than compensation for service. We shall also find that the fringe benefit payments are related to service only to the extent necessary to fulfill the purpose of each.

The non-wage purpose of each fringe payment arising by union demand is to provide workers certain social benefits. These benefits are of three general types: first, the *penalty-premiums* for the purpose of establishing and enforcing a given social standard of working habits; second, provisions for *time off* without loss of customary income for certain activities which are social in nature; and third, benefits we may call *economic-hazard protections* which make outright payment for social benefit, such as those that alleviate the economic hazards of illness, unemployment, and old age.

Penalty-premiums. One of the oldest of premiums is overtime. Since we are concerned here with its purpose or function, we can ignore for the time being that, unlike many of our fringes, it got its impetus through political action and legislation. It is, nonetheless, a social benefit and illustrates the interchangeability of public and private developments of fringes, both being genuinely social in their purpose. The law provides only a minimum standard; both before the law and since, the overtime premium has been a common subject for private negotiations. Let us look at it closely with an example.

If a worker's basic rate per hour, to pay for his actual service, is a dollar and a half, the premium payment for his ninth hour, once the overtime premium is required, adds seventy-five cents. But this is not payment for his actual service. He gave the same actual service during the ninth hour that he gave in each of the preceding eight. Presumably the ninth hour was no more productive than the others; on the contrary it might well have been less productive, considering fatigue. Clearly, the extra half-time, or seventy-five cents in this case, is for a different purpose. It is for a social purpose: to give the worker a cash premium for having sacrificed leisure, under a standard that holds eight hours to be a proper and sufficient length of workday for workingmen. The extra cost to the employer is, as the obverse of the premium, a penalty for deviating from the standard of eight hours, and is required to enforce the social purpose.

Private negotiations on overtime usually intend to shorten hours and increase leisure, however often they may appear to arise out of a desire for more income,[5] but this is not the only social purpose of overtime. When passing the Fair Labor Standards Act, the general purpose in the legislators' minds was to spread work, confirming and broadening the social purpose of overtime—more men would be employed to the limit of forty hours. Again today the same goal can be seen in suggestions for an amendment to that law to require overtime payment after thirty-five hours. The penalty, it is believed, would operate to ease the widespread unemployment problem for the benefit of society as a whole. This broader social purpose is the basis of similar proposals for shorter working hours made by unions bargaining in industries suffering from technological displacement. The goal here is not to increase leisure per se,[6] but to spread the available work in those industries among the unemployed or to prevent further displacement. The

[5]Some workers may wish to increase their income either by working overtime or by seeking an increase in the overtime rate or an earlier onset point for it. This practice has often been noted, but its extent has not been measured. It is probably safe to say that it is a minority practice not more significant than all efforts by some individuals, acting alone or sometimes collectively, to turn fringes into money instead of social benefit. These are exceptions to, and do not change, the basic purpose of the social benefit.

[6]This has been stated clearly by President George Meany of the AFL-CIO in explaining the reasons for labor's campaign for the 35-hour week: "...no one— certainly not the AFL-CIO—maintains that under ordinary circumstances 40 hours a week are excessive on grounds of health, safety or undue restriction of leisure time. On the contrary, the labor movement would be delighted if 40 hours of work were available to all who wanted them. ...a 35-hour week, with increased penalty pay to discourage overtime, is essential to the present and future economic health of the United States and therefore of the free world. Our campaign is unique in that it is based wholly upon the intellectual grounds of the public welfare....We argue only that the prosperity of the United States must be based upon full employment and we believe full employment is possible only if the standard work-week is cut." George Meany, "Introduction," *Shorter Hours: Tool to Combat Unemployment* (Washington: AFL-CIO, 1963), p. 2.

31

private proposals would impose the same social obligation upon this part of industry to accept some of the costs of technological displacement as part of its cost of doing business that the FLSA imposes on industry generally for the more general economic condition—a condition for which, it is felt in both cases, industry bears the responsibility.

For the sake of contrast, take another penalty-premium that, unlike overtime, has no legislative history—reporting pay. Its purpose is also non-wage and social: to compensate a man for the loss of his time if he reports to work when little or no work is available and, as a penalty on the employer, to discourage such unreliable scheduling because it interferes with the worker's life off the job.

Suppose, for a simple example, that the reporting provision requires that if he reports for work, an employee will receive at least four hours' pay. Suppose further that he works only one hour. He receives four hours' pay. Only one of these hours of pay can be called pay for service or wages (even though the worker himself might call all of it "wages," and his employer and the Bureau of Internal Revenue might also call it "wages"). By no stretch of the imagination could it be said that he received six dollars for that one hour of work as pay for the hour of actual service, assuming again his hourly rate to be a dollar and a half. He is receiving one dollar and a half for one hour of work as his wage for that hour and a four dollar and a half non-wage payment, not for service—since no service was given for it—but for the social purpose of compensating him for the inconvenience of coming in for less than a significant amount of work and to discourage the practice by penalizing deviation from the social standard.

Other penalty-premiums, such as night-shift differentials and premium pay for working on Sundays and holidays or during a regularly scheduled vacation period, have the same kind of purpose. If vacation periods or holidays must be worked, an employee may receive double pay for the period, but only half of this is wages for actual service rendered. The other half, the vacation pay in lieu of time off or the holiday premium pay, is a penalty payment to discourage deviation from an accepted social norm in work scheduling and a premium to the employee who is required to sacrifice his actual vacation or holiday. Payments "in lieu of notice" at employment termination state their purpose in the name given them; their non-wage and social nature is apparent—even though these payments may be called "wages in lieu of notice."

Since these penalty-premiums are so often confused with wages, it should also be noted that none of them relates to service rendered in the way that wage payments do. As we will find true of all fringe benefits, penalty-premiums are related to actual service only to the extent necessary to effectuate their social purpose. The overtime premium attaches not to the service in the ninth hour, as does the wage payment, but only to the "ninth-ness" of that hour, since it is the ninth-ness that is to be discouraged and, therefore, brings the premium into existence. The night-shift differential is perhaps most often thought of as part of the wage rate because it attaches to all hours worked on that shift. It is still the "night-ness" of those hours, however, and not the service itself that occasions the additional payment, and it does so for the distinct social purpose of discouraging the scheduling of night work or, where it is scheduled, to compensate the worker for his sacrifice of normal hours during which family and friends are free. Reporting pay arises only upon the occurrence of insufficient work after the employee travels from home to the plant. Similarly, the holiday and vacation pay premiums arise variably with the scheduling of work that is to be discouraged. It is not the service that the payment is for but the occurrence of service at that time. In the case of payments in lieu of notice, it is the failure to give advance notice that occasions the payment.

Calculation of the amount of a premium in terms of wages has also frequently been claimed to be proof that the payment is "wages." But the calculation of premiums as a percentage of the hourly rate or as "regular wages" is simply a matter of convenience and simplicity in administering the premium. It could as easily be a flat amount unrelated to the hourly rate or to the day's or week's wages. As we shall note again of other fringes, the amount of the premium payment, as well as its relation to service, is determined by whatever method will best fulfill the social purpose of the premium.

33

Time Off. In the second category of social benefits are those which make provision for time away from work for some purpose that is social in nature without the worker's suffering loss of income because of his absence. An employee asks for holidays because they are special historical or religious days that he wants to spend with his family, often engaging in community activities. An annual vacation is for the purpose of providing an extensive period away from work to recuperate from the preceding year's continuous service and to enjoy rest and recreation with his family and friends. Sick leave has the obvious social purpose not only of enabling the worker to take proper care of himself without the financial loss to his family which otherwise occurs when illness disables the breadwinner, but also to enable him to stay home instead of exposing others during his illness. Time off for voting and for jury duty are other examples of provision of time off for social use. Personal leave of a given amount and absence from work when there is a death in the family also relate to the worker's life off the job and are thus social in nature.

It seems quite obvious that "regular wages" is usually provided in these payments, often called "wages" for that reason, simply as the best way to effectuate their purpose of providing the time off without loss of regular income. A lump sum or average earnings or a figure calculated by some other method would do as well, provided it approximated customary income.

The fixed relationship between the amount of time off and the full year of service, such as eight holidays per year or so many days of sick leave or vacation time per year, merely expresses the agreed-upon concept of a normal or average need for such an allowance, i.e., the negotiated standard of the social benefit. Beyond setting the standard or extent of the benefit, the payment is quite unrelated to service. Jury duty, voting time, or sickness may or may not occur even though service is given. Thus, the payment may have some or no relation to service, depending upon what may be necessary to effectuate the purpose of the fringe.

There are certain periods of paid time off, often called fringe benefits, that do not have a social purpose and are, in fact, part of wages. The Chamber of Commerce and others list, in a category they call "pay for time not worked," such items as paid coffee breaks, meal periods, wash-up time, and travel time. Despite a superficial appearance that these payments are time-off provisions of the kind just described, they pertain to "on-the-job" conditions rather than to workers' more strictly social needs. Since the time off is in the form of short periods to enable the employee to rest briefly or perform some necessary function often related to or required by the work itself, but in any case now considered necessary to the performance of each day's work, the time periods are more accurately to be considered "work" and their payment "wages."

Negotiation of pay for these on-the-job activities is simply part of the continuing process of redefining what constitutes "service" for which wages are to be paid. Certain minor activities that are not directly productive, from preparatory activities to visiting the rest room, have generally been considered as part of "service" covered by the basic rate per hour. The expanded concept of service may now include trips to the coffee machine or lunch table as well as trips to the rest room, travel inside the plant portal to portal as well as from one machine to another during the day, wash-up time as well as time for checking out, sharpening, or putting away tools. The difference is a matter of degree. Time-study men have seen many such changes over the years and, however they analyze and label the parts, have come to include as an allowance factor whatever is accepted by the parties as constituting paid service.

A distinction may be made between these and other part-of-a-day, time-off provisions such as those for jury duty or voting which are not required by the work itself or in any way related to it but, rather, clearly provide time off for the job for a social use. The regular hourly rate is paid in the one case because these breaks in productive work are part of "service" for which wages are to be paid and, in the other, because the worker is to be assured he may perform these off-the-job functions of a social nature without loss of customary income.

Protection against Economic Hazard. This third type of social benefit makes an outright payment to alleviate the economic hazards of illness, unemployment, old age, and the like. The non-wage, and social, character of this last group of fringes, sometimes extending benefits to cover a worker's dependents, is the most apparent. It is scarcely necessary to elaborate on their social nature and purpose beyond the mention in earlier pages of their similarities to legislated social benefits which they so closely parallel— even though all of these fringes at one time or another have been called "wages."

The payments in this group also occur only as the social need for them arises and they are paid, according to the agreed-upon standard of how much economic hazard will be met with what level of benefits, without reference to service rendered. The amount to be put into or paid out of funds established for these fringes, however, may have some relationship to service, but these decisions depend upon the social purpose for which each fund was established. The amounts contributed to the funds are determined by the necessity to make the funds actuarially sound in order to meet a given and agreed-upon standard of benefits, i.e., in order to effectuate the social purpose of the benefit. Health and welfare, supplemental unemployment, and pension funds are neither invariably built up nor always paid out in relation to employees' past service. SUB funds might build up on this basis to a certain point after which payments into the fund are discontinued. All of the funds are drawn on by some employees but not by others, and by some to a different extent than by others. An employee, in fact, might live many working years and die without receiving a penny from any of the funds, though he may have worked under a contract providing all three of these social benefits.

In these respects, too, the fringe benefits of this third type differ little from their public counterparts. For example, in the case of social security benefits provided employees (in contrast to public assistance, or old-age assistance, provided others), the requirement of so many units of past work merely defines which employees are eligible for benefits and is like the minimum service requirement which exists in most private pension plans to determine eligibility. It may be raised or lowered in either case, depending upon what individuals the law or fringe benefit intends to cover.

36

Even the public benefits are expressed, in rough measure, in terms of earnings. They may seek to represent, as originally conceived, a percentage of average or normal earnings or they may reflect individual differences in past income level. The amount of the benefit, whether it is to be a minimum subsistence standard, or to recognize a past standard of living, or even perhaps to recognize financial obligations such as dependents, is also dictated by the specific social purpose.

If these non-wage fringe payments of the three types we have been discussing are negotiated by the unions to provide social benefits to the workers as a new kind of obligation of the employer, then for what purpose does the employer himself voluntarily make such payments in the absence of a union?

Non-Wages to Increase Work-Force Productivity

Under our "purpose" criterion for distinguishing between wages and non-wages, we must now ask why the employer makes the fringe payments and incurs the labor costs he does. Since not all labor cost items represent income to the employee, and yet an employer's total labor cost is sometimes given as a definition of "wages," we shall begin at this broadest point. Keeping to our same standard for what constitutes wages, we shall here, too, exclude those payments which all, including the employer, agree to be wages paid for the purpose of compensating for actual personal service rendered.

Setting aside for discussion shortly the payments of a social nature that we have just examined, let us consider the remaining labor cost items which employers customarily incur voluntarily and which unions only infrequently seek in negotiations. These items generally do not represent income to the employee and are rarely called either "fringe benefits" or "social benefits." They are considered labor overhead costs, frequently called or included in the term "employment costs." Although employers themselves differ as to what they would include, some of the more common are costs involving personnel administration, training, health and safety programs, a company doctor, nurse and sometimes counsellors, and in some cases (where not understood and agreed to be

37

part of payment for service) special employee gratuities, bonuses, and privileges such as discounts, passes, meals, prizes and awards, ball teams, clubrooms, and other recreational facilities.

These labor costs are clearly non-wage in nature. They are not compensation for actual service, even where they may represent income to the employee directly or indirectly. Their purpose is to maintain an efficient work force in operation, as in the case of the personnel costs, or to increase employee productivity more specifically, as in the case of training and safety programs.

It will be noticed that these costs for the most part pertain to the needs of employees on the job, in contrast to the costs in the social benefit groups, which pertain generally to off-the-job and more strictly social costs. A company doctor and nurse, for example, may care for illnesses that arise or that become acute on the job; sick leave or health and welfare plans, sometimes covering dependents, pertain to off-the-job illnesses.

This distinction is not a hard and fast one, however. A number of the labor overhead costs for the purpose of maintaining an efficient work force may be social in nature, as in the case of recreational facilities for use off the job, counseling programs, and the like.

But their social nature does not change the fact that the employer incurs the cost to increase productivity. Quite the contrary. He is particularly interested in them precisely because of their social effects. Seeking out new parts of the whole man is a time-honored effort to increase productivity. Paternalism is an ancient word in industrial relations, and company social welfare programs have a long history. Ever since industrial psychology became fashionable, the adventures of counseling programs have been famous and their miracles well described in the industrial relations literature.

The fact that the fringes discussed earlier in this chapter are wholly social in nature does not mean that they are not intended by the employer who voluntarily adopts them to be a means of increasing employee or general work-force productivity. In fact, long before the fringe benefit movement and today in the absence of a union, he has been granting fringe benefits for this reason.

Consideration of this purpose has also favorably disposed him, when he is dealing with a union, toward the employees' desire to put part of the available money into fringes.

From the employer's viewpoint, in the prosperous postwar period of rising productivity, putting additional profits into labor costs, which would then be deductible as business expense, was economically wiser than having it taxed as income. As between wages and fringes, however, the organized employer was not altogether indifferent, for reasons to be mentioned shortly, because, for some fringe benefits, as those in Internal Revenue Service-approved trust funds, there were further tax advantages.

But the organized employer's willingness to grant the union's fringe benefit demands did make it necessary for most unorganized employers to follow suit. And when they did so it, too, was for the same productivity purpose. The postwar period was, until recent years, a period of labor shortage. The employer who did not provide a health and welfare program, or pensions, or a liberal vacation plan, soon found his workers leaving for other jobs that did. Fringe benefits, therefore, and particularly those that required employees to build up seniority in order to be eligible for them, have often been voluntarily adopted to keep, or to attract, labor—in other words, for the purpose indirectly of increasing productivity by reducing turnover costs.

But employers also voluntarily incur these costs (or, if organized, yield to the union demands more readily than to wages) in order to increase productivity more directly, and they do so specifically because of the social nature of these benefits. The employee who can stay home and take care of his cold because he has a sick leave plan returns to work with more energy and without having exposed his fellow workers in the meantime. Other fringes have similar advantages, and, in general, the greater freedom from insecurity and worry about the financial problems of old age, unemployment, catastrophic illness, or accidents is felt by some employers to affect production favorably.

Others envision improvements in morale and loyalty to result from the voluntary provision of fringe benefits. The granting of social benefits which unions have won elsewhere is thought useful by some in persuading workers that having a union in the plant is not necessary. The worker who believes that his employer has an interest in him beyond his life on the job is a happier, more productive worker, it is said.

There are still other advantages to the employer in fringes over a further wage increase of equal cost. From some fringes the employer receives a *quid pro quo,* as in the case of severance payments, which relieve the employer of all further responsibility to the employee, or in-lieu-of-notice, reporting, or other premium payments which free the employer to exercise greater flexibility in work planning without stirring up resentments among his employees.

All these advantages of fringes enable the employer to increase the over-all productivity of his work force and are more or less closely calculated in the decision to grant one fringe or another.

Having taken all labor costs—in order to test the validity of our basic wage and non-wage distinction—and classified them (see chart) by the criterion of the purpose for the payment or cost according to the party initiating the action for it, we must also recognize that where the union is involved there may be an area of mutual advantage. A bargain is struck, and who is to say how much results from the employees' economic strength and how much from a compensating benefit the employer sees accruing to himself? We can say only that fringes which are union-initiated are for the *primary* purpose of providing the particular social benefit as such, while in fringes initiated by the employer, the provision of social benefit is a secondary, though essential, consideration; his *primary* purpose in voluntarily incurring the cost is to increase work-force productivity directly or indirectly.[7]

[7]Since a fringe is still a social benefit, whoever initiates it, the discussion in the next several chapters will refer to social benefits as "employer benefits" when voluntarily adopted by the employer for his primary reasons and, when initiated by the union, as "employee benefits."

An exception to the text above which should be noted here is the employer who, out of a genuine social sense, voluntarily incurs the cost of a social benefit expressly and primarily for its benefit to the employee. On the other hand is the occasional union which has sought social benefits primarily because of their value in increasing employee productivity and only secondarily for their social benefit. These exceptional cases are most likely to appear in small firms with only a few workers.

40

Chart. Common Labor Costs Classified by Purpose.

Classification | Purpose of Labor Cost as Intended by Initiator

Wages — To pay for actual service rendered:

Hourly rate, piece rate, incentive earnings, production bonuses, commissions, other payments in money or kind based directly or indirectly upon production or productive service and understood and agreed to be payment for service; pay for brief breaks in work activity for coffee or rest, meal periods, wash-up time, travel time within the plant from portal to portal, etc.

Non-Wages — 1. To provide social benefit as such:

a. Penalty-premiums: overtime, night-shift differentials, Sunday and holiday work premiums, vacation pay in lieu of vacation, reporting or call-in pay, in-lieu-of-notice payments.

b. Time off: vacations, holidays, sick leave, voting time, jury duty.

c. Economic-hazard protections: health and welfare plans, pensions, SUB, life insurance, severance and other dismissal payments; also unemployment insurance, workmen's compensation, and OASDI.

Non-Wages — 2. To increase productivity of the labor force:

a. Social benefits listed above when voluntarily provided by the employer.

b. Personnel administration, training, health and safety programs, company doctor, nurse, counsellors and equipment, special employee gratuities, bonuses, and privileges such as discounts, passes, ball teams, other recreational facilities, prizes, and awards.

This is the two-dimensional nature of the fringe benefit movement, the initiative resting sometimes with the employer and sometimes with the union. The significance of the difference between the two categories of non-wage costs lies only in the extent to

41

which the action taken for a fringe benefit imposes an obligation on the employer to provide it. The employer does not voluntarily incur the cost to fix upon himself any obligation for his employees' social welfare in their lives off the job, whereas this is exactly the sense in which the union makes each fringe secure by inclusion in the contract. Enlarging the concept of the employer-employee relationship, the union adds this new social obligation to the wage obligation the employer has always had. The significance of this important difference which requires the classification of the *non-wage* costs by the criterion of consulting the initiating party's purpose, is discussed again in a later chapter. At this point we need only conclude from the discussion in this chapter that fringe benefits are by their nature and intent not wages to pay for service but non-wages to provide social benefit—whether initiated by the union for its primary purpose of providing the worker a social benefit as such or by the employer for his primary purpose of increasing productivity through the effects of that social benefit on the workers.

If our basic distinction between wages and non-wages and the criterion for making it are useful tools, they should, of course, also meet the test of application to all fringes. Such an application in the necessary detail would be impossible within the confines of one book, but it can be made just as validly when applied to one fringe—if that fringe is paid vacations.

The paid vacation is, and always was, the most universal of all fringes. It also has one of the longest histories. Given to office workers for over a hundred years, vacations were first granted wage earners, who are of primary concern here,[8] about 1910. As we shall see, vacation coverage reached 50 percent of American wage earners several years before the wartime encouragement of fringes

[8]The experience of providing paid vacations for office workers will be discussed at the beginning of the next chapter because it set the pattern for the wage earners' vacation movement. Their movement grew out of that experience and therefore the differences, if their significance is to be realized, must be seen in light of the employers' previous experience with office worker plans. Beyond this origin of the production workers' vacation movement, the following chapters will not discuss office workers as such. Civil service workers, though covered by public legislation and regulations, were granted the same vacation practices as in private industry with the same differences in coverage between office workers and wage earners.

and over 90 percent coverage by the end of the war, when the general fringe benefit movement was just beginning in earnest.

Until recently, paid vacations were the largest cost item of all fringes. During the last twenty years, they have also been the most important fringe in terms of the number of controversial words that have gone into describing what they are. In these words lies the origin of the concept of fringe benefits as "wages." Yet vacations were given a theoretical justification by employers many decades before the wage concept arose. For these reasons and others, no inquiry into fringe benefits could be meaningful without a careful study of this veteran of fringes.

What of the vacation benefit? Did it originate as wages in payment for service? Did it at any point become pay for service? How and why did the wage concept arise? The answers to these questions shed light on the current controversy over all fringes, and we shall return to them again after a look at paid vacations.

Using the criterion of "purpose," but at all times keeping an eye on the paid vacation's relation to wages, let us now take a jump back into the past to examine the circumstances of its origin.

For what purpose were paid vacations started?

PART II

Paid Vacations: Non-Wages to Increase Productivity

The Management Phase, 1910-1940

CHAPTER 3

Employers Experiment with Paid Vacations, 1910-1935

MANAGEMENT initiated the paid vacation movement for employees. It did not do so, however, to compensate employees for their service, nor out of altruistic considerations of social welfare. Employers voluntarily incurred this non-wage labor cost for the purpose of increasing the productivity of the labor force. Individual employers found through experience that annual rest periods for their employees more than paid for themselves in increased employee productivity.

The first paid vacation may have started something like this. An employer whose business was running smoothly took a couple of weeks off, loafed around a bit, hit a few golf balls, and generally forgot his cares. Upon returning to work refreshed and invigorated, he plunged into work, turning out a great deal more than he'd been expecting of himself. A few hours later he lifted his eyes from the cost sheets to notice that old Fred, his faithful bookkeeper, was looking rather wilted. In a burst of insight, he realized that what was tonic for the boss might also be tonic for the bookkeeper. So old Fred was persuaded to take a week off to rest and relax; his pay would continue so that he would not seek other work or worry about financial loss during his vacation rest period. When Fred returned, if he did not burn up the ledger sheets, he at least sat up straighter on his stool and wore his eyeshade at a jauntier angle. And that month the books balanced for the first time that quarter.

The employer little realized, when he extended the vacation idea to a few more of his employees the next year, that he was launching the paid vacation movement in American industry. Though the characters in this incident are fictitious, the plot is not. It runs throughout the management phase of the vacation movement and its traces are still evident in the vacation movement today.

Factors Explaining Early Coverage

The first paid vacations were granted to executives, beginning some time in the middle of the nineteenth century. Other office employees soon followed.[1] Foremen and supervisors on a salary basis in the plant were next. More than half a century after vacations were initiated in offices, the paid vacation movement for wage earners began. It followed the same pattern of gradual extension by groups of employees. First, only the older, high-skilled, and best-known production workers in the most stable industries were given vacations.[2] Some time later, vacations were introduced for other production workers in these more stable industries. The last to receive vacations were workers in industries of the least stable employment where the employer-employee relationship was the most impersonal. Although management did not carry the vacation extension to this last step, it set the pattern.

Employers were not instituting vacation plans or extending them simply on the logic that such a rest period *ought* to make employees more productive. They insisted on seeing the evidence of increased productivity in a measure sufficient to justify the cost of the vacations. Several factors contributed to management's ability to see such evidence, and these factors determined the particular order in which vacations were extended.

The first factor was the closeness to management. Each of the groups of employees favored with early coverage was, as compared

[1] Lee K. Frankel and Alexander Fleisher, *The Human Factor in History* (New York: The MacMillan Co., 1920), p. 131. These authors noted that once vacations were "limited to the management but extended occasionally to the clerical force as well."

[2] U. S. Department of Labor, Bureau of Labor Statistics, *Vacations with Pay in Industry, 1937*, Bulletin R.903 (hereafter referred to as BLS, *op. cit.*) (Washington: G.P.O., 1939), pp. 7–8.

48

with those remaining, closer to the employer both in physical proximity and in the degree to which the employer was acquainted with production records. If the vacation did result in higher productivity, the improvement could be observed at first hand.

Within each group—executives, other office workers, foremen and supervisors, and production workers—the senior employees held first claim on vacations. Not only were they better known but the restorative effect of a rest period on older workers was more evident than it was on younger workers.

But employers not only insisted on seeing the evidence of increased productivity, they also required that the increase be sufficient to justify the cost of obtaining it. If the cost could be kept low, less of an increase would be needed. Thus, the second factor affecting the order in which vacations were extended was the degree to which paid time off could be allowed without a costly loss of production. Where the work load could be lightened, shared, done in advance, or postponed, normal or almost normal production might be maintained, and full replacements for vacationing employees need not be hired. This type of work situation was to be found in offices and for salaried employees generally.[3] Production workers, however, could seldom extend themselves to cover a vacationing fellow's work. Pieceworkers could not do it at all; any absence reflected an equal loss in production. This difference in ability to share the work load reinforced the favored position of salaried workers over production workers, and certain types of production workers over others.

The third factor determining the order of vacation extension was the stability of the employment relationship. In seeking a productivity increase, an employer would not willingly provide paid vacations to employees not continuing their employment in the following year. While the employer could not bind his employees to him as a condition of receiving the paid vacation, he could balance his rate of turnover with the vacation cost and either accept or reject paid vacations as a device for increasing productivity. Throughout the management phase of the vacation movement, employers rejected the idea of paid vacations in industries

[3]John Nelson, "Paid Vacations for Workers," *Iron Age*, vol. 116, 1925, p. 744.

characterized by seasonal or shifting employment where workers are with a single employer for only a short period, even though they may be permanently attached to the industry.[4] Paid vacations came first to industries of stable employment, such as public utilities, retail trade, chemicals, and food manufacturing.[5] Here, management had the best expectation of a return in increased production from the vacation expenditure because steady employment was possible.

Within each group to which vacations were extended, the most stable employees were covered first. This tendency again favored salaried employees and the top skilled and senior production workers whose employment was relatively steady; it inhibited the extension of vacations to production workers generally. It was well recognized that "the better class of jobs in any plant...have a comparatively small percentage of 'quits'."[6] One management magazine put it the other way around: "the average period of service of the wage earner...has been considered as too short and uncertain to warrant vacations,...."[7]

Production workers, in this early period, were much more loosely attached to a company or an industry than they are today. The "day workers," as they were called, were not expected to continue their employment year after year. A management man explained:

We consider him [the accountant] an integral part of the organization, whereas there is a tendency to think of the day-worker as a sort of appendage. When we are evaluating the day-worker we calculate his hourly rate of production, not his annual output, and unless he has proved his stability by holding his job for several years he is in our

[4]Even industries which were somewhat seasonal went without paid vacation provisions, as one editorial noted: "Vacations without pay are the rule in industries which are able to shut down for a certain period of time during the slack period of the year...." An editorial, "Vacations for Wage Earners," *American Machinist,* vol. 63, 1925, p. 142.

[5]BLS, *op. cit.,* pp. 8, 24; see also F. S. Clark, "Give All Workers Vacations with Pay—It Pays!" *Forbes,* vol. 19, 1927, p. 23.

[6]D. C. Wright, "Vacations for Wage Earners," *American Machinist,* vol. 63, 1925, p. 958. Another article noted that office workers have less turnover than wage earners and, of the wage earners, the skilled had less than the unskilled and the older less than the newer workers. "Vacation with Pay for Workers," *Literary Digest,* Sept. 11, 1920, p. 37.

[7]"Vacations for Wage Earners," p. 142.

minds as one who may be here today and gone tomorrow. And the piece worker, because of his semi-independence, seems even more of an outsider, usually, than the day-worker.[8]

In the minds of most employers, little profit could be expected from providing an annual rest to employees thought unlikely to continue working.

All of these factors, the closeness to management, the ability to share the work load, and the stability of the employment relationship, made it easier for the employer to realize a return from paid vacations for salaried employees than for production workers, and served to advance the vacation movement for salaried employees while delaying initiation of the movement for wage earners. Salaried employees were covered by vacation plans in over 10 percent of manufacturing plants by 1900, in more than one-third by World War I, and in about 80 percent or more by 1935, the end of this early period.[9] On the other hand, practically no vacations were provided wage earners before 1900 and very few before 1910.[10] Only about 10 percent of manufacturing plants provided vacations for any of their wage earners in 1935.

Psychological Gap

These large discrepancies in vacation coverage between salaried and production workers indicate more, however, than just the effects of the three factors discussed above. A deeper cause was the psychological gap between managements and their manual workers. The most significant effect of this psychological gap was that it kept management from even considering the idea of extending paid vacations to wage earners, despite its long experience with vacations for salaried employees.

Charles Mills noted that "prior to the War, vacations were regarded as being necessary for 'white collar' workers but were

[8]"Factory Vacations That Help instead of Hinder," *Factory, the Magazine of Management*, vol. 32, 1924, p. 829.

[9]BLS, *op. cit.*, pp. 4 and 9. These figures are estimates calculated from Table 4 with reference to data in Table 2, p. 4, and checked against all data available from other sources.

[10]Charles M. Mills, *Vacations for Industrial Workers* (New York: The Ronald Press Co., 1927), Table 23, p. 277.

seldom discussed for manual workers."[11] Scarcely a word of reference to paid vacations can be found in the literature on industrial relations before the 1920's. D. C. Wright observed that "since the earlier days of industry" it had

been rather taken for granted that the salary-drawing portion of an organization was to get a vacation, but any suggestion that the "hands" were to be similarly blessed, was carefully avoided.

Just why it should ever have been originally conceived that a "white collared" clerk was ordinarily so exhausted by his strenuous desk work as to require revivifying, while the actual producer, who put in long hours at shop work that frequently was exhaustingly heavy, was expected to draw his renewal from some inner fount, is hard to explain.[12]

Mills reveals the difference in psychological attitude toward plant workers with the explanation that early coverage for salaried employees was "partly because they were 'brain workers' and as such needed annual periods of rest." He explained the growing coverage of wage earners in 1927 by adding: "However, today, as much mental effort may be required of the manual worker as of the clerk or minor salaried employee,...."[13] Another writer said that vacations were granted executives and foremen because of their heavy responsibilities, "but, as labor increasingly proves itself an intelligent and trustworthy partner, it is bound increasingly to receive the perquisites and privileges that relationship implies."[14] It was common throughout this period for writers to assume that vacations for salaried employees were essential to their work, but for wage earners they were a "privilege."[15]

[11]Ibid., p. 24.   [12]Wright, op. cit., p. 958.   [13]Mills, op. cit., pp. 24–25.
[14]A. M. Kennedy, "Two Weeks with Pay?" Factory and Industrial Management, vol. 75, 1928, p. 777.
[15]In 1955, Barbara Wooton commented, "...no one who looks at the picture as a whole can fail to be struck...by the degree in which the incidental advantages of different employments vary positively, not inversely, with the monetary remuneration that these employments carry: the rule is that to him that hath shall be given, rather than the opposite. The security of tenure, the length of notice to be given and often also the duration of paid holidays enjoyed by professional and salaried employees are normally superior to what is customary in wage-earning employments: indeed it is only since the First World War that it has become customary to provide any paid holiday at all for manual workers in general." She finds the answer for these advantages enjoyed by clerical over manual workers in "the superior social standing of clerical, as compared with manual, work,..." Barbara Wooton, The Social Foundations of Wage Policy (London: George Allen & Unwin Ltd., 1955), p. 55.

The best evidence of management's "double standard" for manual workers came from the employers themselves. One employer stated:

I believe that vacations for industrial workers have no good effect since they add nothing to their industry, efficiency or loyalty, but might have directly the opposite effect.[16]

Other employers said simply, "I don't think employees working on an hourly or piecework basis are entitled to vacations," or "Our pieceworkers are all of foreign extraction and wish to work full time. Vacations do not appeal to them."[17]

Some of these employers could have rejected vacations on the basis of high costs relative to a productivity increase—on the basis, in fact, of any of the three factors which make the profitability of vacations for wage earners less apparent. But the fact of the matter was that most employers simply did not consider vacations for their plant workers. Whatever management thought of the benefits in increased productivity deriving from paid vacations for office and salaried workers, the logic of the argument did not carry to the shop floor. Formidable differences in psychological attitude stood in the way.

But the psychological differences began to break down with World War I, and vacation plans then appeared in noticeable numbers for the first time. The vacation movement for wage earners can be said to have had its beginning at this point.

World War I

It was said of the period prior to World War I that "management thinking about the conditions for wage earners has not been sufficiently in scientific and physical terms to bring annual rest periods into wide use."[18] But during the war, a national concern over increasing production focused management attention on ways and means of increasing employee productivity and stimulated an interest in paid vacations for production workers.

For example, industrial fatigue studies conducted on a large

[16]"Do Factory Vacations Pay?" *Factory*, vol. 26, 1921, p. 1086.
[17]*Ibid.*
[18]Ordway Tead and Henry C. Metcalf, *Personnel Administration: Its Principles and Practice*, 1st ed. (New York: McGraw Hill Book Co., Inc., 1920), pp. 76–77.

scale during the war had shown the distinctly favorable effect of rest upon production.[19] Also, employers who had adopted vacation plans during or shortly before the war had found them profitable. "We believe it is good business," said one, "...the expense of the vacation plan is more than compensated by the results obtained." "A mighty fine investment," said another of his plan adopted in 1918, "...a production increase is always noted." Some also explained:

Few employees can do their best without a periodical rest. The company benefits in the way of production in receiving the employees' renewed energy upon their return from vacation.[20]

A new interest in industrial relations was also beginning to bridge the psychological gap between management and its production workers. Many companies, particularly the larger firms,[21] were now ready to consider the idea of paid vacations for production workers. By the end of the war, about 5 percent of manufacturing plants had permanent vacation plans for some of their wage earners.[22] It was a small beginning, but the word was getting around. For the first time, articles occasionally appeared in management publications, extolling the advantages of providing paid vacations to plant workers. Employers were told, early in 1920:

A year of continuous hard work decreases to an appreciable degree the vitality and alertness of a worker. His former measure of effectiveness can be restored by a short period of rest.[23]

[19]Mills, *op. cit.*, p. 64.

[20]*Ibid.*, pp. 239, 271, and 269. Charles Mills surveyed 199 firms' vacation plans in effect during 1924–1926 and asked the employers what value they had found in their plans and other detailed information. The employers' replies, shown in Table 18, pp. 236–275, are used in illustration of various points throughout this chapter.

[21]"Vacations for Factory Workers," *Management and Administration,* vol. 8, 1924, p. 52. Although it might seem that small firms should have been the first to observe the beneficial effects of paid vacations on either office workers or plant workers, larger companies were financially better able to experiment with the various features of the new industrial relations programs. "...what the enthusiast often fails to take into account is the solid fact that it is only the amply financed company, like the amply financed man, which can take advantage of all the economies and make money by spending it." Kennedy, *op. cit.*, p. 776.

[22]BLS, *op. cit.*, pp. 4, 9. Calculated from Tables 4 and 2. The estimate is a rough one in the absence of reliable data. More plans than this were in effect but did not survive the 1921–1922 recession. They will be discussed, along with the rationale for them and the reasons attributed to their abandonment, later in this chapter.

[23]"Vacation Arrangements That Don't Upset Things," *Factory,* vol. 24, 1920, p. 1550.

Later in 1920, the first survey of vacation plans reported that despite the differences in employment stability and pay basis between salaried and hourly workers, vacations for wage earners were coming about largely through an extension of existing salaried employees' plans:

The advantage and desirability of giving office workers an annual vacation with pay have long been recognized, and now, without any apparent concerted action, vacation with pay for factory workers is slowly becoming established practice....The present tendency to accord the same privilege to factory help is doubtless due to the belief that what is good for office employees should also be good for the manual worker....[24]

These early reports on the wartime experience opened up the question and launched a decade of experimentation and discussion of paid vacations for plant workers.

The 1920's

Management proceeded slowly and, as noted in the 1920 survey, "without any apparent concerted action" in extending vacation coverage beyond salaried workers. Employers' insistence upon an assurance of productive return from the vacation cost often dictated extreme caution, as this comment shows:

Our plan of vacations serves as a reward for continuous service and prepares the individual for another year of strenuous work. We hope some day to extend the privilege down the line to hourly rated men who have ten or more years of service.[25]

Of the employers who were somewhat bolder and willing to try vacations for wage earners generally, many had a wait-and-see attitude, such as the one who provided vacations for 95 percent of his plant workers, cautioning that the plan was "not to be considered as a precedent for future years." He added, "It is being tried as an experiment with the feeling that...[the employees] will be more efficient for having this rest."[26]

Slowly, one by one, many of these employers were finding the experiment profitable:

[24]Vacation with Pay for Workers," p. 37.
[25]"Factory Vacations That Help instead of Hinder," p. 886.
[26]Mills, *op. cit.*, p. 269.

We inaugurated a vacation plan for our employees last year, for the first time, and we believe that it was money well spent. We shall certainly continue the practice.[27]

The testimonials grew in number. "Our experience shows that production for the year is increased,"[28] became a common report. Articles in management magazines passed the experience along, no doubt encouraging other employers to try for a productivity increase with such urging as: "What about the man in the shop? Some companies (and they are increasing in number) seem to think that he, too, is better off, and a more effective worker, if he spends a week or two of each year away from his work."[29]

But while employers continued to extend vacation coverage from employees closest to them outward to production workers, they also kept one eye on the cost of this extension. Although many were finding that "there are few instances where the absence on account of vacation does not require the substitution of workers,"[30] paid vacation plans were still found profitable. Others found that some work sharing was possible. An employer reported:

By planning vacations well in advance we have been able, in nearly all instances, to carry through the vacation period with the necessity of employing very few extra men—quite an accomplishment when you consider that 67% of those on our mill payroll are entitled to receive vacations.[31]

"Many of our employees," ran a typical comment, "work considerably harder during the vacation period in order to make the vacation possible for their fellow employees."[32]

Not only could workers be persuaded to absorb some of the work load by redistributing it, but they were also persuaded, in some plans, to contribute directly to the cost of their vacations. In some companies, savings clubs were formed by payroll deductions to partially finance the vacation.[33] In several cases, employees

[27]*Ibid.*, p. 265.   [28]*Ibid.*, p. 259.
[29]"Factory Vacations That Help instead of Hinder," p. 829.
[30]Mills, *op. cit.*, p. 239.
[31]Morris Harrison (personnel director, Hammermill Paper Co., as told to L. I. Thomas for *Factory*), "It's Time for Vacation-Planning!" *Factory, the Magazine of Management*, vol. 38, 1927, p. 675.
[32]Mills, *op. cit.*, p. 253.
[33]*Ibid.*, pp. 59–60, and "Factory Vacations That Help instead of Hinder," pp. 890, 892.

were permitted to work an hour or two of overtime (at straight-time rates) each week until they had accumulated a week of "earned" vacation which was then matched by a "merit" portion granted by the employer, in one instance on the basis of one day per year of service with the company up to six days to provide a second week of vacation.[34] All of these schemes had one aim: to provide, at the least possible cost, a rest period free from financial worries in order to secure the restoration of an employee's productive efficiency.[35]

To the extent that such plans were contributory, however, the employees were simply purchasing some leisure time for a vacation rest out of the wages paid to them for service. Such plans were truly deferred wages. Plans not financed by the employer were in no way paid vacations as contemplated here and played little part in the vacation movement. By 1930, in fact, it was noted that only three out of more than two hundred plans surveyed involved any employee contributions at all.[36]

Employers, however, were very much concerned with securing a maximum productivity increase from any allowance of vacation time off, and this required that the time be paid to assure that the worker would take the vacation. It also required the assurance that he spend his vacation period at rest and play.

One way to do this was to include, as most plans of this period did, a flat prohibition against working for the same or another employer during the vacation period. One company, adopting this as "an inflexible rule," commented: "The purpose of the plan, of course, would not be carried out if exceptions were made,

[34]Merrill R. Lott, "50-50 Vacations for Workers by the Hour," *Factory, the Magazine of Management,* vol. 36, 1926, pp. 649ff, and Mills, *op. cit.,* p. 60. Occasionally plans were found in which the employees paid for their vacations entirely, either through savings clubs or by working overtime, without management contribution of any kind, except possibly the payment of interest on the money held until the vacation period. Such a wholly earned vacation, at the rate of 20 minutes of overtime work per day up to 50 working hours, is described by E. A. Terrell, "Vacations with Pay," *American Machinist,* vol. 57, 1922, p. 692.

[35]Some employers felt that work sharing detracted from the benefits of vacations. One suggested that the shutdown type of plan was better than overburdening those workers not on vacation. All employees, then, would go at once, he said, and return "full of vim for the year's tasks ahead." F. I. Charles, "Can a Business Shut Down for Vacation?" *System,* vol. 43, 1923, p. 593.

[36]"Pertinent Facts about Vacations," *Factory and Industrial Management,* vol. 79, 1930, p. 1359.

for there would be no rest for such workers."[37] Another employer was equally specific:

Vacations are given for the good they do employees as such, not as opportunity to make extra money. So a worker may not decline to take his vacation and still receive his vacation pay—that would make it a sort of bonus rather than a vacation plan.[38]

Some employers feared that even though workers refrained from taking other employment, vacations might not be properly used for rest and recreation, as this one who commented:

We do not believe that a vacation benefits a factory worker unless he actually goes away somewhere to the country. If they just use their vacation to hang around the corners, they had much better be at work. We presume that not over 25 per cent of our men actually go away.[39]

To assure their return from the vacation cost, a number of large companies even went to additional expense to see that their employees did rest and relax. They established recreation clubs, built clubhouses, and bought vacation grounds and rest camps. These were made available to employees during vacations either free or for a small fee. At many of the rest camps, workers were permitted to bring their families. The purpose for this additional expense was made clear by one company:

We believe the Ranch to be an excellent investment. Not only are our employees better physically as a result of its experience, but their families are profiting even more...mother and children may spend as much time as they wish where pure water, air and sunlight will ward off illness for the entire year. Naturally, the less illness there is at home, the nearer to one hundred per cent efficient the man of the house becomes at the plant.[40]

Frequent articles reporting on company vacation camps appeared during the 1920's. Pictures of workers on vacation at camp had captions such as:

Some factory managers try to place their workers in such an environment as this during their vacations, believing that healthy outdoor

[37]Nelson, *op. cit.*, p. 744.
[38]Harrison, *op. cit.*, p. 675.
[39]Mills, *op. cit.*, p. 67.
[40]"Keeping Employees Fit with Pay," *American Industries*, vol. 26, 1925, p. 27.

living and wholesome recreation will better fit them for renewed efforts on their return.[41]

But as vacations were extended more broadly, other safeguards had to be added. Although generally vacation pay was given prior to the vacation period (in 61 percent of mid-'20 plans),[42] many employers withheld part or all of the vacation pay until the employee returned or until he had put in a minimum amount of service following his return, as for example the employer who announced that "everyone [qualified]...who returns to work on July 12 and remains during the balance of the month of July will be paid full wages for the vacation period. ..."[43]

Strict eligibility requirements excluded on the average about half of the wage earners in a plant.[44] Employers continued to favor the higher-skilled, higher-paid, and senior workers because of their more stable employment relationship and, hence, the greater likelihood of their continuing employment to yield employers the benefit of the paid rest period. Present employment and continuous service were the limiting requirements: "The employee must have been on the payroll prior to June 1, if he be one of those with an uninterrupted record of service."[45] Since vacations were only for continuing employees, no allowance was paid, of course, to a worker whose employment was terminated for any reason, "even if the discharge be on the eve of an expected vacation, ..."[46] Providing a social benefit to employees was not the purpose of these paid vacation plans. The idea underlying them was that vacation time, since paid for by the company, belonged to the company, as the following comment indicates:

During the vacation period, the salesman is expected to take a good

[41]"Do Factory Vacations Pay?" p. 1087. A similar picture in another article was captioned: "They'll go back ready for work. A vacation spent like this brings back the 'pep' lost in a year of toil." Of this company's "efficiency" vacation, as management called it, it was noted: "Foremen in the stockyards plant declare that buoyant spirits, better vitality, and consequently increased efficiency results from these 'health trips' of workers." "Vacation Arrangements That Don't Upset Things," pp. 1551–1552. See also "Vacations with Pay," *Monthly Labor Review*, vol. 22, 1926, p. 944, which described vacation camps and a Vacation Bureau Service in New York City, to which industrialists went for suggestions on where to send their employees on vacation.

[42]Mills, *op. cit.*, p. 56.
[43]Charles, *op. cit.*, p. 690.
[44]Mills, *op. cit.*, p. 63.

[45]Nelson, *op. cit.*, p. 743.
[46]*Ibid.*

rest and prepare for a hard season ahead. Houses generally are coming to feel that the salesman's time is not his own during his vacation period—that inasmuch as he is being paid, he is expected to do what the vacation is meant for, namely, rest up. He is not expected to take a short time job and make extra money.[47]

Temporary Plans of the 1920's

While the plans we have been describing were clearly instituted for the purpose of increasing employee productivity, there were other plans adopted in great numbers during the 1920's under a slightly different rationale. They, too, were non-wage costs incurred for the purpose of increasing productivity, but they sought to do so, not directly through the physical effects of a rest on the worker, but indirectly through reducing labor turnover and other employment costs. The idea underlying this second type of plan was that the vacation was for the employees' sake as a reward for certain behavior which would, in turn, benefit the employer.

Industrial relations programs came into great popularity as employers sought to improve their competitive position in the tight labor market of the prosperous '20's. The shortage of labor dictated a new concern for the wage earner. Paid vacations were instituted expressly to attract and keep labor, to reduce absenteeism, and to increase employee morale and loyalty. Since the purpose of these plans was to stabilize the work force, they had to be aimed of necessity at the very groups of workers who had the least stable employment relationship.

To attract labor, vacation coverage was extended broadly to cover all workers in the plant work force. Even the pieceworkers, who required 100 percent replacement during vacation periods to maintain production, were granted vacations despite the high cost deterrent. As one employer said, "we find that giving a vacation to pieceworkers has enabled us to secure help even in the most difficult time...."[48]

To keep labor, vacations were provided to the least stable of the work force as an incentive to stay with the company. One employer observed that his plan was

[47]"Shall Salesmen Be Given Vacations?" *Printer's Ink,* vol. 132, 1925, p. 20.
[48]Mills, *op. cit.,* p. 273.

very beneficial to the company in that labor turnover has been reduced considerably since adoption. Men are rather hesitant to change positions for fear of losing this advantage as other industrial plants do not give vacations.[49]

Not only did this view bring vacations to "day workers" in general, but it brought them, particularly and purposely, to the newer and younger employees largely excluded in the earlier, highly graduated plans. Shorter service requirements were urged. "It is necessary to teach the unstable worker to stand still a little while before you can persuade him to remain a long while...,"[50] explained one writer on vacation plans.

To reduce absenteeism, employers again appealed to the least stable of the work force with paid vacations as the bait. Rather detailed house rules were written governing both attendance and tardiness, the paid vacation being tied directly to the level of performance on both scores. Some plans provided for the deduction of one day of vacation for each day taken off without notice during the preceding year, or for a specified number of late days. Management claims for the results of these devices ranged from the general statement that "our vacation plan tends to...make our production steady on account of the desire to make their attendance just as perfect as possible"[51] to the more precise formulation: "It has reduced our total absenteeism from about 10 percent to less than 4 percent."[52]

To increase employee morale and loyalty, vacations were also provided broadly to all wage earners in the work force. It appeared that the only requirement for coverage under these plans was that the worker be a human being. Thus, vacation plans were enthusiastically recommended as "showing that the management is interested in the welfare of the workers and recognizes them as human beings in giving opportunities for recreation in this way."[53] One can catch the flavor of this new management view of the usefulness of paid vacation plans from employer comments:

[49]*Ibid.,* p. 247.
[50]"Factory Vacations That Help instead of Hinder," p. 830.
[51]Mills, *op. cit.,* p. 273.
[52]*Ibid.*
[53]*Ibid.,* p. 241.

61

The workingman is beginning to be recognized as a human being and one who appreciates a vacation with his family just as much as the man who wears the white collar in the office.[54]

It has done more to prove our real human consideration of our employees than almost any other of our industrial relations endeavors.[55]

This was the language of employers whose plans were instituted principally in the early 1920's, the heyday of the American Plan. Paid vacations designed to "make the employees realize that the company is interested in them beyond the mere fact of the pay envelope"[56] received during the mid-twenties more publicity than did plans instituted for any other purpose. They were described as "almost a requirement of modern industrial social welfare"[57] and "one of the most worthwhile ideas in industrial welfare work."[58]

So far, we have been describing plans adopted during the 1920's as falling into one or the other of two categories, those instituted to increase employee productivity and those intended to stabilize the work force. Although employers probably adopted their plans without conscious awareness of the fact, there were several inherent differences between the two types of plans. Those adopted solely with a view to stabilizing the work force put the principal emphasis upon what the employee did before, rather than after, the vacation. These were based upon a reward concept; if a worker stayed long enough or with a minimum of absenteeism, he got his reward. On the other hand, the employer who said, "At the inception of the plan the theory was advanced that to break the year by a period of rest and recreation would prove beneficial to both body and mind," was specific as to where he would look for the expected return:

No false impression has been created that this is a form of the kind of paternalism which the average American workman dislikes. The Norton men understand fully that the plan operates to the mutual

---

[54] *Ibid.*, p. 253.
[55] *Ibid.*, p. 237. Both this plan and the preceeding one were adopted in 1924.
[56] *Ibid.*, p. 239.
[57] *Ibid.*, p. 247.
[58] *Ibid.*, p. 271. In 1924 it was reported of vacations that "the movement is fast approaching the interest held by industrial medicine, accident prevention, and stock purchases." "Vacation Plans for Wage Earners," *Iron Age,* vol. 114, 1924, p. 1518.

benefit of the company and themselves. They realize that returning to the plant refreshed, they are able to do more and better work.[59]

Although a few employers knew what they were after, the dichotomy in philosophy justifying these two types of plans was rarely so sharp in practice as it has been presented here. Plans were more often adopted for a multiplicity of reasons and the self-serving statements of employers about the value of their plans is a poor clue to the real motivations behind their adoption. The welfare publicity and language of the day in itself often obscured the expression of motivations.[60] In some cases, employers may have had little more reason for their adoption of a plan than going along with the latest wrinkle in industrial relations programs. However, Mills concluded from his survey of 199 plans evaluated by the employers themselves:

The employer who contemplates the introduction of a plan or is checking up on the results of a plan already operating in his plant is primarily interested in the way it affects his business. Only as such plans can be shown to pay their own way do they seem advantageous to him.[61]

The value of all these plans adopted during the 1920's, whatever their underlying justifications, was always under question. A firm of attorneys making a survey of vacation plans in 1924 made this observation:

Probably at no other time have American industrialists been so keenly in quest of personnel policies of proven value as incentives to increased production and stabilized forces. Never before in the development of the modern industrial relations program has there been a more searching demand for an analysis of the costs and other economic factors involved.[62]

[59]Nelson, *op. cit.*, p. 743.

[60]In one survey of 1,500 factories, interest in the popular motives was so great that no mention at all was made of the possibility that increased employee productivity might result from the physical rest of a vacation. The employers, this article said, "reported that vacations given to the factory force increased loyalty to the firm, reduced turnover, and tended to make more contented workers, while they also stated that vacation policies stood for fair play and good business." "Vacations with Pay for Office and Factory Workers," *Monthly Labor Review*, vol. 21, 1925, pp. 272–273.

[61]Mills, *op. cit.*, p. 21.

[62]"Vacation Plans for Wage Earners," p. 1471.

As between the two types of vacation plans, employers more often questioned the value of those adopted primarily to stabilize the work force. The use of paid vacations for this purpose was based on the questionable assumption that there was no deeper cause for work-force instability than could be overcome by such attractions as paid vacations. Since the broad coverage which these plans required to be effective made them costly, employers examined them carefully even during the '20's and particularly as the labor market eased somewhat. Some found their highly advertised advantages to be of doubtful value.

This was particularly true of plans based on the least precise standard, those intended to raise the general morale and increase worker loyalty to the company. Some employers were finding that the worker's appreciation of their interest in his welfare was not always forthcoming. Comments on this ranged from "probably helps but employees seem to think it is due them"[63] to "they are hostile to it as they are to all paternalism."[64] Plans designed to reduce absenteeism were also thrown into question as the decade wore on. At its close, a survey of vacation plans reported that "only 45 percent said granting vacations with pay reduced absenteeism."[65]

Nevertheless, most employers in the '20's believed that they were finding a profitable return either in increased production or reduced labor costs from all of these plans, and this belief was enough to persuade them to keep their plans in force. Events of the next few years put all paid vacation plans to a severe test, however, and quickly sorted out those with a lasting value from the others.

Early Depression Years, 1930–1935

It has been estimated that up to half of the vacation plans existing in the 1920's were dropped during the early depression years, 1930 to 1935.[66] Plans adopted to attract or keep labor or

---

[63]Mills, op. cit., p. 257.

[64]"Factory Vacations That Help instead of Hinder," p. 888.

[65]"Pertinent Facts about Vacations," p. 1359.

[66]National Industrial Conference Board, Vacations with Pay for Wage Earners, Studies in Personnel Policy No. 215 (New York: N.I.C.B., April 1935), p. 10. Coverage

otherwise stabilize employment were quickly weeded out in these years of surplus labor. The grim events of the depression had a far greater effect on worker morale than gestures of management toward recognizing workers as human beings. As the labor force stabilized itself, there was no need for high-cost schemes for that purpose. A vacation plan adopted to encourage "a desirable class of workers to apply for employment"[67] or kept on the grounds that "it steadies the men"[68] or "stimulates regularity"[69] was no longer needed. The depression did all these things for the employers.

Because of their high cost, these plans were given a searching reappraisal by companies seeking ways of retrenching in these lean years. Unless a plan clearly paid for itself in some form, it was likely to be scrapped even before wages were cut, since elimination of paid vacations would reduce labor costs without reducing the employee's total money income for the year.

Information on the abandonment of vacation plans by type of plan is not available, but Mills' report of what happened during the 1921–1922 recession provides a clue. Employers at that time had dropped certain of their vacation plans, according to one, "as part of a wage reduction."[70] One firm which had adopted a plan in 1920 "in order to retain the employees and secure their cooperation in the work" found that "business for the next 2 or 3 years did not justify a continuation of the plan."[71] Another whose plan had been instituted in 1919 dropped it in 1921, explaining:

We found it necessary to discontinue the plan because of the depression....In the years in which it was used, the demand for labor exceeded the supply and it was perhaps of considerable benefit to us in securing help and retraining an ample force. It was made to reduce frequent absences of employees from work.[72]

Were similar data available on plans existing in the late 1920's, showing which were dropped and which were kept during the depression of the early 1930's, the same discrimination undoubtedly would have been evident. Of all the 1920 plans, the type best

---

under plans also was affected. Many workers were automatically eliminated by failure to qualify on account of layoffs and short time.

[67]Mills, *op. cit.,* p. 269. [70]*Ibid.,* p. 281.
[68]*Ibid.,* p. 247. [71]*Ibid.*
[69]*Ibid.,* p. 263. [72]*Ibid.*

able to ride out the depression was one whose purpose was the provision of a rest period to restore productive capacity. Such a plan, in fact, might well have been considered even more valuable, especially with longer hours being worked, in a period of economic hardship when a company's concern was with maximizing the productivity of the employees kept on the payroll. Most likely to have kept their plans were those employers who said they found that vacations had "a recuperative effect on the force"[73] or that the workers "will be more efficient for having this rest."[74]

The figures on vacation plan adoptions in the years from 1930 to 1935 also indicate that employers were finding vacation plans worthwhile for a reason unrelated to labor market conditions. Despite the loss of many plans at the outset of the depression, the paid vacation movement was not only making steady progress but even appeared to be picking up speed. In fact, the per-year rate of adoption of permanent plans seemed to be somewhat greater during these years than it had been during the 1920's, particularly in industries of relatively steady employment where the employer had more assurance of realizing the return from his vacation cost.[75] After a few years' silence, articles on vacation plans began to reappear, increasing in number each year. "The movement is coming back, perhaps stronger than ever," said an article in 1935 in reporting the results of a vacation plan survey. "Industry is recognizing," the survey had commented, "that shop as well as white-collar workers should have paid vacations to break the routine of year-round employment,...."[76]

Vacation coverage of wage earners in permanent plans, which was somewhere around 5 percent in 1920 and had grown to close to 10 percent by 1930, was somewhat over 10 percent by 1935. Compared to the approximately four-fifths coverage of salaried workers by this time,[77] however, wage earners had made only a small beginning.

[73]*Ibid.*, p. 251. [74]*Ibid.*, p. 269.
[75]BLS, *op. cit.*, p. 9. Calculated from Table 4. N.I.C.B., *op. cit.*, pp. 10–11.
[76]"Vacation Policies," *Forbes*, vol. 35, 1935, p. 20. The survey reported here had been made by Princeton University's Industrial Relations Section.
[77]BLS, *op. cit.*, pp. 4, 9. As noted earlier, these figures are estimates based on Tables 2 and 4, employment figures for these years, and all other data available from surveys of vacation plans. By "permanent plans" is meant plans which, though

No Union or Employee Demand for Vacations

The years up to 1935 may be called the period of management origin of paid vacations. During it, as we have seen, two types of plans arose with somewhat different characteristics. Plans of the second type, based on vacations as a reward, generally did not survive the economic period of tight labor markets which had called them forth. But even had the depression not brought the end of these plans, their survival was doubtful. Plans using vacations as a social benefit reward necessarily presumed some demand for them on the part of the workers, but no such demand yet existed. The age of social benefits had not yet arrived and, in fact, was not to come for some time. Employees, in this early period, were notably uninterested in paid vacations.

The contrast of this attitude with experience in Europe during the same period was striking. Mills, who studied both the European and American experience with paid vacations in the mid-20's, observed: "In the short space of seven years, from the beginning of 1919 to the close of 1925, the vacation movement in Europe approached the 8-hour day or the 48-hour week in importance."[78] There, paid vacations were being won in legislation as a direct result of trade union pressures. But of America, where he found the initiative to be coming from employers whose attitude was that vacations were profitable to business operations, he commented:

This attitude, combined with the traditional American reluctance to enact social legislation as a curb for industrial ills, and the comparative indifference of trade unions, has resulted in leaving the development of the vacation movement in the United States largely with employers.[79]

In the United States, no significant pressure to adopt vacation plans came from either organized or unorganized employees. Although employers frequently noted that their employees "appreciated" the paid vacations, there appeared to be little actual employee demand for them. A great deal of public and employee

---

adopted earlier, were still in effect in 1937. This calculation omits plans adopted for a short period or which failed to survive the depression of the early '30's.

[78]Mills, *op. cit.*, p. 15.

[79]*Ibid.*

relations had gone into selling the employees on paid vacations as a measure which demonstrated management's real concern for their social welfare, but these efforts were not always considered successful by the employers themselves, as noted earlier. One employer claimed that most of his workers preferred to work during the vacation and draw double pay. He instituted a Christmas savings plan to replace the vacation plan.[80]

Organized workers, too, had little interest. The extent of paid vacation plans in union agreements was almost insignificant. Vacation plans were rarely found in union agreements before the 1920–1929 decade. Their appearance in that decade followed logically upon the preceding period of union growth and the wartime governmental recognition of collectively bargained contracts.[81] Some of these agreements merely spelled out vacation plans previously instituted by management.[82] The Bureau of Labor Statistics reported that "agreements received by the bureau in 1925 show that provision was made for paid vacations in division or local agreements in 11 cases" and that from 1926 to 1929 it had received only 71 trade agreements providing for vacations with pay.[83] With the help of the Department of Labor, the American Federation of Labor, and trade associations, Mills could find only 175 contractual plans, even some of these by informal agreement, "and each affects a relatively small number of employees."[84] Of these 175, the majority were not with private employers but with government units; 71 plans in locals of the firefighters, plus a scattering for the street railway workers, steam and operating engineers, and the blacksmiths, were in agreements with municipalities. Many of the contractual plans, furthermore, covered employees on a salary-like pay basis, who historically had received earlier coverage than wage earners generally because of their relatively stable employment and ability to extend themselves to do the vacationing employees' work. This suggests that some of the union

[80]"Pertinent Facts about Vacations," p. 1359.
[81]BLS, *op. cit.*, p. 8.
[82]For example, see Mills, *op. cit.*, p. 76.
[83]"Vacations with Pay," p. 945; "Vacations with Pay under Collective Agreements," *Monthly Labor Review*, vol. 28, 1929, p. 31.
[84]Mills, *op. cit.*, pp. 35, 70. In contrast there were several thousand company plans in the U. S. during the 1920's, as estimated from Mills' Table 22, p. 277, and BLS, *op. cit.*, Table 4, p. 9.

plans had originated not with the unions but with the companies or in regulations governing employment conditions in the municipalities. Mills noted that "in general, vacation provisions in collective agreements do not differ materially from those granted in individual companies."[85]

This was also apparent from the 1929 BLS report on union vacation provisions, many of which were the same clauses that were characteristic of company-instituted plans, limiting vacations to the same groups favored by management. For example, the brewery workers' contractual plans covered only engineers, watchmen, and stablemen. Four BLS file agreements provided vacations for electrical workers "on monthly salaries without overtime pay." A typographical workers' agreement allowed a week's vacation "providing the remaining force will use every effort to get out the edition regularly." One teamsters' plan required employees to reciprocate by giving the employer one week in overtime during the year. Nine other teamster plans, however, provided for vacation pay in lieu of the time off in certain cases where an employee was unable to take the time off or had left his employment. Informal arrangements between company and union were noted by the BLS in both 1925 and 1929, including some typographical workers' plans "through verbal agreements with the newspaper proprietors."[86]

Illustrative of union disinterest in vacations was this report from an impartial chairman in a Chicago clothing industry case, in which the union sought and won the abandonment of a vacation plan: "The theory of the union is that workers want their reward in the pay envelope."[87]

During this early period, vacation coverage did not correlate either by industry or occupation with union organization. Many of the most highly organized crafts and industries were marked by a total absence of paid vacations. Forty-four percent of the total union membership at this time was employed in industries such as mining, leather, clothing, textiles, and building trades, where seasonal and cyclical fluctuations in employment were of

[85]Mills, *op. cit.*, p. 72.
[86]"Vacations with Pay;" "Vacations with Pay under Collective Agreements," pp. 31–34.
[87]Mills, *op. cit.*, p. 76.

considerable importance. Management would see little value in a vacation rest as a boost to productivity because of the discontinuity of employment; the unions were more concerned with higher wages and more work-time for their members.[88]

Paid vacation coverage came first to office workers and to other predominantly salaried occupations such as retail trades which were neither organized nor seriously threatened by unionization. The industries which had given the earliest coverage to hourly paid workers were still unorganized in this period. A few companies in the chemical industry provided paid vacations for the older employees as early as 1900–1910. More plans appeared in chemicals in the 1920–1929 period, along with other relatively stable industries: food, rubber, crude petroleum, and machinery, particularly electrical machinery. Only paper and printing, receiving its earliest coverage in the 1910–1919 decade, had any degree of, or threat of, union organization. But although unionization continued in this industry, it subsequently failed to maintain its lead in vacation coverage. By the end of the period it had relatively low coverage.[89]

Even during the early 1920's, when the antiunion drive was of prime interest to many employers, few gave any indication of adopting vacation plans as a result of either direct or indirect pressure from unions. Although management publications occasionally suggested that a lack of leisure might be a cause for strikes,[90] none of the articles on vacations during this entire period mentioned any use of paid vacations in more directly forestalling union organization. Of the 199 employers commenting on the value of their vacation plans in the mid-1920 survey

[88]*Ibid.*, p. 70. For example, an agreement made in 1922 between the Cleveland Garment Manufacturers' Association and the locals of the International Ladies' Garment Workers' Union provided for a vacation plan and 40 weeks' guaranteed employment. In the second year of the agreement, when vacations were to become effective, a new agreement was made in which the vacation provision was traded for an extra week of guaranteed employment. *Ibid.*, p. 76.

[89]BLS, *op. cit.*, pp. 7–8. The Bureau of Labor Statistics also notes here that this early coverage provided vacations only to the older employees and was not extended to the rest of the wage earners until later.

[90]William S. Hobbs, "Employees' Vacation as an Asset," *Power*, vol. 68, 1928, p. 270; "Vacation with Pay for Workers," p. 37.

by Mills, none mentioned vacations as a deterrent to unionism.[91] Of course, this possible deterrent effect was implicit in much of the general interest in industrial relations programs, particularly where employers said they sought to make employees more loyal. But evidence of direct links with paid vacations is scarce.[92]

Vacation Pay Not Wages

Without even an employee interest in paid vacations, the full credit for initiating the movement must go to the employers. It was obvious that they incurred this expense as a non-wage labor cost. The only employers who saw paid vacations as wages were those, it might be said, who did not offer vacations at all. This might have been true of the employer who said, "We have no vacation plan in effect. When I take a vacation, it is at my own expense and I see no reason why other vacations should not be on the same basis."[93] Or the employer who said, "Factory workers are now prosperous enough to take vacations at their own expense."[94] These employers saw vacations as coming out of the wages an employee earned during the rest of the year; but such time off was employee- not employer-financed, with the employer simply allowing permission for the unpaid leave.

Nonetheless, vacations were, in certain instances, called "an important addition to compensation." This idea was put forth in the early period principally to explain the discrepancy in vacation coverage between office workers and plant workers. It was frequently said, for instance, that one of the reasons office employees were granted vacations was because they seldom received payment for overtime hours. Others, reversing the field, said that office workers were not given overtime payment because they had vaca-

[91]One employer, however, commented that strikers who returned to work were denied their vacation privileges, "and this seemed to mean more to them than the loss of standing in life insurance." Mills, *op. cit.*, p. 241. But Mills himself commented, "The psychological results of such accumulation of tiredness may be a critical factor in many labor troubles," *ibid.*, p. 24.

[92]Occasionally, the existence of a union contract in itself was cited as a bar to institution of a paid vacation plan, as in the case of the employer who said, "Under our arrangement of collective bargaining with organized labor, it would seem inadvisable to consider." "Do Factory Vacations Pay?" p. 1086. Another said, "Our labor agreement and piecework system make vacations inadvisable." *Ibid.* Still another company cited "the excessive union scale of wages" as "the determining factor" in the abandonment of its vacation plan. Mills, *op. cit.*, p. 281.

[93]*Ibid.*, p. 68.　　　　　　　　　　[94]*Ibid.*

71

tions.[95] The idea that, as one employer put it, "factory workers are paid well enough that they can take a vacation without pay as well as office workers can with pay,"[96] implied that vacations somehow represented a form of income which could redress an adverse wage differential.

In the first place, of course, it did not represent an increase in total income. Where an employer had to hire substitutes for the employees on vacation, his annual labor cost was increased by roughly 2 percent per week of paid vacation granted. Yet, for the employee, the paid vacation was not an addition to total income for the year unless he had previously taken an annual vacation without pay, a practice sometimes permitted but hardly more widespread than unpaid leaves are today. This payment in leisure time could not be converted into additional income except by taking employment elsewhere during the vacation period, an alternative neither contemplated by employers nor, in most plans, even permitted.

In the second place, the available data on vacation coverage do not support the contention that vacations were used to narrow wage differentials. In each group receiving coverage, the already higher-paid employees had received vacations first. Executives received vacations before the lower-paid office workers and top-paid production workers before the rest of production workers. Virtually no vacation plans existed in low-wage areas or industries.[97]

Had the employers who originated the paid vacation movement with permanent plans viewed vacations as wages in payment for service, they would or could have offered the workers a choice. But such a choice between a wage increase and paid vacations was rarely offered. Employers seeking to increase employee productivity adopted their vacation plans independently of wage increase considerations or employee desires.

Nor did employees view the vacations as pay for service. On the contrary, their lack of interest in paid vacations as a social benefit reward led both organized and unorganized workers to suggest that the employer put the same cost into a wage increase. For example, of a company plan adopted in 1925, the employer

[95]*Ibid.*
[96]"Do Factory Vacations Pay?" p. 1086.
[97]BLS, *op. cit.*, p. 4.

noted, "generally the expressions have been favorable, although," he then acknowledged, "a limited number of employees have indicated they would prefer an equivalent raise in rate of pay."[98] An employer with a contractual relationship with his employees commented: "Under agreement with the union, that organization wishes all privileges converted into pay and placed in the worker's envelope."[99]

Since vacation pay would also have appeared in the pay envelope, it was clear that in declining vacations the employees were asking that they be permitted to work the full year and that the money which vacations would have cost the employer be given to them in increased wages for that service.

In noting the comparatively few collective agreements containing vacation provisions, Mills commented:

There are doubtless several reasons for this situation, the most commonly accepted one being the fact that organized labor had made no concerted attempt to obtain such provisions. The more basic demands for shorter hours and high wages have been the first interest of labor leaders. Where the desired standards have been obtained, effort is concentrated on maintaining them.[100]

Workers were not likely to take paid vacation plans to their hearts as long as surveyors could say, as Mills did, that the company adopting a vacation plan "does not do so because 'it is good thing for the men' or because 'it promotes health' or is 'socially just' or a 'reward,' but because it tends to increase efficiency and make greater profits."[101] Employees and their unions probably, and apparently, accepted the purpose of paid vacation plans to be just as management intended: not to pay wages for service and not to provide social benefits, but to increase employee productivity.

Summary

The vacation movement for wage earners was originated unilaterally by management up to 1935, as a non-wage cost for the purpose of increasing the efficiency of the work force. The movement progressed only as fast as individual employers came to recognize from experience that paid vacations would increase

[98]Mills, *op. cit.*, p. 261.
[99]"Do Factory Vacations Pay?" p. 1086.
[100]Mills, *op. cit.*, p. 70.
[101]*Ibid.*, p. 66.

employee productivity. Despite the flurry of temporary plans during the 1920's, vacation coverage reached only a little over 10 percent of wage earners by 1935, compared with 80 percent coverage for salaried workers.

The factors influencing the extension of coverage to wage earners during this period favored certain groups of employees, particularly the senior workers, the higher-skilled, and the higher-paid. First, their production records were personally known to the management and the productivity increase resulting from the rest was likely to be immediately obvious to the employer. Second, these groups of workers had greater ability to share the work load and thus reduce the employer's vacation cost. Third, vacations were granted where the employment relationship was the most stable and employers had greater assurance of a return on their vacation cost, again favoring the same groups of workers. Newer and younger workers and all employees in industries of irregular employment had no vacation coverage.

Although paid vacations were finally extended to wage earners, the psychological gap between management and its production workers was the fourth factor still limiting vacation coverage in this period. Evidence of it was apparent in most of the articles on vacations—ranging from the 1921 comment that extending vacations to the plant workers might, in one management view, have an adverse effect on their industry, efficiency, and loyalty,[102] to this observation in 1930:

Vacations for office workers and executives are taken very much for granted; but a good many employers are a little afraid of granting vacations with pay to production workers, especially those on incentive plans—it seems they would rather let the other fellow try it first.[103]

However small it was and however slowly it moved under the auspices of management alone, the paid vacation movement had at least begun for production workers. Although the marked employee disinterest in vacations was to continue, the movement suddenly quickened its pace in the next period, 1935–1940, as the unions—entering the picture as a new but quite indirect force—affected management decisions about paid vacations.

[102]See above, p. 53.
[103]"Pertinent Facts about Vacations," p. 1358.

CHAPTER 4

Vacation Coverage Surges
to 50 Percent, 1935-1940

IN CONTRAST to the slow-footed progress of the early period, the vacation movement in 1935 quite suddenly gained momentum. In the three years, 1935–1937, the number of vacation plans for wage earners tripled over those in existence in 1934.[1] Even the business recession of 1937–1938 appeared to have no effect upon this progress. Vacation plans were neither abandoned, suspended, nor significantly revised as they had been in the recession of 1921–1922 and the early depression years.[2] During this five-year period from 1935 to 1940, vacation coverage for wage earners reached the 50 percent mark.[3] Of equal significance was the fact that many of these newly adopted plans covered all workers in a plant rather than only the favored few.

What had occurred? What new force had arisen to cause the vacation movement to abandon its slow pace and limited coverage?

Coincident with the adoption and extension of vacations after 1935 was the sharp growth in union membership and the intensive organization of production workers. Forty percent of all wage-

[1]United States Department of Labor, Bureau of Labor Statistics, *Vacations with Pay in Industry, 1937*, Bulletin No. R.903 (hereafter referred to as BLS, *op. cit.*, (Washington: G.P.O., 1939), p. 8.

[2]Eugene Whitmore, "Current Vacation Policies of 500 Companies," *American Business*, vol. 8, 1938, pp. 14–15.

[3]No figures are available to show the exact time when vacation coverage reached the half-way point, but it would appear from the studies and estimates available that this point was reached by the end of 1940.

earner plans existing in 1937 were adopted in that year alone[4]—
the year marked by the establishment of the Wagner Act's con-
stitutionality and the rise of the CIO. Coverage in manufacturing
industries, historically trailing non-manufacturing, began to catch
up.[5]

The first paid vacations for wage earners in the basic steel
industry were adopted in 1936 by a majority of the large steel
companies. Management's institution of these plans came at the
height of the unionization drive by the Steel Workers' Organizing
Committee. "The widespread movement is without precedent in
the history of the industry," exclaimed one report. "This is the
first time," it said of U.S. Steel's coverage of its 100,000 workers
all at once, that "the Corporation has extended vacations with pay
to this class of workers."[6] Of the plan instituted by the Jones and
Laughlin Steel Corporation, it was explained: "The management
granted a petition which had been transmitted through employee
representatives several months ago."[7] The *Weirton Steel Employees' Bulletin* told workers that its plan "is the result of several
months' work and cooperation on the part of the employees' representatives and management."[8]

What was happening in steel was also happening in other industries now receiving attention from union organizers. The General
Electric Company plan, adopted in 1929, had been dropped in
1932 but was put in force again on January 1, 1936. The International Harvester plan, also adopted in 1929, was liberalized in
1936.[9] These were actions typical of those in hundreds of companies during this period, 1935 to 1940. Vacation plans were being

[4]BLS, *op. cit.,* p. 8.

[5]*Ibid.,* pp. 2–4, 8.

[6]"Vacations with Pay Offered to 200,000 Steelworkers," *Steel,* vol. 98, 1936, p. 16.
This action by the steel industry brought its employees into third ranking order
among the industries which had been pioneers in the vacation movement (chemicals, crude petroleum producing, food, rubber, and machinery) from virtually no
coverage at all. BLS, *op. cit.,* p. 3. Mills had found iron and steel to have only 1.1
percent of its employees covered in 1925. Charles M. Mills, *Vacations for Industrial
Workers* (New York: The Ronald Press Co., 1927), p. 277.

[7]"Vacations with Pay Offered to 200,000 Steelworkers."

[8]"Weirton Employee Vacation Plan," *Iron Age,* vol. 137, 1936, p. 78.

[9]"Selected Plans of Companies Granting Vacations with Pay to Wage Earners,"
Management Review, vol. 25, 1936, p. 221.

adopted and extended by management in response to threats of unionization.

Dual Value Vacation Plans

Yet, as will be shown later in this chapter, there was still no interest in paid vacations by employees, organized or unorganized. Workers were demanding union recognition and wage increases, not paid vacations. Employers responded to the threat of unionization by voluntarily incurring the cost of providing paid vacations because vacations had a dual advantage to the employer. Not only would they demonstrate the employer's interest in his workers' welfare, but they would pay dividends by increasing productivity in the process.

Once again paid vacations were advertised as they had been in the 1920's as "a practical way of recognizing and rewarding continuous and faithful years of company service."[10] One writer in 1935 noted the shortening of the work day and work week and observed, "If the vacation is looked on only as a needed period of recuperation after a year's work, there seems to be less need for such a policy now than a few years ago. But," he continued:

if the vacation policy is actuated by a desire to erase a distinction between factory and office personnel, to provide an incentive for continued service, and to make possible a period of complete freedom in which the employee may get away from customary tasks and surroundings and secure a new point of view, as well as relaxation and rest, there is fully as much reason for granting vacations with pay today as in the past. Particularly at a time when more thought is being given to maintaining cordial relations with employees, a vacation policy merits consideration, since it is certain to arouse the spontaneous approval of employees.[11]

Some of the new plans adopted in response to organizing drives were justified as a means of providing supplemental income. This might take the form of paying for some of the layoffs due to work shortage as "vacation." Or use of vacations as a bonus or income

[10]Charles E. Payne, *Developments in Company Vacation Plans,* The Conference Board Studies in Personnel Policy, no. 13 (New York: National Industrial Conference Board, Inc., April 1939), p. 6.

[11]"Vacations with Pay for Wage Earners," *Monthly Labor Review,* vol. 40, 1935, p. 1497. This was a report on the N.I.C.B. 1935 study mentioned in Chapter 3.

supplement might be accomplished by allowing a choice between the vacation or pay in lieu of it—i.e., double pay for working during the vacation period. The N.I.C.B. reported:

...the motive for granting vacations can hardly be for rest and relaxation...if employees have had reduced working schedules and layoffs during the year. On the contrary, some vacation plans have been continued under such conditions for the express purpose of supplementing workers' earnings, and employees are granted the option of remaining at work and receiving the vacation allowances in addition to regular pay.[12]

The Weirton Steel Company plan, adopted in 1936, permitted a choice between a vacation with pay or pay in lieu of a vacation.[13] The Aluminum Company of America, adopting a plan in 1939, had a similar provision.[14] The Republic Steel plan of 1936 provided that employees who preferred to work rather than take vacations could collect their "vacation pay" with interest at Christmas time.[15]

But the use of vacations as a bonus or income supplement appears to have been a new and not very common practice. The N.I.C.B. observed that the provision for taking pay in lieu of vacation time not only was "rarely found in former years" but, even in 1939, existed in only 7 of the 210 plans it studied that year. "A majority of the companies...definitely state that no option shall be granted except under unusual circumstances," it said.[16] Another survey of 425 company vacation plans in Southern California found that only 125 employees out of 206,750 covered by the survey had received pay in lieu of time off in 1939. "In no case," reported this survey, "was this practice a general provision of the vacation policy, but was a special arrangement granted to a small number of employees."[17]

---

[12]Charles E. Payne, *Trends in Company Vacation Policy*, Supplement to *The Conference Board Management Record*, Studies in Personnel Policy No. 21 (New York: National Industrial Conference Board, Inc., 1940), p. 7.

[13]"Weirton Employee Vacation Plan."

[14]"Aluminum Company Gives Vacations with Pay," *Iron Age*, vol. 143, 1939, p. 85.

[15]"Vacations with Pay Offered to 200,000 Steelworkers."

[16]Payne, *Developments in Company Vacation Plans*, pp. 5, 15.

[17]"Vacations with Pay in Southern California," *Monthly Labor Review*, vol. 51, 1940, p. 648. Summary of V. V. Veysey and Everett D. Hawkins, "Vacations with Pay in Los Angeles County."

Productivity Increase Is Main Value

For most employers, such a clause would defeat the essential purpose of providing the vacations. Vacation plans had value over a wage increase or other benefit of equal cost in meeting unionization threats only because of the productivity increase that employers could expect from vacations to repay part or all of the cost. As one employer stated, "A vacation is assigned for the benefit of the service and not as an opportunity to earn extra wages."[18] A vacation rest for workers "might stimulate them to greater efficiency," reported the N.I.C.B. in its 1939 survey of company motives for adopting vacation plans.

Doubt was expressed about the public relations aspect of the dual value. A survey conducted in July 1936 of plans designed for the "purpose of eliminating the distinction between office and factory personnel and providing incentives and rewards for continued meritorious service," reported that in "their influence on employee relations, the record is far from being unreservedly favorable." Over half of the surveyed companies reported that vacations had no effect or only temporary effects on employee loyalty or morale.[19]

The priority given the productivity-increase purpose of these dual value plans was clearly evident both from employer statements and from the vacation plans themselves. "The two basic principles leading to a substantial period of annual absence at rest and recreation, with pay," reported one writer on vacation plans, "are: first, that a vacation for an employee, whatever his rank or line of work, is an investment in health, strength, and efficiency for the year ahead; second, that it is a varying reward for continuous service."[20] The emphasis was also to be found in the current handbooks of many companies. The General Foods Corporation booklet on "Principles of Personnel Administration and Employee Relations," for instance, contained this statement:

[18]National Industrial Conference Board, *Company Vacation Plans*, The Conference Board Management Research Memorandum No. 1 (New York: N.I.C.B., 1939), p. 3.
[19]"Vacations with Pay," *Mechanical Engineering*, vol. 60, 1938, p. 257. This article reported on a survey conducted by the National Metal Trades Association and reported in the *Metal Trades Digest*.
[20]H. E. Fleming, "No Vacations for Various Classes of Workers This Summer," *Printers Ink*, vol. 195, 1941, p. 42.

"Vacations with pay are granted to regular employees as a recognition of continued service and for the value of a period of recreation in preparation for future service."[21]

The companies that felt the need or desire to point out the value of a vacation plan as they faced unionization of their plants were more vocal than the many companies, both smaller in size and without unionization threatening, that were also continuing to adopt vacation plans without fanfare for the same reason as in the earlier period. These employers were more specific in saying that the vacation "is a period of rest and recuperation and is meant to be used as such."[22]

Evidence that this was still management's primary motivation for adopting vacation plans could be seen in the selective provision of vacations to certain workers. Although coverage was extended more rapidly and broadly in this period, employers carefully excluded from coverage those who might not be expected to continue employment year after year in order to yield the productivity increase from annual vacations.

In industries where the work was highly seasonal or where workers frequently changed employers and would not be returning to the same employer in the period following the vacation, virtually no vacation coverage existed. This was generally true of mining, lumber, leather, clothing, textiles, longshoring, and the building trades. In these situations, a paid vacation looked like a bonus or wage increase. One employer, for instance, argued that the provision was not really a vacation but "merely a wage increase in disguise, for the plant would shut down normally due to seasonal fluctuations in business."[23] These employers preferred to put the money into a wage increase rather than into paid vacations.

Even where an employer in one of these industries considered paid vacations out of a genuine social sense, the result was the same. One such employer in the textile industry wrote a brief article expressing an interest in vacations for the wage earners in his industry. "It always has seemed foolish to me," he said, "that so many mills seem to think that anyone who works out in

[21]*Ibid.*
[22]Payne, *Developments in Company Vacation Plans*, p. 15.
[23]*Ibid.*, p. 7.

80

the mill shouldn't get a vacation." Yet his own mill had no vacation plan for these workers. "We do, however, see that the overseers are treated the same way as the office help when it comes to vacations."[24] The attitude was typical of employers in the origin of the movement, when vacations were being granted only to those close to management. But in this period, the gap in coverage persisted for an economic reason; the unlikelihood of any productivity increase from paid vacations in irregular-employment industries kept them from being instituted. Surveyors frequently pointed out, as one put it, that employers "have come to realize the importance of vacations with pay in industries where the employment relation is relatively stable."[25]

Yet even in the relatively stable-employment industries, great care was taken to provide vacation coverage only for the most regular employees. This was done in two ways. The first was to require a worker to have been with the company a given number of years, from one up to five years in most plans, before becoming eligible for the first week of vacation. Graduated plans, which predominated throughout this period, based longer vacation allowances upon even greater length of service.[26] Any employee who stayed with a company for the required number of years would be considered to have demonstrated that he would continue his employment during the period following the vacation.

The other way in which employers assured themselves that only regular employees would be granted vacations was to require further that an employee work a given amount of time during the year immediately preceding the vacation period. This service minimum was usually set high enough to exclude any employee who worked less than full time. While "continuous service" had been sufficient to describe a full-time, regular employee in plans for office workers and the favored groups of production workers, the extension of vacation coverage to the rest of the plant workers brought an increased interest in additionally spelling out the

[24]John Williams, "Vacations with Pay," *Textile World*, vol. 86, 1936, p. 1651.
[25]"Vacations with Pay in Southern California," p. 647.
[26]Payne, *Developments in Company Vacation Plans*, pp. 9, 11. At one early point in this period, graduated plans showed a temporary drop as a sudden influx of uniform plans came with the wholesale wage earner coverage in manufacturing industries, but at no time did graduated plans lose their majority status.

qualifying requirements in terms of hours, days, or weeks of
service. Among the steel company plans, U.S. Steel's plan was
noted for its detailed interpretation of continuous service.[27] The
N.I.C.B. noted in 1940 that one of the problems "which may
delay some establishments in adopting a uniform policy for all
employees" (same vacation allowances for both office and plant
workers) was "the difficulty of stablizing employment for workers
in the wage earning group."[28] Employers were still taking no
chances on granting a vacation and receiving no productivity
increase from the employee thereafter if they could help it.

The vacation plan provisions themselves were designed to see
that employees actually took the time off for rest. "Split vacations,
accumulated vacations, and pay in lieu of vacations were looked
upon with disfavor by companies."[29] Company handbooks frequently made additionally clear to the employees what the purpose
and requirements of the vacation plan were, as this one did:

It is the desire of the company that all employees entitled to vacations
should enjoy this time for recreation, refreshment and relaxation. Consequently, except in very unusual circumstances, employees will not
be paid vacation money and be allowed to work for additional regular
pay during the vacation period.[30]

Employers, though responding to union organizing drives with
advertisement of vacations as a welfare benefit for employees,
maintained a strong proprietary attitude toward their vacation
plans. Evidences of management desire to keep control of the
vacation plan in its own hands appeared and reappeared. For
instance, the N.I.C.B. reported:

Many plans state that the right of interpretation of provisions is held
exclusively by management and that the continuation or revision of
the plan is subject to future conditions and at the discretion of the
company.[31]

[27]"Selected Plans of Companies Granting Vacations with Pay to Wage Earners,"
p. 222.
[28]Payne, *Trends in Company Vacation Policy*, p. 19.
[29]"Vacations with Pay in Southern California," p. 650.
[30]Fleming, pp. 42, 47, quoting Ritter Dental Manufacturing Co. handbook. The
Crown Zellerbach Company handbook stated similarly: "No employee is to have
the privilege of drawing the vacation pay and continuing to work in lieu of taking
a vacation." *Ibid.*, p. 47.
[31]Payne, *Developments in Company Vacation Plans*, p. 16.

One company, with a regular plan for salaried employees, had granted wage earners vacations in eight of the previous ten years, but instead of a formal plan left the question to the Board of Directors to be decided anew each year.[32] Another company stated in its handbook that "the vacation is a company custom only and is not a part of its contract with employees."[33]

As will be shown, employers were unduly apprehensive, if not about what unions could do with control over the plans, at least about the immediate likelihood of union control. Unions were still giving management no competition, making no challenges to its complete hegemony in the paid vacation movement during this period.

Union Disinterest in Vacations

Unions were apparently a significant factor in the eyes of some employers, but they were not entering the vacation movement as a direct force. Very little demand for paid vacations existed among the unions. Yet employers, particularly those who used their plans as demonstrations of an interest in wage earners' conditions, generally assumed such a demand. Surveyors of vacation plans, attempting to explain the rapid adoption, also assumed that workers were interested in vacations as a social benefit. One said:

Employee and public relations have assumed added importance in the minds of industrial executives, with the result that more careful attention has been given to working conditions and to the desires of employees.[34]

The desires of employees, however, in these industries to which paid vacation plans were so suddenly and broadly extended, were for union recognition and wage increases and not at all for the adoption of paid vacation plans.

For instance, a company reported:

When we were negotiating a union contract, we offered one week's vacation with pay or a 2% increase in wages in lieu of a week's vacation with pay. The union voted in favor of the 2% increase in wages.[35]

[32]"Vacation Policies in the Textile Industry," *Management Review*, vol. 28, 1939, p. 448.

[33]N.I.C.B., *Company Vacation Plans*, p. 3.

[34]Charles E. Payne, "Trends in Company Vacation Policy," *The Conference Board Management Record*, vol. 2, 1940, p. 37.

[35]"Vacation Policies in the Textile Industry," p. 447.

One of the firms with a provision for choice between a paid vacation and pay in lieu of the time off reported that "such a small proportion of workers took vacations...that the vacation plan will be abandoned."[36]

The preference for a wage increase was especially marked in industries which were highly seasonal in nature. Here, the employers had the least interest in granting paid vacations, and any such provision would usually amount to a cash payment at layoff time. A survey of vacations for union members reported that in the building trades vacations were not being asked for because, as one member put it, "We have too many vacations now. The only trouble is that they are without pay."[37] The idea of paid vacations simply had not caught on with workers even in situations where it appeared to represent the increase in income which they might be expected to favor. These workers preferred to have the money in their wage rates, increasing the pay for their service.

For most workers, shorter hours seemed to have greater appeal than paid vacations. In reply to a question put by *Fortune* in 1936 asking whether longer vacations or a shorter working day were preferred, it was reported that 75 percent of workers chose the latter.[38]

Vacations were rarely a contract demand during these years. It is therefore not surprising that there still was no positive correlation between vacation coverage and unionization.

Non-manufacturing industries, with little union organization or threat of it, had higher vacation coverage than manufacturing. Ninety-one percent of the employees in public utilities worked under vacation plans in 1937, 88.2 percent in retail trade, 82.9 percent in wholesale trade, and 63.6 percent in hotels and restaurants.[39]

On the other hand, many highly organized industries had little or no vacation coverage. Coal mining, for instance, which had had less than 1 percent wage-earner coverage in 1937,[40] was still without coverage by the end of this period. Clothing manufactur-

[36]Payne, *Developments in Company Vacation Plans*, p. 7.
[37]"Vacations with Pay in Southern California," p. 651.
[38]"The American Vacation," *Fortune*, vol. 14, 1936, p. 161.
[39]BLS, *op. cit.*, p. 28, Table 1.
[40]*Ibid.*, p. 2, Table 1.

ing, railroad transportation, building construction, longshoring, and the entertainment occupations, including actors and musicians, were also well organized and had a long history of collective bargaining, but "were marked by an almost complete absence of paid vacations in union agreements."[41] The fact that union organization was high in these industries, which, with the exception of railroad transportation, were characterized by irregular employment and hence provided no incentive to employers to adopt vacations, only underscores the dominant management role in determining vacation coverage and the union disinterest in pressing for vacations where they did have bargaining strength.

Vacation coverage was lower for organized workers as a whole than for wage earners as a whole. At the close of this period, when coverage reached the 50 percent mark for all wage earners, the Bureau of Labor Statistics reported that only 25 percent of organized workers had paid vacations.[42]

Contractual Plans Originated with Management

Almost all of the vacation plans in union agreements during this period had originated, in fact, not with the unions but with the companies. This point bears emphasis; ten years later it was to become a crucial but forgotten historical fact, and the ignorance of it led to an incorrect interpretation of contractual vacation plans by arbitrators and courts. The N.I.C.B. had found that prior to 1937 only 4 percent of companies surveyed had their plans in a union contract and that by 1939 one-third of the plans were subject to union agreement, with only a small percentage at either time having originated with the unions.[43] Similarly the Bureau of Labor Statistics reported that while 72.1 percent of rubber workers, about 86 percent of petroleum workers, and 71.2 percent of steel workers were provided vacation coverage in 1937, plans in these industries largely antedated the collective bargaining relationship.[44] The basic steel industry's plans instituted en

[41]"Vacations with Pay in Union Agreements, 1940," *Monthly Labor Review*, vol. 51, 1940, p. 1071.
[42]*Ibid.*, p. 1070.
[43]Payne, *Developments in Company Vacation Plans*, p. 6.
[44]BLS, *op. cit.*, p. 2; "Vacations with Pay in Union Agreements, 1940," p. 1071.

masse in 1936 were included in the first agreements in 1937 which brought most of the industry under contract. In the textile industry, too, contracts with the large companies "formally acknowledged the practice of paid vacations."[45]

Some of the contractual vacation plans of these years, furthermore, were undoubtedly company plans as judged by control as well as by origin, particularly in those cases where the agreements were with employee groups organized with the assistance of the company. For example, one company reported, in a survey of vacation plans, that to be eligible for vacations "employees must have membership in the mutual welfare group."[46]

Evidence of the extent to which contractual plans were originally company plans simply added to the contract without change lay also in two additional facts. First, contractual plans were most common in the industries high in company-plan coverage (thus correlating with vacation coverage generally rather than with union organization); and, second, contractual plans bore the same characteristics as company plans.

The largest proportion of contractual plans was in the industries that were leaders in the vacation movement, whether or not there was a significant extent of organization in them. Thus, vacation plans in union agreements were found most often in petroleum and rubber and were fairly common in retail trade in 1937. Contractual plans were common also in the salaried occupations, among licensed ship officers and in newspaper offices, and in street railway and bus lines, often municipally-owned and provided with paid vacations by law or regulation. "Elsewhere," reported the Bureau of Labor Statistics of union agreements in 1937, "vacation provisions are the exception rather than the rule."[47]

By 1940 there was a sizeable number of contractual vacation plans, but also high vacation coverage generally, in iron and steel, rubber, aluminum, wholesale and retail trade, telegraph and radio,

[45]"Paid Vacations under Agreements in the Textile Industry," *Monthly Labor Review*, vol. 53, 1941, p. 415.
[46]"Report on Vacation Plans of Typical Companies," *American Business*, vol. 9, 1939, p. 39.
[47]"Vacations with Pay under Union Agreements," *Monthly Labor Review*, vol. 44, 1937, p. 1486.

meat packing, petroleum production and refining, light and power, and chemicals.[48]

And, finally, contractual plans showed the same characteristics as company plans which, as we have seen, were designed to assure the employer a return on his investment. Almost as many contractual vacation plans as company plans prohibited taking vacation pay in lieu of the vacation or splitting vacations.[49] The same language providing vacations to "regular employees" was to be found and the same general exclusion of employees whose employment was less stable.[50] Vacation coverage was no broader in contractual plans than elsewhere. One survey in 1940 showed that although "all" workers were eligible for vacations in about half of the contractual plans surveyed, in almost a third eligibility was limited to "some" or "only a few."[51]

Most significant of all was the fact that contractual plans were little different from all vacation plans in that they usually contained no allusion whatever to terminated employees, either to specify their ineligibility to vacation pay or to allow it. In the few instances that terminations were mentioned in union agreements, about as many prohibited terminal vacation pay as provided it.[52] No such clauses were needed or desired where employers did not consider vacations for such workers and where workers without experience in receiving terminal vacation pay did not expect it. Vacation plans had never effected their limited coverage by specifying exclusions from coverage. The initiative to grant vacations lay in management hands, and vacations were specifically provided only for certain employees in the employ of the company at vacation time. Almost standard was this type of language: "All employees on the payroll on June 1 who have been in continuous

[48]"Vacations with Pay in Union Agreements, 1940," pp. 1070–1071.

[49]*Ibid.*, pp. 1076–1077; "Vacations with Pay in Southern California," p. 652. A mirror image of the occasional company prohibition against an employee's working during the vacation showed up in the BLS 1937 file of union agreements—this time with the union doing the enforcing. Two vacation plans covering tailors provided that any tailor found working during his vacation must turn over his earnings during that time to the union. "Vacations with Pay under Union Agreements," p. 1487.

[50]"Vacations with Pay in Union Agreements, 1940," pp. 1072, 1071.

[51]"Vacations with Pay in Southern California," p. 650. "Almost half of the employees were eligible for paid vacations" in the company plans. *Ibid.*, p. 648.

[52]"Vacations with Pay in Union Agreements, 1940," p. 1075.

service for at least two years and who have worked a minimum of __ hours, in the preceding year to June 1, will be eligible for 1 week of vacation."

As the 1940 survey mentioned above observed, in discussing vacations in union agreements, "...where jobs are relatively steady, the principle of vacations with pay flourishes" and "Agreements for vacations with pay have been obtained, as a rule, from those firms which employ a regular force of workers"[53]—i.e., where management found it profitable to grant them.

The vacation movement continued to be management-led without direct pressure from an employee or union demand for paid vacations, whether or not management was adopting the plan in response to the pressure of union organizing and whether or not its plan was subsequently incorporated into a union agreement. But the story would not be complete without taking special note that, when it did occur, a union demand carried a view of paid vacations sharply different from the employers'.

New View of Vacations

Most of the relatively few union demands for vacation plans were probably won without a struggle. Some employers may have welcomed the request, at least in preference to some other union demand. In such cases, however, the union's concept of paid vacations would not be a matter of record and we can only assume that these demands represented a strong employee conviction about paid vacations. To find expression of it, one must turn to the even rarer cases when a union persisted in its vacation demand against employer opposition to the point of a strike. Although strikes for paid vacations were unheard-of in either this or the earlier period, some of the disputes did go to arbitration. Since it is here that the union view of vacations is recorded, it is important to examine such cases carefully. Taking one that was reported in Mills' study of paid vacations in the mid-twenties and two of the few that occurred in the 1935–1940 period will serve here to show that whenever unions did take positive action to secure paid vacations, they introduced a new concept.

[53]"Vacations with Pay in Southern California," p. 651.

Employees who were not interested in vacations had simply not come to the feeling that an annual rest was essential to their continued well-being; they expressed no disagreement with management's desire to assure itself a return but simply accepted the vacation as a gratuity the employers were willing to grant. But those who did have a positive interest in securing paid vacations knew what they were after. Unconcerned with whether or not a benefit also accrued to the employer, these workers desired the vacation rest time for their own benefit. The vacations were sought, at the employer's cost, with the belief that the employer had an obligation to provide for the recuperation of energies of each worker whose services he used.

This view of the employer's obligation was expressed by the arbitrator in the earlier case, in 1924, a case in which the Commercial Telegraphers were demanding continuation of a plan that management wished to drop. The arbitrator recommended retention of the plan, saying:

The pay for vacation is as much wages as pay for actual work, because the rest is indispensable to conserve continued physical and mental condition. . . . "Vacations with pay" are not a gift, much less a bonus, but a part of the earned wage conserved for vacation needs. . . . [54]

The view which this arbitrator held for the employees was not wholly in conflict with management's view. In this case, he found them consistent, continuing as follows:

The rejuvenation due to the vacation rest shows itself in the more efficient work of the rested worker. All employees should exercise their right to their vacation period. Those not doing so and accepting the pay therefor, in addition to the pay for work done during their vacation period, are converting the proposition into one of a "bonus" and defeating by their reduced efficiency the beneficial purpose of the principle. . . . [55]

[54] Mills, *op. cit.*, pp. 73–74. This case involved a new working agreement between the Commercial Telegraphers' Union and the United Press, International News Service, and Universal Service. Mr. Hywel Davies, the arbitrator, contradicted his opinion that vacations were part of the earned wage conserved for vacation needs by following it with these words: "and no corporation even considers that the 2/52 year pay for the vacation period should be added to the 50 weeks of actual work to arrive at the actual average pay for each of said 50 weeks." *Ibid.* Mr. Davies' emphasis was apparently on the employer obligation which he felt was owing as much as wages.

[55] Mills, *op. cit.*, p. 73.

In some respects, the employee view was merely the reverse side of the same coin. Certainly this arbitrator saw the benefit as a mutual one. Both parties, he recognized, saw the purpose of vacations to be provision of a physical rest.

But there were evident contradictions between the employee and employer views. While both wished to conserve the human machine, the employee desired it for his own sake and the employer for his firm's benefit. While management might voluntarily incur the cost of conserving the human machine because it found the cost would be repaid in greater productivity—not unlike the cost of conserving its metal machines—it saw no obligation to do so. Management reserved the right to determine which employees should be rejuvenated by a paid vacation. It did not view this conservation as a right of the employees.

Yet this was precisely how the employees saw paid vacations where they actively sought coverage: provision of paid vacations was a management obligation and the right of every worker. As another arbitrator, in this period (in 1938), expressed it:

...a loyal, conscientious employee is making a substantial contribution to his employer's business with each year's service. In these positions which require considerable physical exertion, each succeeding year takes a greater toll of the reserve physical energy of the employee. To compensate for this, the employee should have a physical rest each year and this period of rest should be increased from time to time as the employee grows older in the service of his employer...there is an obligation to employees who have given years of service to the business of the employers...this obligation should be recognized and met.[56]

There was a further difference in the two views of vacations. Employers were interested in the rest only as it affected productivity in the *following* year whereas the employees felt vacations were owed them because of the service in the *previous* year, the service already given which had created the need for rest. In this sense, the *right* to an annual rest had been *earned*, the employees felt.

This "earned right" concept held clear implications for vaca-

[56]California Bakers' Association of San Francisco and Bakery Wagon Drivers and Salesmen's Union, Local No. 484, J. E. Brenner, chairman, Board of Arbitration, June 9, 1938. File copy of award, National Labor Bureau, Seattle, Washington.

tion plan provisions. If earned by the preceding year's service, the vacations could not be allowed at management's discretion to some workers and not to others, or for some service but not all service. Any employer who used a man's services had, by taking a toll on his energies, incurred a commensurate obligation to provide for its restoration.

If an employee's employment were terminated, he would have to be paid his accrued vacation pay proportionate to the amount of service given the employer prior to the termination. However, as noted earlier, such provisions were quite rare in any vacation plans, contractual or company, in either of these early periods. Nevertheless, the significance of the provision was remarked shortly after the close of this period when the *Management Review* in an article in 1941 noted first that until now the prevailing philosophy had been that vacations were "a feature of the health program of a company instituted for its presumed beneficial effects on future service" and then commented as follows:

The fact that some companies grant vacation pay to employees discharged for cause would seem to indicate a trend toward regarding vacation pay as an emolument earned by past service.

"This practice, however," it then added, "would appear to be still relatively uncommon."[57]

Although a new phenomenon in the vacation movement, conflict between management and labor over their different views of vacations and over provision for terminal vacation pay in particular was inevitable. Such a case arose toward the end of this period culminating in an arbitration award on June 25, 1940. Local 1–34 of the Ship Clerks' Union, International Longshoremen and Warehousemen's Union, demanded paid vacations of the Waterfront Employers' Association of San Francisco. These workers were employed on a casual basis by many different employers and would not necessarily be returning to the same employer to render him any increased productivity from the vacation rest.

However, these workers, seeing vacations as an employee benefit, were not concerned by the fact that the employer who paid the

[57]"Vacation Pay for Discharged Employees?" *Management Review*, vol. 30, 1941, p. 190.

vacation's cost might not receive the benefit. Without expectation of such a return, the employers put forth the argument, which had always been advanced by employers in industries of seasonal or intermittent work, that vacations were not needed. The BLS reported it as follows:

The absence of vacations in these industries is partially due to the contention that cumulative fatigue, which may justify vacations for year-round workers, is not a factor in casual or intermittent employment, which by the nature of the work provides opportunity for rest and relaxation.[58]

But Wayne Morse, the arbitrator to whom this dispute was submitted, had this to say of the employers' argument:

The fact that a clerk may take time off at his own expense does not provide him with a true vacation privilege....It isn't much of a vacation for a clerk to be out of a job intermittently and during that time be under the economic pressure of maintaining contacts each day with the hiring hall in the hope that he may be dispatched to another job.[59]

The plan which was devised for these workers included all the requirements of a plan based upon vacations as an earned right: vacation pay for all service and all employees, and necessarily allowed at employment terminations. A vacation fund was set up to be jointly administered by the union and the employers' association. Employers were to contribute to this central fund an amount based on the length of service rendered by each employee. The pro-rated amounts thus pooled were to provide the employees with vacations or partial vacations in direct proportion to the total service rendered during the year.

Although this type of plan shared both the cost and the benefit of paid vacations among the employers, opposition to paid vacations in these industries continued almost unabated throughout the rest of the vacation movement, as succeeding chapters will show. From the employer's viewpoint, vacations continued to be, as they were in the origin of the movement, a matter of individual employer recognition of a return benefit.

For the employer who recognized no return, as noted earlier,

[58]"Vacations with Pay in Union Agreements, 1940," p. 1071.
[59]*Ibid.*

vacations were simply a bonus or "wage increase in disguise." But the employees who made these early vacation demands did not see it that way at all. They were not asking for pay in lieu of a vacation or for a wage increase out of which to buy their own vacations. Their demands were for time off in which to rest and recuperate without loss of regular income—an employee benefit, social in nature, which the employer owed them by reason of his use of their services.

However interesting these rare cases of employee demand might be, throughout these two early periods they had no observable effect on the vacation movement in terms of numbers or philosophy; they are of note only as a harbinger of things to come. Up to this point neither employees nor their unions were seriously interested in vacations, either as an employee benefit or an employer benefit. In some cases they appeared hardly to understand the idea of paid vacations. In 1941 the mineworkers won a provision for one week off in the summer with a $20 bonus check at Christmas time. When the employers granted the week off, since it appeared to be without pay, 91,000 miners called it a lockout and milled around the pit-heads demanding that they be allowed to work. Sixteen-hundred miners stormed the Pennsylvania State Unemployment Compensation Bureau office to file claims for unemployment compensation, even after it was explained that this was a paid vacation won for them in negotiations.[60]

Where there was any general union expression relative to paid vacations, it echoed the employers' view. William Green, president of the American Federation of Labor, in 1927 had said:

As the evidence accumulates that vacations with pay are good business we should certainly expect to see an extension of this practice. Vacation benefits the worker physically and mentally and certainly makes for better industrial relations.[61]

[60]"Vacations Resented," Business Week, July 19, 1941, pp. 48–49. It is not surprising that the miners did not recognize their "vacation" as such. Twenty dollars at Christmas did not put food on the table in July. Management in other industries usually paid employees their vacation pay in advance to assure that the rest time would be free from financial worries, a condition necessary for relaxation.

[61]"Vacations with Pay for Industrial Workers," Monthly Labor Review, vol. 24, 1927, p. 902.

Labor certainly then did see an extension of the practice, but not by a direct effort on its own part. Unions, with other issues more pressing, generally left both the initiative and philosophy up to the employers.

Summary

During the years 1935 to 1940, the paid vacation movement had taken a sudden leap forward. Thanks to the attention that union organizing drives focused on wage earners, the psychological gap that had long prevented even consideration of vacations for the production workers was now gone, and with it two other factors limiting early vacation coverage to certain groups of employees. No longer was either the closeness to management or the ability to share the workload a major factor determining who would get vacations; all workers in a plant might now be eligible. In 1939 the N.I.C.B. reported that a little over one-fourth of vacation plans covered 100 percent of the production workers. Almost four-fifths covered at least 80 percent, and only 3.5 percent covered less than 50 percent of the workers in a plant.[62]

Only one of the factors was still operating to determine which employees would receive vacations: the stability of the employment relationship. Workers in industries of irregular employment had no vacation plans, and in industries of relatively stable employment high minimum service requirements excluded all but the most regular employees, even where the plan technically covered all workers in a plant.

The sudden increase in and broadening of vacation coverage in this period came almost entirely as a result of management voluntarily incurring this cost in union and non-union industries alike. Coverage continued throughout this period to be highest in industries with neither unionization nor serious threat of it. But even where unionization threatened and employers were looking for ways of responding to the union organizing drives, they had good reason, they believed, to choose vacations: here was a benefit that would yield them a return in increased productivity to offset the cost. Given the disinterest of both employees

[62]Payne, *Developments in Company Vacation Plans,* p. 7.

and their unions in paid vacations, unions played a part in the faster pace and broader coverage only indirectly.

Nevertheless, the indirect effect of the unions was a lasting one. Presumably, had the organizing drives not been successful, some of these plans would have been dropped, as the plans used as temporary expedients in the 1920's had been. But in this case that alternative was not available to employers. Unionism was successful, and most of the company plans were incorporated into the labor agreements, making permanent the swift advances in plan adoption and broadened coverage.

This, in turn, had further significance to the future of the movement. It hastened the day when paid vacations would become an active employee demand. Once a sizeable number of employees had paid vacations, a demand for them on the part of the rest of American workers was inevitable. At the start of this period a little over 10 percent of industrial workers had vacation coverage. By the end, 1940, it had reached the 50 percent mark. This extensive coverage was also to influence government policy which, in the next period, became a factor in wartime industrial relations.

Ironically, perhaps, management was creating a demand for vacations as an employee social benefit and an obligation of industry, despite the fact that it had adopted these plans for its own benefit and without any intention of thereby assuming an obligation for employee social welfare. Although the employee view of vacations as an earned right to a social benefit was scarcely observable in this period, the extensive coverage now reached, combined with the upsurge of unionization, indicated that this view was one to be reckoned with in the years ahead.

PART III

Paid Vacations in Transition

The War Period, 1941-1945

CHAPTER 5

The War Labor Board Adopts Employer View of Vacations

BEGINNING in 1941 the government became an important factor in the vacation movement. Its wartime economic policies and specific vacation policies were to bring the movement to a significant turning point by the end of 1945.

The first sign of governmental influence came early in 1941. Employers in defense industries had been concerned during 1940 about the government's attitude toward vacations as a possible interference with defense schedules. In response to an inquiry, the Office of Production Management issued a statement on May 2, 1941, recommending that employers with vacation plans in plants making munitions or essential war materials give their employees vacation bonuses rather than time off, except where vacations would not interfere with defense production.[1]

From this point onward, the government played an increasingly greater role in the vacation movement. Following the demise of the National Defense Mediation Board, which handled a few cases involving vacations during its nine stormy months ending with the close of 1941, the National War Labor Board was established with wide support and strong powers of enforcement. In administering wartime economic policy in the field of industrial relations, this Board rapidly advanced the paid vacation movement.

It did not do this directly, however. Though a significant factor

[1]National Industrial Conference Board, *Vacation Policy and National Defense,* The Conference Board Reports, Studies in Personnel Policy, No. 34 (New York: N.I.C.B., 1941), p. 17; H. E. Fleming, "No Vacations for Various Classes of Workers This Summer," *Printer's Ink,* vol. 195, 1941, p. 47.

in the movement, the government was necessarily an indirect force. Government boards instituted no vacation plans and made no improvements on their own motion; positive action depended upon the initiative of management or unions required to submit their vacation plans or demands for War Labor Board approval. The government thus merely responded to the forces already at work in the vacation movement.

Employers Favor Wartime Vacations

Management continued to push the vacation movement throughout this period under the same view that had always guided its actions. The N.I.C.B. reported in 1942 that the general view was still that, "as in the case of salaried employees, vacations provide rest, recreation and change that is reflected in the employee's better work upon his return, and that, consequently, vacations are a sound investment."[2]

The government was to respond to the employer view of vacations by adopting and adhering to it until it was no longer tenable. However, the first official position on vacation policies—the OPM recommendation of May 2, 1941, to grant pay in lieu of vacations to essential defense workers—presented some conflict, and management accepted it only with reluctance. While conceding it to be necessary in some cases, this caution was added:

Let it be recognized, however, that when a company gives a vacation bonus and keeps employees at work...both the employer and the individual employee are losing the return from an investment in health and strength. Some extra money admittedly will not give that same peace of mind which comes from a two weeks' period away.[3]

Even earlier in the defense effort, 1940, "the view was expressed by executives that the vacations were needed bcause of the fact that workers have been under pressure for some time and may be under even more pressure in the coming year."[4] After the war had been on for a year and a half, employers were saying:

We believe vacations even under present war conditions are good for production....[5]

2"Vacation Policy," *The Conference Board Management Record,* vol. 4, 1942, p. 105.
3Fleming, *op. cit.,* p. 47.
4N.I.C.B., *Vacation Policy and National Defense,* p. 2.
5Elmer W. Earl, Jr., *Wartime Influences on Vacation Policies,* The Conference

Vacations with pay should be granted to all war workers. Experience has clearly demonstrated that proper vacations will increase output....[6]

Under this view, considered as valid in time of war as in peacetime, the majority of employers continued to favor the adoption of paid vacation plans, even when they were not pressed to do so. But several factors were now adding pressure: the intense competition for workers, the prevalence of cost-plus contracts, and the increasing expectation of War Labor Board approval of employee demands for paid vacation plans.

Despite this, however, there still were many employers in industries of relatively steady employment who did not recognize any value from paid vacation plans. As from the start of the movement, there were also the employers in industries of irregular employment who steadfastly opposed vacations because no return could be expected from the many employees whose employment did not continue. These were the employers who received special attention in this period.

Union Vacation Demands Begin

Unions, for their part, were now beginning to reflect the first observable employee demand for paid vacations. In the steel industry where vacations had been in effect since 1936 and where defense requirements were now making pay in lieu of vacations common practice, an informal survey reported that 80 percent of the employees were found to prefer the actual time off. While the Steel Workers' Organizing Committee agreed to permit pay in lieu of the time off where management found it necessary, it stipulated that "to the greatest degree possible...eligible employees shall receive the benefit of vacation from work."[7]

The fact that the majority of workers were now under paid vacation plans undoubtedly added to the interest in vacations among those not covered. Although also noting that most companies adopted their plans voluntarily, an article early in 1941

Board Reports, Studies in Personnel Policy, No. 56 (New York: National Industrial Conference Board, Inc., 1943), p. 5.

[6]Ibid.

[7]"Vacations and Defense Studied in Steel Mills," Iron Age, vol. 147, 1941, p. 87.

was subtitled with the first direct statement: "Unions now demand paid vacations."[8]

But the demand for paid vacations in 1941 and most of 1942, with few exceptions, was not yet an important one. Unions were still more interested in recognition, wages, and hours. Despite the majority coverage, the idea of paid vacations had not really caught on with the workers. Indicative of the lack of demand was the fact that coverage for union members, which had been considerably behind that for wage earners as a whole in 1940, did not catch up until 1944.[9]

Furthermore, the demand that did exist was still being expressed in the terms of an employer benefit to increase productivity rather than flatly as an employee benefit. For example, one of the early union demands on behalf of a large body of workers, the non-operating employees of the railroads, was won in December 1941 after a long and difficult dispute. The final award of the Railway Emergency Board expressed the employee-benefit view of the unions in combination with the employer-benefit view (which the carriers in this case did not support), finding:

That the paid vacation in industry has become an important element in our American standard of living,

That it is necessary to the maintenance of physical and mental well-being of workers,

That productive efficiency tends to be enhanced by a periodic respite from labor, and vacations with pay greatly improve labor morale,

That the cost of vacations is offset in part, at least, by the increased productivity resulting therefrom,

That the increasing strain upon the individual produced by the defense effort accentuates the need for an annual leave....[10]

[8]"Trend to Paid Vacations for Hourly Workers," *American Business*, vol. 11, 1941, p. 17.

[9]U.S. Department of Labor, Bureau of Labor Statistics, *Vacations with Pay in American Industry 1943 and 1944*, Bulletin No. 811 (Washington: G.P.O., 1945), pp. 2, 20.

[10]*Report to the President by the Emergency Board Appointed September 10, 1941, under Section 10 of the Railway Labor Act, to Investigate the Facts as to the Dispute between Certain Common Carriers by Rail and Certain of their Employees Respecting Vacations with Pay, Rules of Service, and Wage Increases and to Report Thereon.* Nov. 5, 1941. (Washington: G.P.O., 1941), p. 60; Wayne L. Morse, "Award of Referee in the Matter of a Controversy between the Fourteen Cooperating Railroad Labor Organizations and the Carriers Involving the Terms

But if the interest in paid vacations on the part of employees and their unions was still in an embryonic state early in this period, it was to grow enormously almost overnight when the wartime economic stabilization policies set a limit on wage increases. Still without an interest in vacations per se, the unions, seeking contract improvements for their established locals and for the newly organized, saw vacations as an employee benefit that could be secured even though wage increases were foreclosed. In addition, unions could skillfully use their knowledge of Board procedure to illustrate, in their organizing drives, the value of union representation, inasmuch as workers had to act concertedly in applying to the War Labor Board for vacations or other improvements.

The War Labor Board was also to respond to the growing union demand for paid vacations, but, despite the obvious basis for the demand, without acceding to the union view that vacations were primarily for the benefit of employees.

WLB: Vacation Pay Is Not Wages

Vacation coverage, standing at 50 percent of all wage earners at the start of the war period, rose to over 90 percent by the end of 1945.[11] The story of how this came about is the story of a series of pressures and counter-pressures put upon the War Labor Board. As will be seen shortly, the Board responded to the demand for extension of vacations to the rest of American workers by continually liberalizing its vacation policies. It responded to the counter-pressure from the remaining employers opposing vacation plan adoption by adopting the employer-benefit view of the justification for paid vacation plans. First, however, the Board had to confront directly the question of whether vacation pay was wages or not.

The War Labor Board was established on January 12, 1942, as a dispute-settlement agency to minimize strikes and lockouts in wartime. Although it was not given its wage stabilization functions

of a Vacation Agreement." Chicago: Dec. 17, 1941. The final agreement provided a plan with the same characteristics as company plans in general.

[11]National Industrial Conference Board, *Vacation and Holiday Practices*, The Conference Board Reports, Studies in Personnel Policy, No. 75 (New York: N.I.C.B., 1946), p. 4. The N.I.C.B. found that by the end of 1945, 92.9 percent of the companies it surveyed had paid vacation plans.

officially until October 3, 1942, the Board had been entrusted with wage stabilization by President Roosevelt on April 27, 1942, when he issued his seven-point program to combat inflation. On July 16, 1942, in settling a dispute in the steel industry, the Board announced the Little Steel Formula setting a 15 percent limitation on wage increases (calculated from January 1, 1941, to match the rise in the cost of living since then) and extended it almost immediately to apply to the rest of industry. The Board felt its wage stabilization responsibilities strongly; union demands for vacation plans or their liberalization, which began to come to the Board soon after its establishment, were increasingly denied as being part of the wage problem.

In a June 1942 case, the Board unanimously approved a panel report which said, "The panel considers the demands for an extra week's vacation with pay [and higher overtime premiums] as demands for wage increases" and denied the vacation request as inconsistent with the wage stabilization program.[12] In an August 12 case, the employer, like most employers opposing vacation demands, saw vacations simply as an additional cost item. The Board appeared to agree, finding that the employees were not entitled to vacations with pay where the company was found unable to further increase costs and was already granting "vacations" without pay wherever possible. This employer had said that vacations with pay were "simply a variation of the wage increase problem," and the Board discussed the issue under the heading "Wages."[13] On August 18, the Board pointed out in a case involving vacations that "the responsibility of the National War Labor Board for wage stabilization is explicit and direct."[14]

[12]*In re* American Brass Co. *and* International Union of Mine, Mill and Smelter Workers, Locals 251, 445, 423, CIO. June 25, 1942. Bureau of National Affairs, *War Labor Reports, Wage and Salary Stabilization Reports of Decisions and Orders of the National War Labor Board and Subsidiary Agencies* (hereafter referred to as *War Lab. Rep.*) (Washington: BNA, 1942–1946), vol. 1, pp. 268–269.

Throughout the war period, the subject of this and the next chapter, shifts in War Labor Board policy and philosophy, in rough chronology, are illustrated by cases reported in the *War Labor Reports*.

[13]*In re* Cambridge Tile Manufacturing Co. *and* Federation of Glass, Ceramic and Silica Sand Workers of America, CIO. August 12, 1942. *War Lab. Rep.*, vol. 2, p. 276.

[14]*In re* Aluminum Co. of America *and* United Mine Workers of America, District 50, CIO; American Magnesium Co. *and* Aluminum Workers of America, Locals 2, 3, 9, 11, 16, 23, and 24, CIO, and United Automobile Workers of America, Local

The Board's attitude toward vacations in these cases was expressed in a case on August 5. The Board rejected a request for more than one week of vacation on the grounds that a one-week vacation was "reasonable" considering area practice and should *not* be liberalized "in view of the war emergency and the need for maximum production."[15]

Yet shortly afterwards, on November 20, the Board was holding that a *more* liberal vacation was *essential* to maximum production, explaining, "The necessity for occasional rest and rehabilitation becomes more rather than less important in time of war,. . ."[16]

This abrupt reversal in views as to the vacation's effect on production followed a gradual tightening of wage controls in cases decided during the summer, and a November 6 policy statement reaffirming continued Board use of the Little Steel Formula prohibiting further wage increases. Unions, beginning to chafe under these wage controls, clamored for some form of concession. The War Labor Board was now directly in the line of fire. Under this growing pressure, it could not continue to hold that paid vacations were wages and therefore unstabilizing.

The Board first began to yield on September 1 in the Association of Team and Truck Owners case when it upheld a panel recommendation granting a one-week vacation plan, saying cautiously:

It is made very clear, however, that the decision is based solely upon the facts of this case and does not establish a rule that vacation pay is never to be considered as a wage increase.[17]

But just such a rule was on the way. Three weeks later, on September 23, the Board approved a panel recommendation which

---

808, CIO, and National Association of Die Casting Workers of America, Local 2, CIO. August 18, 1942, *War Lab. Rep.*, vol. 2, p. 311.

[15]*In re* General Cable Co. *and* International Brotherhood of Electrical Workers, Locals B868 and B1164, AFL. August 5, 1942. *War Lab. Rep.*, vol. 2, p. 233.

[16]*In re* Fifteen Clay Sewer Pipe and Hot Top Manufacturers *and* United Brick and Clay Workers of America, District 9, AFL. Nov. 20, 1942. *War Lab. Rep.*, vol. 4, p. 410.

[17]*In re* Association of Team and Truck Owners *and* International Brotherhood of Teamsters, Chauffeurs, Warehousemen and Helpers of America, Locals 600 and 729, AFL. Sept. 1, 1942. *War Lab. Rep.*, vol. 3, p. 12. The Panel, in its report, had said, "We see no reason for any departure from the Little Steel Formula, but in view of the recent orders of the Board...we think it should be used to its full length—particulary that the paid vacation which theoretically adds 2 percent to the employers' wage bill (but actually probably adds less) should not be reckoned a wage increase." *Ibid.*, p. 14.

stated, "The argument that the union's demand would result in inflation may be dismissed summarily...."[18] On December 3, 1942, the Board reversed a decision against vacations with this chastisement:

...we are of the opinion that here, too, the referee was impeded by his apprehensions over the dangers of inflation from making the necessary contribution toward a uniform practice....[19]

WLB Adopts Employer Rationale

That paid vacations were not wages and not unstabilizing became the official position of the Board for the rest of the war period. In the spring of 1943, after a clarification of policy from the Director of Economic Stabilization, the Board announced that vacations were not part of basic wages, but rather were working conditions which could be improved without adding to inflationary pressures. By the fall of 1943, it was stating flatly:

The National War Labor Board has always rejected the argument so frequently advanced by employers, as in this case, that vacations should be considered a part of the wage structure....
It is universally recognized that the question of whether or not the employees in a given case should be granted vacations with pay should be considered independently of any wage issue.[20]

The matter was far from "universally recognized," however. Employers bringing dispute cases to the Board never ceased insisting, for the duration of the war, that vacation payments were part of the wage increase problem, inflationary and unstabilizing. The Board was particularly sensitive to the charge that its policies were unstabilizing. The intensity of the opposition from these employers who saw vacations only as a cost item caused the Board to adopt a theoretical justification for paid vacations, thereafter awarding vacation plans as "a stimulus to production through

[18]In re Harbison-Walker Refractories Co., Kentucky Fire Brick Co. and North American Refractories Co. and United Brick and Clay Workers of America, Locals 702, 510, 448, 456, and 504, AFL. Sept. 23, 1942. War Lab. Rep., vol. 3, p. 280.

[19]In re Pacific Wood Products Corp. and Lumber and Sawmill Workers, Local 589, AFL. Dec. 3, 1942. War Lab. Rep., vol. 5, p. xxx.

[20]In re Aluminum Co. of America and International Union of Mine, Mill and Smelter Workers, Torrance, Alcoa Workers' Union, Local 609, CIO. Nov. 27, 1943. War. Lab. Rep., vol. 12, pp. 451–452.

the beneficial effect" of the vacation rest on workers.[21] It confronted the laggards with management's own view that:

...the employer is partially compensated for the expense involved
by the freshness and renewed energy with which the employees return
to their jobs.[22]

Thus, not only did paid vacations not add to income,[23] but
they were not inflationary because their cost to the employer was
offset by an increase in production. Believing, as the Board said
in its Termination Report, that vacations "increase the physical
well-being and morale of workers, thereby leading to increased
production,"[24] it approved plans recommended by its panels and
Regional Boards. In other cases the National Board expressed the
view itself.

To assist the Board in popularizing this view in support of its
vacation policies came a statement from Chairman Donald Nelson
of the War Production Board that:

...the volume of production is increased if the workers can restore
their energies through periods of physical and mental rest, change
and relaxation. After a brief vacation a worker should be in better
shape to contribute to the increased effort which our war program
makes necessary.[25]

The War Manpower Commission also added support for the
Board's vacation policies with this statement about wartime vacations: "Our objective is production. Maximum output is the
measure of a policy."[26]

[21]*In re* Timpte Brothers Auto Trailers *and* United Automobile Workers, Local
186, CIO. May 27, 1943. *War Lab. Rep.,* vol. 9, p. 6.

[22]*In re* Semet-Solvay Co. *and* United Mine Workers, District 50, Local 12308.
March 19, 1943. *War Lab. Rep.,* vol. 7, p. 128.

[23]Unlike most of the fringe issues which the Board came to permit—sick leave,
night-shift bonuses, holidays, etc.—vacations did not represent a net increase in
the worker's income unless he had previously taken vacations without pay (an
unlikely event) or unless he worked during his vacation for the same or another
employer.

[24]U.S. Department of Labor, *The Termination Report of the National War
Labor Board, Industrial Disputes and Wage Stabilization in Wartime* (Washington:
G.P.O., 1947), vol. 1, pp. 348–349.

[25]Press release issued by the Office of War Information, April 12, 1943. Quoted
by Earl, *op cit.,* p. 5.

[26]*Ibid.*

WLB Permits Pay in Lieu of Vacation

By this logic, however, paid vacation plans under which employees were kept at work and paid a vacation allowance in lieu of the time off must be considered inflationary. They both added to workers' income and raised employers' costs without an offset in increased production. On the other hand, pay in lieu of vacations was considered necessary in some cases, not only for the skilled or essential workers in a plant but sometimes for whole plants. Where adequate replacements could not readily be secured, an even greater production loss might result from "bottlenecks" caused by some of the vacation absences from work. The necessity of allowing pay in lieu of time off in these cases was recognized by many employers who fully believed in the value of their paid vacation plans.[27] But employers of all persuasions, when confronted with demands for plans in plants where vacations were "out for the duration," challenged the Board's policies with arguments strengthened by the Board's own logic. Under these circumstances, they said, adoption of a paid vacation plan would be merely a cost item and a wage increase, both unstabilizing.

Unlike the Office of Production Management in its 1941 recommendation, the Board from its inception had opposed vacation payments in lieu of time off, consistent with its stabilization responsibilities.[28] But it began to yield as the pressure mounted for vacation plans in plants which could not allow the time off. Employees in these plants felt that their being more essential workers was no valid reason for denying them a benefit others were receiving as (in their view) a substitute for a wage increase.

[27]The N.I.C.B. commented that this policy was "adopted reluctantly by many companies, because they had become convinced that vacations promoted efficiency." Gertrude Reynolds, *Vacation Policy in 1945,* The Conference Board Reports, Supplement to *The Conference Board Management Record* (New York: The National Industrial Conference Board, Inc., 1945), p. 8.

[28]In some cases the Board granted vacations with a prohibition against taking pay in lieu of the time off, as, for example, Employers' Negotiating Committee *and* International Woodworkers of America, CIO. June 16, 1942. *War Lab. Rep.,* vol 2, p. 5. In others it permitted it only where necessary, as in Bower Roller Bearing Co. *and* United Automobile Workers, Local 681, CIO. March 12, 1942. *War Lab. Rep.,* vol. 1, p. 71. In this case, the company asked to be allowed to pay in lieu of time off when production required workers' continued service and the Board cautioned the company to do so sparingly and to consult the union when the need to work during the vacation periods arose.

The Board soon found it necessary to approve plans allowing pay in lieu of the time off, attempting, as it did so, to answer the employer opposition:

On the one hand, vacation pay is clearly a part of a company's labor costs. If the vacation is not taken—as in wartime it frequently will not be—the vacation pay certainly constitutes an addition to the employees' equal earnings. On the other hand, a universal rule that vacation pay is to be considered as equivalent to a wage increase would often work manifest injustice. It would logically result in lesser rate increases being given where vacation pay is granted than where it is denied; in fact, therefore, the employees would not be receiving vacations with pay.[29]

But beyond recognition of a "manifest injustice," the Board had no philosophy to support its action. Responsible as it was for wage stabilization, the Board was not willing to admit that, as the employers charged, these vacation plans were being granted strictly as an employee benefit in substitute for denied wage increases.

Sometimes the Board dodged the issue, as when a month later it released a panel report that observed: "The mediators do not feel it necessary to indulge in a philosophic discussion as to whether the subject of vacation pay is a 'wage issue.' "[30] On other occasions it yielded to the employers' arguments, as in the March 1943 case denying a request for a one-week vacation and adopting its panel's recommendation:

...since the national emergency will in all probability make it necessary to waive vacations, the demand of the union is tantamount to a demand for a 2% increase in wages....[31]

But employees were not to be denied vacation plans other workers were getting just because they could not be spared from their jobs. Less than two weeks later, the Board received, and could hardly fail to approve, this panel recommendation:

Using as a basis for evaluation the statement of [N.W.L.B. Chairman] Dr. George W. Taylor in the case of the Association of Team and

[29]*In re* Association of Team and Truck Owners, p. 12.

[30]*In re* Chrysler Corp. *and* United Automobile Workers, CIO. Oct. 2, 1942. *War Lab. Rep.*, vol. 3, p. 447.

[31]*In re* Lane Cotton Mills Co. *and* Textile Workers of America, Local 351, CIO. March 19, 1943. *War Lab. Rep.*, vol. 7, p. 284.

Truck Owners...it is fairly clear that in this instance there is justification for a vacation with pay.[32]

A week later, the Board was again confronted with its own past decisions and this time put itself officially on record by approving this mediator's interpretation of its policy:

The union argues in support of its proposal that the National War Labor Board has adopted the policy of granting vacations with pay to war workers even when it is apparent that such workers will be unable to take off any time and will merely be given a wage bonus in lieu of vacation....

The company...states that the union's vacation proposal is merely a device to increase wages....

The mediator believes that the union has correctly stated the Board's policy in regard to vacations with pay and that the company has not established any sound grounds for refusing to grant a paid vacation to its employees. The government's policy is to encourage the taking of vacations whenever this is possible. The policy of granting a week's pay in lieu of vacation when it is impossible for employees to take time off is becoming more and more widely accepted by industry throughout this country.[33]

With occasional exceptions, this became the War Labor Board policy. It not only permitted employers to grant pay in lieu of time off whenever they felt it necessary, without seeking WLB approval, but it also held that such payments were not to be considered in computing average earnings for the purpose of applying the Little Steel Formula.[34]

The Board had weathered the storm with the position, as stated in its Termination Report, that "the establishment of the vacation principle, regardless of whether vacations could actually be taken, was the primary consideration."[35] In holding that paid vacations in themselves were not unstabilizing and, when paid in lieu of the time off, were "simply a fair and equitable determina-

[32]*In re* Donaldson Iron Co. *and* International Molders and Foundry Workers of America, Local 18, AFL. March 31, 1943. *War Lab. Rep.*, vol. 8, p. 188.
[33]*In re* Hospital Supply Co. and Walters Laboratories, Consolidated *and* United Electrical, Radio and Machine Workers of America, Local 1225, CIO. April 7, 1943. *War Lab. Rep.*, vol. 7, p. 536.
[34]U.S. Department of Labor, *Termination Report*, vol. 2, pp. 237, 651-654.
[35]*Ibid.*, vol. 1, p. 349.

tion of an employee's reasonable rights in the situation,"[36] the Board had succeeded in making the necessary expedient concession by granting this demand for vacation pay, clearly an employee-benefit, without having to desert its employer-benefit rationale. In fact, it found it useful to reaffirm this latter view even while making the concession to employees, as, for example, in releasing the following recommendation from its referee who approved the practice of vacation pay in lieu of time off:

The fact remains that the contract provision is not intended under normal conditions to provide a bonus in lieu of vacations. The basic objective is to provide for an actual vacation and for pay to the worker while on his vacation with a view to increasing his efficiency and improving his well-being. The fact that during the present abnormal period, by reason of the labor shortage, it is not practical to take vacations does not change this basic principle. The desirable condition is to have every worker take a vacation and return to his work rested and refreshed without suffering a financial penalty or loss.[37]

Adherence to this view, which the industry representatives often agreed with,[38] no doubt eased the acceptance of the policies the Board had found necessary. By its use, the Board was able to answer employer attacks without appearing to make an exception to wage stabilization which might have opened the door to other demands more inflationary and unstabilizing than vacations were even when paid in lieu of time off.

Having armed itself with this philosophy and having succeeded, it thought, in separating vacations from the restrictions of wage stabilization, the Board could respond to the numerous employee

[36]*In re* Federal Shipbuilding and Drydock Co. *and* International Union of Marine and Shipbuilding Workers, Local 16, CIO. Sept. 15, 1943. *War Lab. Rep.*, vol. 11, p. 232. The opinion in this case was given by the Board's Shipbuilding Commission.

[37]*In re* Bower Roller Bearing Co. *and* United Automobile Workers, Local 681, CIO. May 31, 1943. *War Lab. Rep.*, vol. 9, pp. 26–27.

[38]For example, a panel industry member concurred in a recommendation of a plan allowing pay in lieu of vacation with this reminder: "I do not approve of vacations to workers as a means of raising wages or fattening the purse. The human kind needs rest from toil for a sufficient period to relax and repair the sinews of the body. The actual vacation should be a requirement of management wherever possible. Management should go to great lengths to arrange its schedules to provide it." *In re* Mead Corp. *and* United Mine Workers of America, District 50, Locals 12244 and 12281. May 20, 1943. *War Lab. Rep.*, vol. 8, p. 486.

demands now coming for extension of paid vacation plans to the rest of industry and the liberalization of plans already in effect.

WLB Adopts "Standard Plan"

In yielding to these demands, however, the Board found itself restricted by the prevailing-practice criterion it had been using. Through the summer of 1942 the Board had granted vacation plans only where there was a showing of similar area practice. The tightening of wage controls and the increased demand for vacations very quickly required a break with so restrictive a criterion. It came in the Association of Team and Truck Owners case of September 1, 1942, but in a cautious way: "Rather than attempt...to lay down a general rule," said the Board, it would "decide the question in each instance upon the peculiar facts of the case then before us."[39]

But the most peculiar fact about the cases now coming to the Board was that the employees demanded plans and liberalizations strictly as an employee-benefit—"across the board" as the wage controls had been applied—regardless of any prevailing practice. Not willing to adopt this view of vacations as simply a wage-increase substitute, the Board attempted to maintain general rules requiring some showing of prevailing practice, revising the criterion only when it had to. First it added consideration of industry practice to area practice and gave its regional boards express permission to approve vacation plans "which do not exceed the sound prevailing practice in the industry and area."[40]

But the Board continued to make exceptions both before and after the new rule was laid down, granting plans or improvements where, as in one case, the company was a "leader in its industry"[41] or where, as in another instance, a large competitor had a more liberal plan.[42] Thus, a few months after the Board had denied a vacation plan better than one-week for five years' service on the ground that "if the Board were to direct a more liberal policy, it

[39]*In re* Association of Team and Truck Owners, pp. 12–13.

[40]Instructions to Regional War Labor Boards: Operation under Executive Order 9328 and under the Supplementary Directive of May 12, 1943. *War Lab. Rep.,* vol. 8, p. xxvi.

[41]*In re* Phelps Dodge Copper Products Corp. *and* United Electrical, Radio and Machine Workers of America, CIO. Sept. 10, 1942. *War Lab. Rep.,* vol. 3, p. 136.

[42]*In re* Harbison Walker Refractories Co., p. 280.

might well be regarded as tantamount to the introduction of a vacation policy into the industry,"[43] it was doing just that. It was liberalizing a plan beyond the one-week industry practice on the ground that a two-week provision was "not at all uncommon in American industry."[44]

The Board's decisions throughout 1943, mostly rendered without comment, appeared to be establishing a pattern of one week for one year's service and two for five years. "This vacation pattern is now common over the nation," was a June 1943 comment from one of its mediators, and the Board seemed to be willing to go along with the finding even though it was not the practice in the particular industry.[45] But it was not until the Fulton Iron Works Co. case in April 1944 that this came to be its "standard" plan which could be approved or, in dispute cases, ordered by its Regional Boards

...without being rigidly bound by the fact that this growing practice may not have extended to the majority of plants in a particular area or industry at the time the dispute comes before the Regional Board.[46]

The Board had now yielded to the employee demand for paid vacations and virtually in the terms they were demanded: as substitutes for the wage increases denied workers. And if workers already had a plan, it was liberalized. In yielding to this employee demand, however, the Board did not also have to admit that vacations were simply an employee benefit. And it did not do so.

[43]*In re* U.S. Coal and Coke Co. *and* United Mine Workers, District 50, Local 12340. Nov. 27, 1942. *War Lab. Rep.*, vol. 5, p. 33.

[44]*In re* Universal Atlas Cement Co. *and* International Union of Mine, Mill and Smelter Workers Union, Local 309, CIO. April 13, 1943. *War Lab. Rep.*, vol. 7, p. 480. In another case it was admitted that "the two weeks provision is in many respects breaking new ground in the ...industry...but it is a policy which is by no means unusual." *In re* Federal Shipbuilding and Drydock Co., p. 230.

[45]*In re* American Brake Shoe and Foundry Co., Brake Shoe and Casting Division, Plants E and G, *and* United Steelworkers of America, Locals 1285 and 1814, CIO. June 24, 1943. *War Lab. Rep.*, vol. 9, p. 436. The Board's practice here is reminiscent of the Pullman porter who is alleged to have told the unseasoned traveller that his average tip was a dollar and, when he was given a dollar, thanked the donor for being the first to come up to the average.

[46]U.S. Department of Labor, *Termination Report*, vol. 1, p. 340. More liberal plans might be granted if supported by prevailing practice, but less liberal plans could be allowed only where compelling evidence indicated the propriety of such a restriction. *Ibid.* Also see Fulton Iron Works Co. *and* International Brotherhood of Electrical Workers, Local 1, AFL. April 6, 1944. *War Lab. Rep.*, vol. 15, pp. 230–231.

Development of the Board's rationale for so broadly granting vacations resulted from the counterpressure of employer opposition.

The unpredictability of the Board's criteria during the search for a reliable standard probably could not have been avoided, developing as it did not only from the Board itself as it worked its way through the new job of wage stabilization in wartime, but from its numerous panels, commissions, referees, mediators, and Regional Boards, whose recommendations were often given considerable publicity before the National Board's review approved or revised them.[47] And, in any case, the very flexibility of changing criteria had distinct advantages where the Board, buffeted between pressure and counterpressure, wished to proceed, but to proceed slowly.

On the other hand, the uncertain standards invited dispute cases as employers opposed to vacations or liberalizations sought to have the Board deny the demands by one criterion or another. While by this time the number of employers opposing vacation plan adoptions was relatively small, the number opposing liberalizations was large. Those who believed in the value of annual vacations did not necessarily believe that there would be a correspondingly greater value from longer vacations.

In plants where vacation time off could not be taken, the addition of a second week's allowance appeared to employers simply as a wage increase in the form of an additional vacation bonus; because it was neither supported by prevailing practice nor offset by a productivity increase, the extended allowance was attacked as "an unwarranted increase in production costs" and therefore unstabilizing.

Where vacations were taken, employers opposed the second week on the grounds that reducing time spent at work was contrary to the war manpower policy of increasing the workweek and man-hours available for productive work for the war effort. Industry representatives who had gone along with the Board's policy on vacation plan adoptions now began to dissent from its policy of lengthening vacation allowances.[48]

[47]U.S. Department of Labor, *Termination Report,* vol. 1, pp. xxiii–xxv.

[48]See, for example, V.-O. Milling Co. *and* American Federation of Grain Processors, Local 21830, AFL. June 1944. *War Lab. Rep.,* vol. 16, p. 482.

To secure the maximum acceptance for its decisions, the Board had applied each of its successively broader criteria, including even its final desertion of prevailing practice for a "standard" plan, with the flexibility which the pressure and counterpressure in each case required. But as the Board made exceptions to each new criterion used, a storm of protest rose from employers, and particularly each time the exceptions verged upon acknowledging vacations as primarily an employee benefit. In reaction, therefore, the Board rejected the kind of thinking occasionally suggested, as in the following case, by its panels. This panel stated (a full year before the Board's adoption of the "standard plan") that it believed that all American workers should have vacations uniformly "because the basic physical and psychological and humane considerations which underlie any vacation policy are the same. The panel supported this view of vacations as an employee benefit, "social" in nature, by observing:

Under normal conditions collective bargaining would undoubtedly operate to extend and enlarge vacation privileges in the area in question. The panel feels that it should not adopt a negative position and prevent by means of governmental decree, a development which seems not only healthy but also natural in view of observed trends in industrial relations.[49]

Alarmed by the implications of such talk, employers continued to protest that vacation grants and liberalizations were "inconsistent with the Government's program of not using the war effort to secure new gains."[50] Criticism also came from the Board's own

[49]*In re* Mead Corporation, p. 481. The Panel had recommended one week after a year's service and two weeks after two years. The Board revised this to require five years for the second week. In several cases this approach, anticipating what the gain might have been under free collective bargaining, was used. In an earlier case, a referee wanted to grant vacations but found in the past history of collective bargaining that the weakness of the union had required it to give up vacations many times to gain other points and protections and concluded that he should avoid "interfering with the bargaining processes of the parties." But the National Board granted a one week plan. *In re* St. Louis Cutting Die Cos. *and* International Association of Machinists, AFL. Nov. 9, 1943. *War Lab. Rep.*, vol. 12, p. 322. In another, a Regional Board granted a vacation plan despite past bargaining history in which the union, repeatedly given a choice of vacations or a wage increase, had always taken the wage increase, most recently, in fact, in the preceding year, 1942. This case apparently did not go to the National Board. *In re* American Fork and Hoe Co. *and* United Steelworkers of America, Local 2189, CIO. Nov. 24, 1943. *War Lab. Rep.*, vol. 13, p. 352.

[50]*In re* Thirty Michigan and Northern Wisconsin Lumber Companies *and* the International Woodworkers of America, Locals 15, 125, 142, 184, 220, 261, 327, 342, 347, CIO, and United Brotherhood of Carpenters and Joiners, Locals 1006, 2540, 2616, 2858, AFL. June 8, 1943. *War Lab. Rep.*, vol. 9, p. 507.

industry representatives. In the Fulton Iron Works case, which was to set the "standard plan" as Board policy on vacations, they said:

The Board's wartime function is to stabilize not to standardize labor relations....We believe that it is not within the province of the government to change existing collective bargaining agreements except when changes seem to be required for the winning of the war.[51]

The Board's response to the counterpressure was predictable; it was dictated by the character, and the source, of the criticism. In an opinion written by Chairman George Taylor, the Board held that vacations and their improvements were necessary to the war effort. According to management's own view:

We take serious issue with this argument [quoted above]. We had thought that it was well recognized that the maximum productive efficiency cannot be obtained from workers without some opportunity for vacations in which to build up their energies for the coming year. It is our view that it is even more necessary during a war period than in normal times to provide reasonable vacation periods as an aid to securing maximum war production.[52]

A "reasonable vacation period," according to the Board, was the one week for one year, two for five, of its "standard" plan. This allowance should therefore be granted regardless of prevailing practice in any specific industry since, the Board said, it was

...a normal practice in American industry throughout the country... voluntarily instituted by a vast number of companies as a sound management practice in order to secure maximum efficiency on the part of workers.[53]

The employer-benefit view, in providing an answer to employers, enabled the Board to discard the prevailing-practice criterion, which the union demand for vacations in substitute for further wage increases required it to do.

By early 1944, with the considerable help of the WLB, the "standard" allowance came to be a prevailing practice in industry generally and the extent of vacation coverage reached 81 percent

[51]*In re* Fulton Iron Works Co., vol. 13, pp. 638–639. The industry representatives' dissent was dated Jan. 3, 1944.
[52]*Ibid.*, April 6, 1944, vol. 15, p. 231.
[53]U.S. Department of Labor, *Termination Report,* vol. 1, p. 340. This statement was made in the same case.

of all American wage workers.[54] However, the remaining 19 percent included an important group of workers, ignored by management from the origin of the movement, who now sought vacation coverage.

Employers Protest Extension to Seasonal Workers

In industries of seasonal or irregular employment, the prevailing vacation practice at this mid-war point was, for the most part, no practice at all.[55] Yet workers in these industries were also under the wage controls and they also sought the vacation benefits granted other workers. Now from this quarter reality had begun to press in upon the War Labor Board. Its reliance upon the employer-benefit view of vacations was to be seriously challenged by the employers for whom it could not be convincing.

Employers in industries of seasonal or short-term and shifting employment, whose employees frequently did not return after layoffs, shared the workers' view of vacations as entirely an employee benefit and rarely were willing to make voluntary or joint requests to the Board for paid vacations. Most of the vacation cases in these industries came to the Board as dispute cases.

The employers buttressed their opposition with several types of arguments. First, they pointed to the lack of any showing of industry practice. Second, they argued that since vacations could not be granted during the busy season, a vacation plan amounted to a bonus paid at layoff time and "must be considered a wage issue."[56] Employers pointed to the fact that the Board itself had said this of seasonal industries on occasions. For example, in an early case the Board had denied a plan in the shipping industry, saying that vacations were not feasible during the season, "so that the demand for a vacation with pay amounts to pay for a period of time after the close of the season when the seamen are no longer employed."[57]

Third, the employers argued that where the layoff was temporary, it provided an adequate rest; and where employment was

---

[54]BLS, *Vacations with Pay in American Industry 1943 and 1944,* p. 2 This figure is calculated after excluding office workers from the figures given.

[55]*Ibid.,* pp. 1, 2, 20.

[56]*In re* Thirty Michigan and Northern Wisconsin Lumber Companies, p. 507.

[57]*In re* Detroit and Cleveland Navigation Co. *and* International Seafarers Union, AFL. July 3, 1942. *War Lab. Rep.,* vol. 2, p. 73.

short-term with workers shifting from one employer to another, they could take their own vacation between jobs if and when they desired.

A fourth type of argument involved the administrative difficulties of providing vacations to those who worked only part of a year. The irregular character of its operations, one employer argued, "makes it impossible to calculate eligibility for vacations."[58] Another complained that "such a vacation plan is complicated and creates extra expense to the company in the form of extra bookkeeping."[59]

And, finally, employers in these industries argued that no vacation was due their workers because "vacation is only for employees" and "when a person ceases to be an employee...he is not entitled to a vacation."[60] Employers simply could see no possible value to themselves in providing a paid vacation to those whose employment was terminated and would not be returning to yield them any benefits of a paid rest period.

WLB Grants to "Regular" Seasonal Workers

Although it might appear that the Board would have a difficult time, under the circumstances, with its argument that vacations were an employer benefit, it recognized that vacation plans could not be denied these workers. Under this necessity, it rose to the occasion. The Board divided the problem in two and confronted the easier half first. It made a distinction between those situations in which the workers could reasonably be expected to continue their employment after a temporary, seasonal layoff and those situations in which, by the nature of the work, employees could not be expected to return to the same employer, either because layoffs were too long or because work was casual or short-term.

The Board began by yielding only to the demands of workers whose layoffs were temporary, thus avoiding the administrative

[58]*In re* McLean-Arkansas Lumber Co. *and* International Woodworkers of America. Local 337, CIO. Sept. 18, 1943. *War Lab. Rep.,* vol. 11, p. 211.

[59]*In re* Saginaw Pattern and Manufacturing Co. and Wolverine Pattern and Manufacturing Co. *and* Pattern Makers' Association of Saginaw. Jan. 10, 1945. *War Lab. Rep.,* vol. 21, p. 303.

[60]*In re* Central States Employers' Negotiation Committee *and* Central States Drivers' Council, International Brotherhood of Teamsters, Chauffeurs, Warehousemen and Helpers of America, AFL. Oct. 14, 1942. *War Lab. Rep.,* vol. 4, p. 135.

difficulties of devising a plan for workers of highly irregular and diverse employment. More importantly this action avoided the necessity of granting vacations to workers permanently off the payroll of the employer who paid for the vacation. It was pointed out, as in one case, that "such workers as work steadily over a period of time are entitled to some vacation regardless of the industry."[61]

Although this policy of granting plans only to the year-round workers in a plant excluded some workers in most seasonal industries and almost all workers in the highly irregular or short-term employment industries, it enabled the Board to grant plans on a basis more acceptable to employers.

In the lumber industry where operations required considerable time off during the slack seasons, the union had asked for vacations prorated on the basis of all hours worked during the year, but the plan granted by the Lumber Commission and approved by the Board established a minimum period of work for eligibility to vacations in order that the vacation "be of value to the employer as well as to the employee. . . to encourage workers to stay with an employer through a definite period."[62] Fourteen hundred hours of work during the year were required for a full week's vacation and 840 hours for half a week.[63] The Board directed that employees who were regular enough to qualify for the full week could receive it even if on layoff at the end of the year, but that employees of less service who were eligible for only half a week *had to be in the employ of the company at the end of the vacation year.*[64] If this latter requirement were not made, the Board said, policing the vacation clause would have required administrative machinery which the Lumber Commission did not have and "even if the Commission had attempted to provide such machinery, such an order would have been beyond its power and jurisdiction."[65] This was, from the origin of paid vacation plans, the employer's

[61]*In re* Thirty Michigan and Northern Wisconsin Lumber Companies, p. 507.

[62]*In re* Employers Negotiating Committee, p. 18.

[63]*Ibid.; In re* Employers Negotiating Committee *and* International Woodworkers of America, CIO. June 26, 1942. *War Lab. Rep.,* vol. 2, p. 19. For loggers the requirement for half a week's vacation was 700 hours.

[64]*In re* Lumberman's Industrial Relations Committee, Inc.; Crown Zellerbach Corp. *and* International Woodworkers of America, Local 7–140, CIO. Nov. 19, 1943. *War Lab. Rep.,* vol. 12, pp. 229–230.

[65]*Ibid.,* p. 237.

requirement to assure that vacations go to those employees most likely to continue employment to yield the employer a return.

Similar plans were granted in other seasonal industries preserving the customary employer requirement, common to vacation plans from the origin of the vacation movement, that the employee be on the payroll at vacation time or at the end of the qualifying year but allowing exception for some layoff time during the qualifying year. For example, a week's vacation allowance was approved in part of the trucking industry for those employees who were in employment on November 15 and had worked 60 percent or more of the preceding year's total working days.[66] The requirements of plans varied with the type of work situation, but they had one thing in common: they provided paid vacation allowances only for the most steady employees in the seasonal industries. One Regional Board noted of its award:

Generally, cannery workers are casual labor. Few will qualify for vacations under our award, and those who do will probably be full-time year-round employees...the provision [for counting overtime hours along with straight-time hours to meet the 1600-hour work requirement to qualify] may in a few cases permit a vacation to other than year-round employees.[67]

In these cases the Board had no philosophic difficulties in applying the employer view that vacations' purpose was to increase productivity and it sometimes had the support of its industry members. But if it had thus far avoided trouble by designing plans that were not in conflict with that view by covering only those most likely to continue employment and yield the employer some benefit to offset his vacation cost, the trouble was not to be avoided much longer.

"Irregular" Seasonal Workers Get Plans

The rest of the workers in these industries, so irregular in employment that they were unlikely to be on the payroll on the date marking the end of the qualifying year, were impatient with

[66] *In re* Southeastern Area Employers Negotiating Committee *and* International Brotherhood of Teamsters, Southeastern Joint Teamsters Council. Dec. 10, 1943. *War Lab. Rep.*, vol. 12, pp. 666, 751.

[67] *In re* Associated Producers and Packers, Inc., *and* Washington State Council of Cannery Unions, AFL. June 21, 1945. *War Lab. Rep.*, vol. 25, p. 497.

the argument that for vacation purposes they were not "employees." In general, they saw vacations simply as an employee benefit given in lieu of a wage increase and could see no reason for their exclusion. But in any case, the Board itself had answered the objections of their employers that layoff time provided sufficient rest. It approved and often requoted in later cases this panel opinion:

Though the company argued that this is a seasonal industry where the workers do not work the entire year and that the vacation with pay is a bonus that has little to do with the idea of a vacation, the panel feels that a vacation or a layoff without pay is not a vacation; the purpose of a vacation is to give an employee a feeling of freedom and relaxation.[68]

The demand for vacation plans to cover these workers had been present in some measure throughout the war period, but it began to build up pressure when these workers saw vacations being granted in their industries to their more regularly employed fellow workers. Dissatisfaction with the plans, in fact, had been voiced by the excluded employees even at the time of adoption, as in the west coast lumber case where, it was noted in a later lumber case, the union

...was then insisting on a vacation with pay based on various numbers of hours of work within the year but with no requirement that they must be working at the end of the vacation year. The union contended that all workers in the industry should be entitled to a vacation and that, because of the irregularity of employment, many workers would not qualify for a vacation....[69]

Under these pressures, the Board soon found that the administrative problems it had described as "beyond its power and jurisdiction" were no obstacles at all, when vacations had to be granted. In the lumber industry, for instance, the Board finally overcame the "obstacles" by merely ordering a clause providing prorated terminal vacation pay to workers who were laid off, saying:

The giving of vacations with pay has become a generally accepted principle in American industry. We find no good reason for with-

[68]*In re* Burlington Dyeing and Finishing Co., Inc. *and* Textile Workers Union of America, Local 297, CIO. Dec. 31, 1942. *War Lab. Rep.*, vol. 5, pp. 520–521.
[69]*In re* Lumberman's Industrial Relations Committee, Inc., p. 231.

121

holding it now from the comparatively few operations that do not already have it.[70]

Other plans were devised to suit various types of work situations. Either the Board ordered a vacation plan and left the arrangements to be worked out between the parties, or, especially where the parties were unable to agree, it worked with them on the task. In men's and boys' clothing and in women's clothing, plans were devised by the parties and submitted to the Board for approval, providing a model for some of the later plans.[71] In these central vacation funds, set up by the union and the employers with whom they dealt, vacation payments based on the amount of service given each employer were pooled for all covered employees. These schemes followed the general pattern of the one devised by arbitrator Wayne Morse for the Ship Clerks in 1940. This was particularly true of the longshoremen's plan granted by the Board in 1945.[72]

Whether the vacation allowance was paid to the employee directly under a terminal vacation pay clause or into a fund from which he annually collected his accumulated vacation pay, it was in all cases paid at employment termination, in proportion to the amount of service given, and the worker was not required to be "on the payroll" of any one of his several employers as of any certain date. This exception to the usual practice under vacation plans was necessary, of course, to provide vacations at all to workers who could not, by the irregular nature of their work, stay with one employer long enough to qualify under any of the customary service minimums.

But allowance of vacation pay at employment termination, for workers without a regular or continuing employer-employee relationship, sometimes after as little as thirty days' work, brought immediate and forceful protest. The employers' strongest argu-

[70]*In re* Northwest Fir Companies and Northwest Pine Companies *and* International Woodworkers of America, CIO, and United Brotherhood of Carpenters and Joiners of America, Lumber and Sawmill Workers' Union, AFL. March 4, 1944. *War Lab. Rep.*, vol. 14, p. 503.

[71]*In re* New York Clothing Manufacturers' Exchange *and* Amalgamated Clothing Workers Union, CIO. Feb. 12, 1944. *War Lab. Rep.*, vol. 14, p. 803; BLS, *Vacations with Pay in American Industry 1943 and 1944*, p. 20.

[72]Waterfront Employers Association of the Pacific Coast *and* International Longshoremen's and Warehousemen's Union, CIO. August 18, 1945. *War Lab. Rep.*, vol. 26, p. 531.

ment was based firmly on the employer benefit view of vacations which the Board had been expressing as the justification for its vacation policies. Dissenting industry representatives reminded the Board of this fact, as for example:

Board policy on vacations for production workers is well known. Such vacations are ordered not as a wage increase but as a period of rest to be provided by an employer for an employee after a year of service in order that he may return refreshed.[73]

The Board majority in this case confronted the problem honestly and directly. First, it frankly admitted its own responsibility for the situation it now faced and then acknowledged that it could not deny vacations to these workers. It said:

The employers point out that no vacation is provided under any longshore contract. However, the instant case involves a large segment of the national longshore industry and covers a great area over which vacations have become practically universal. The extension of the paid vacation in that area as elsewhere has been achieved largely through the practice of the Board. The question is whether longshoremen should be excluded from the benefits of that practice.[74]

In deciding that no workers could be excluded, the Board appeared to be close to acknowledging that vacations were to be allowed to all workers as an employee benefit granted in lieu of wage increases. But the Board was making no such concession. It budged only slightly from its past position that vacations were primarily an employer benefit for the purpose of increasing productivity, despite the frontal attack by employers in situations where they thoroughly believed no benefits could return to them.

The Board fell back upon the national outlook it had frequently expressed. As noted above, the Board had said in the Fulton Iron Works case, when it made the "standard plan" WLB policy, that vacations were "even more necessary during a war...as an aid to securing maximum war production." Furthermore, having said, as in an earlier case, that vacations "contribute heavily to the efficiency and output of any industry,"[75] it was but the next logical step to hold that the value from paid vacations returned to industry as a whole and did not necessarily have to accrue to

[73]*Ibid.*, p. 532.　　　　　　[74]*Ibid.*
[75]Kaul Clay Manufacturing Company *and* United Clay Products Workers, Local 1193, CIO. August 20, 1943. *War Lab. Rep.*, vol. 10, p. 524.

each individual employer who paid the bill. This aggregate value concept had first been expressed by the National Defense Mediation Board, January 3, 1942, and was quoted by a WLB panel some months later to justify a terminal vacation pay clause in the N.D.M.B.-granted vacation plan for truck drivers whose employment often did not last to or through the vacation season. The panel, whose recommendation was subsequently approved unanimously by the National Board, said:

From the point of view of the public interest in manpower, a driver should have a vacation whether he continues working for one employer or shifts to another. As the Mediation Board said: "The work of the over-the-road driver is arduous and tiring. We believe that the industry as a whole will benefit if for a short period once a year the drivers are relieved of the constant strain and responsibility of their work and allowed a few days of rest and relaxation."[76]

In a later expression of the concept of aggregate employer benefit, this explanation was made:

...the future, rather than the former, employer would benefit from the restoration of the employee's efficiency resulting from the fact that the receipt of the vacation pay would enable the employee to take his vacation between jobs. Nevertheless, the assuring of the vacation would also serve to maintain the efficiency of operations of the original employer.[77]

Although employers had made clear by their opposition that they did not see themselves in the aggregate and looked for a return to their individual company operations, the Board held firm to the national view of the salutary effect of such measures on the total war production effort.

Supported by this rationale, the wartime WLB policy extended vacations to the last group of American workers for whom management had not voluntarily provided coverage and brought virtually to an end the adoption phase of the movement. By the end of the war period vacation coverage of wage earners was over 90 percent—an extent of coverage no other fringe benefit even approached.

[76]*In re* Central States Employers' Negotiating Committee, p. 136.
[77]Sullivan Drydock and Repair Corporation *and* Industrial Union of Marine and Shipbuilding Workers of America, Local 13, CIO. Feb. 29, 1944. *War Lab. Rep.,* vol. 14, p. 289.

Summary

The high percentage of vacation coverage attained by 1945, as well as the extensive liberalizing of plans, had come about under the view of vacations as a non-wage labor cost incurred for the purpose of increasing the productivity of the work force. During most of this period of rapid progress, management acted voluntarily. Employer and joint applications for WLB approval of adoptions and liberalizations of vacation plans far outnumbered dispute cases.[78]

Management had been pushing the vacation movement as it had originated it, on a practical, tough-minded theory of return value in increased productivity. To the extent that it ceased to see a return from vacation expenditure, it ceased to push further development of the movement. It was at this point that the unions entered the vacation movement as a major force.

Though a major force, the unions nevertheless pressed for vacations in collective bargaining with an eye to what was allowable under government controls. In the final analysis, it was the wartime economic policies of the government, in restricting wage increases but permitting fringe benefits, that provided the motivation and the WLB that provided the machinery, by which the unions extended paid vacations to the rest of American workers.

While the Board undoubtedly was sincere in holding to the employer-benefit view to justify establishing vacations as national policy on the principle that they increased production, it nonetheless used this view skillfully to gain acceptance of the policies which actually were dictated by practical considerations. But, in any case, it was unnecessary as well as unwise to go further and make an outright admission that vacations were a substitute for wage increases. Such an admission might have been fatal to wage stabilization, but it was an open secret[79] and the WLB virtually

[78]U.S. Department of Labor, *Termination Report*, vol. 1, pp. 801, 822.

[79]The BLS commented, "During the war period, in which wage increases have been controlled by the Government, one of the most important benefits that a union could obtain for its members has been a new and more liberal vacation arrangement." BLS, *Vacations with Pay in American Industry 1943 and 1944*, p. 20. In its final report, Region X of the WLB noted the effect of the "wage freeze" and how it was interpreted at the time by both industry and labor. It said, "Immediately after Executive Order 9328 [the April 8, 1943, 'hold the line' order restricting approval of wage increases to the Little Steel Formula] both industry

admitted as much after the war in its Termination Report in summarizing the Regional Boards' comments on the usefulness of allowing fringes. It said:

The regions agreed that the use of fringe adjustments helped them to hold the stabilization line on basic wage rate adjustments. These adjustments were referred to as a "safety valve" and "a useful cushion" which helped to offset "the rigidity of our controls over basic wage rates" that might have created pressures that would "blow the lid off of stabilization."[80]

At the time the cases were decided, however, the Board merely yielded to the demand and did its talking not to the employees but to the protesting employers and to the public.[81]

Nor did the unions challenge the use of the employer-benefit rationale throughout the adoption phase of the movement. In seeking vacation plans, in fact, they often argued the productivity increase view, not because they were concerned with whether management received a benefit from vacations but because it was so obviously the argument the Board was responding to favorably. The earned-right view was not used by unions to win vacation plan adoptions or liberalizations. It may be presumed they realized that to do so might endanger their case; the earned-right view, as expressed in cases before the war, suggested that vacations were earned along with service like, or as a part of, wages. The Board was granting vacations only because they were not wages.

If there is a question as to how much of the union demand for paid vacation plans was based on a genuine desire for the rest period to meet a "social" need involving the workers' health and general well-being and how much was simply a desire for a "fringe benefit" other workers were getting, one thing is nevertheless clear: neither employees nor their unions during this period saw vacations as wages in payment for their actual service but rather as a substitute for an increase in the hourly rate for that purpose.

---

and labor looked upon fringe adjustments as a substitute for further increases." U.S. Department of Labor, *Termination Report*, vol. 1, p. 753.

[80]*Ibid.*, p. 596.

[81]In its *Termination Report*, however, the WLB noted the benefits that its policies on vacations, and on fringes generally, yielded to workers. Region X, for instance, observed, "Fringe adjustments probably are more permanent in character than wage adjustments. The public members of the Board were well aware of this fact, as well as the social and economic advances which may have been made through fringe adjustments." *Ibid.*, p. 753.

In fact, the paid time off which they received instead did not increase their income except in special and temporary cases.

The Board, too, had taken great pains to make a distinction between vacation pay and wages. The matter was crucial to wage stabilization from the cost side as well. The employer-benefit view with its emphasis on the productivity increase was the only rationale that would clearly free vacations from conflict with wage stabilization: the productivity increase, in off-setting their cost, kept vacations from being inflationary.

Without doubt, the employer-benefit view had served the vacation movement long and well. It had been the guiding force throughout the adoption phase from the origin of the movement for wage earners before World War I to its close near the end of World War II. But if the earned-right view of vacations as a social benefit primarily for the employee's sake had played little or no part in this progress, a turning point had now come, marking the end of an era in the vacation movement.

When it granted vacations to the last group of workers by providing prorated vacation allowances at employment termination, the Board itself laid the basis for a new concept of vacations which, even before the war period was over, was to bring the War Labor Board to the point of denying that vacations were primarily employer benefits intended to increase productivity. On an issue other than vacation plan adoptions, the unions were now to argue that vacations were an earned right. The Board's carefully held position that vacations were not wages was now put to a severe test.

CHAPTER 6

The War Labor Board Shifts
Its Rationale

ONE of the results of the government's wartime wage stabilization policies, in freezing wages and permitting fringe benefits, had been to make vacations by the end of 1944 "one of the most active subjects in collective bargaining negotiations."[1] Union workers, who had always been behind wage earners as a whole in their vacation coverage, caught up in 1944.[2]

Although most vacation plans had been instituted by management, they were soon included in union contracts. Some employers had opposed the inclusion,[3] and others had indicated that they

[1] Gertrude Reynolds, *Vacation Policy in 1945*, The Conference Board Reports, Supplement to *The Conference Board Management Record* (New York: The National Industrial Conference Board, Inc., 1945), p. 11; see also U.S. Department of Labor, *The Termination Report of the National War Labor Board, Industrial Disputes and Wage Stabilization in Wartime* (Washington, G.P.O., 1947), vol. 1, pp. 753, 774.

[2] In 1940, union workers had 25 percent coverage compared to about 50 percent for all workers. In January 1943, they had 60 percent coverage compared to 81 percent for all workers during the year April 1943 to April 1944. By November 1944, 85 percent of employees under union agreement had vacation plans. Although figures are not available on total coverage as of this precise date, it may be assumed that union workers had caught up. U.S. Department of Labor, Bureau of Labor Statistics, *Vacation and Holiday Provisions in Union Agreements January 1943*, Bulletin No. 743 (Washington: G.P.O., 1943), p. 1; "Vacations with Pay in Union Agreements, 1940," *Monthly Labor Review*, vol. 51, 1940, p. 1070; U.S. Department of Labor, Bureau of Labor Statistics, *Vacations with Pay in American Industry 1943 and 1944*, Bulletin No. 811 (Washington: G.P.O., 1945), pp. 2, 20.

[3] For example, see Burlington Dyeing and Finishing Co., Inc., *and* Textile Workers Union of America, Local 297, CIO. Dec. 31, 1942. Bureau of National

felt vacations to be a matter of company policy rather than a subject for local bargaining.[4] But the trend toward including vacation plans in union agreements continued largely unopposed, reflecting both the increase in union organization and the wartime union interest in paid vacation plans. Prior to 1937, only 4 percent of vacation plans were in contracts. The figure jumped to 26 percent in that year and to 64 percent in 1943. By 1945, 80 percent of companies surveyed by the N.I.C.B. reported their plans were embodied in agreements with employees.[5]

These figures indicate the extent to which paid vacations had become contractual rights of the employees. The significance of this fact was noted in an early 1942 arbitration case as follows:

Vacation rights are not something which can be given by an employer with one hand and taken away with the other at the employer's discretion or whim, but they are in fact vested rights. Once granted in a labor contract, they become a property right; they become a legal obligation owed to the employee by the employer.[6]

Although about half of the vacation plans of that year were included in union contracts, the "right" was carefully restricted to those employees who were most likely to be continuing their employment: those on the payroll at vacation time and who had given continuous service in the preceding year. In actual practice, an employee who had completely fulfilled the year's service requirement received no vacation or vacation pay if he were laid off before actually taking the vacation, even if the layoff came the day before his vacation was to begin. Employers had almost never granted such pay. As noted of the period preceding the war years, very few vacation plans, contractual or company, contained any

---

Affairs, *War Labor Reports, Wage and Salary Stabilization Reports of Decisions and Orders of the National War Labor Board and Subsidiary Agencies* (hereafter referred to as *War Lab. Rep.*) (Washington: BNA, 1942–1946), vol. 5, p. 520.

[4]For example, see American Can Co. *and* United Steelworkers of America, Locals 1861, 2113, 2049, 1478, 2067, and 2041, CIO. Jan. 14, 1944. *War Lab. Rep.*, vol. 13, p. 651.

[5]National Industrial Conference Board, *Vacation and Holiday Practices*, The Conference Board Reports, Studies in Personnel Policy, No. 75 (New York: N.I.C.B. 1946), p. 5.

[6]*In re* Crown Mills of Portland, Oregon, *and* Flour and Cereal Workers Union No. 20160. Arbitrator: Wayne Morse. Jan. 18, 1942. File copy of award, National Labor Bureau, Seattle, Washington.

reference at all to terminated employees, either to provide or deny them vacation rights, although employers sometimes allowed vacation pay on an individual basis in certain circumstances. It was reported in 1943 that 70 percent of employers surveyed by the N.I.C.B. required specifically that employees be on the payroll at the time of the vacation period.[7]

At the same time, however, if an employee were called into military service, the figures were reversed: 80 percent of employers gave him a vacation payment when he left—not only the full vacation for the preceding year of service but even a prorated amount for part of a year's service rendered in the current year.[8] This led the N.I.C.B. to report "two distinctly different views as to the nature and purpose of vacations:"

The first is that vacations are granted for the purpose of allowing employees a rest period in which to reequip themselves physically for the tasks they must face in the ensuing year. According to this view, vacations are *privileges* which are granted to employees at the option of management.

The second view is that vacations are *basic rights,* that they are periods in which to recuperate from the tasks already accomplished during the past year and that they are therefore associated with compensation just as actual work performed is associated with wages.[9]

But the majority of employers clearly held the former view. The anomalous allowance of vacation pay at termination for military service was the only exception they were willing to make, and they did so rather on the basis of patriotism than as a matter of the philosophy of paid vacation plans.

Between the two views of vacations—as an employer benefit, only for employees who would continue employment to yield the increased productivity resulting from the rest, and as an employee benefit, due all employees as a right regardless of subsequent employment status—the battle was about to be joined. The War Labor Board found itself squarely in the middle. Faced with

[7]Elmer W. Earl, Jr., *Wartime Influences on Vacation Policies,* The Conference Board Reports, Studies in Personnel Policy, No. 56 (New York: N.I.C.B., 1943), p. 14.
[8]*Ibid.,* p. 15; "Weirton Liberalizes Vacation Plan; Pays Former Employees Now in Service," *Steel,* vol. 110, 1942, p. 58.
[9]Earl, *op. cit.,* p. 14.

demands for terminal vacation pay, the Board started out by yield-ing only one step at a time without acknowledging any new con-cept of vacations as an employee right.

Vacation Pay Granted at Military Leave as Bonus

The earliest demands for terminal vacation pay related prin-cipally to leaves for entry into the armed services and arose when workers not granted the allowance by their employers saw most other workers receiving such payments. Aware of the common practice of allowing vacation pay at these terminations, the Board granted it on the same basis management had—as a bonus.

In the first case involving military leave, in April of 1942, the Board denied a request for a three-months' bonus to workers leav-ing for military service provided they were granted accrued vaca-tion pay.[10] Then, in June 1942 when the WLB originally granted a vacation plan in the lumber industry, its award specified:

...when employees are drafted or enlist in the armed forces, but for such workers only, that a vacation allowance be granted for the weeks worked during the year, the allowance to be a fraction of the full yearly vacation pay...pro-rated....[11]

The Board made this policy, however, not on the view that vacations were an "earned" right, despite the occasional language to that effect from its lower bodies, such as this from a panel:

We believe if he has earned his vacation pay, he should not be required to forego it because he is inducted....[12]

Rather, vacation pay at entry into military service was granted out of patriotic motives quite without regard to any philosophy. For example, in a later case which well described the underlying motivation, the Shipbuilding Commission noted that granting

[10]*In re* Babcock and Wilcox Co. *and* United Electrical Workers, Local 439, CIO. April 6, 1942. *War Lab. Rep.,* vol. 1, p. 133.

[11]*In re* Employers Negotiating Committee *and* International Woodworkers of America, CIO. June 16, 1942. *War Lab. Rep.,* vol. 2, pp. 5–6. This had been the recommendation by the WLB arbitrator, unanimously approved by the National Board in its directive order.

[12]*In re* California Wire Cloth Co. *and* United Steelworkers of America, Local 1798, CIO. Dec. 30, 1943. *War Lab. Rep.,* vol. 14, p. 74.

such allowances "will be readily understood as a partial expression of our sense of debt toward those who are so called."[13]

For all of the Board's opposition to vacations as a bonus, it was the bonus idea and not an earned right concept that inspired its policies relative to terminations for military service. In some cases the Board granted not only the vacation that might appear to have been "earned" by partial service in the current year but even allowed the full year's vacation which the employee had not yet earned in any sense of the word, but for which he would have become eligible if he had continued his employment until the end of the year.

The Board had taken its lead from the employers who had been willing to give vacation pay at military leave. Although this first type of terminal vacation pay presented no problem to the WLB, the precedent it established soon did. Workers not only now saw the practice of terminal vacation pay for the first time, but they saw an official government endorsement of it. Employees and their unions began to ask for it for other terminations.

Vacation Pay Granted at Layoffs as Severance Pay

Terminal vacation pay at layoffs had been an occasional union demand since the beginning of the war period and, of necessity, had been demanded by the unions to provide vacation coverage to workers in industries with seasonal or irregular employment. For workers in regular employment industries, however, it did not become a common demand until late in the war. During the last year of the war particularly, many workers began to worry about reconversion layoffs. Their unions commented on the increasing irregularity of operations and noted that "forces may be reduced at any time."[14] They now began aggressively to seek vacation pay for layoff terminations, to provide not paid vacation time off but severance pay, as the following illustrates:

[13]*In re* New York Shipbuilding Corp. *and* Industrial Union of Marine and Shipbuilding Workers of America, Local 1, CIO. Feb. 8, 1945. *War Lab. Rep.*, vol. 21, p. 628.

[14]*In re* U.S. Cartridge Co. *and* United Electrical Workers, Local 816, CIO. Oct. 2, 1945. *War Lab. Rep.*, vol 28, p. 281.

The worker suffers direct loss of earnings during the layoff and should not be asked to bear the additional loss of a decrease in vacation pay, it [the union] argues.[15]

To buttress their demand for vacation pay at layoffs, the unions came up with a clear and insistent expression of the earned-right view, requiring not only pay for vacations already qualified for by a full year of service up to the eligibility date at or near the vacation time, but also prorated pay for partial service in the current year where an employee had not yet reached the qualifying date before his layoff. The unions were explicit about the full import of the earned-right view:

The union...contends that no person shall be deprived of his vacation...which would be the case unless prorating of vacation pay is included in the contract. Those men who are laid off before having completed a full 40 weeks of work in any given year will be deprived of that part of the vacation period which has been earned.[16]

This view assumed that the nature of vacations was such that they were earned as the service was being rendered, day by day or month by month. The similarity to the earning of wages was obvious, and the unions occasionally supported their earned-right argument with the new, but, they thought, compelling argument that vacation pay was due as part of wages.

If these unions had shifted ground from the union position that vacation plans could be granted despite the wage freeze because vacation pay was not wages, then employers, too, had shifted. In the earlier days employers were arguing that vacation payments were wages and as such were not allowable except as part of the permissible wage increase of the Little Steel Formula. The employers now protested that "Vacation pay is not part of wages...."[17] and that

vacations should not be considered as additional compensation which an employee earns in the same manner as he earns wages.[18]

[15]*In re* Bendix Aviation Corp., Philadelphia Division, *and* United Electrical Workers, Local 114, CIO. Oct. 31, 1945. *War Lab. Rep.*, vol. 28, p. 569.

[16]*In re* American Radiator and Standard Sanitary Corp. *and* United Automobile Workers, Local 344, CIO. Nov. 1, 1945. *War Lab. Rep.*, vol. 28, p. 750.

[17]*In re* Atlas Powder Co., Weldon Spring Ordnance Works *and* International Brotherhood of Firemen and Oilers, Local 6, AFL. August 6, 1945. *War Lab. Rep.*, vol. 27, p. 127.

[18]*In re* American Radiator and Standard Sanitary Corp., p. 750.

Even though no productivity increase would result from this vacation cost, some employers were willing to go along with requests for vacation pay at layoffs more or less as a severance bonus. Others were not so kindly disposed, saying, "a vacation contemplates continuous employment and shouldn't be used as severance pay...."[19] Some industry representatives on Regional Boards and panels also registered strong protests in their dissents against both the demand and the earned-right argument on which it was based. One pointed out that the union was merely after "protection, that is, severance pay if the plant closes, not vacation benefits."[20] Another, on more philosophical grounds, argued that:

The vacation is not payment for work performed during any past period but is solely a reward for continuous service given in expectation that the employee will continue with the company.... The incentive for continuous service as a result of granting vacations with pay would be destroyed if vacation pay was made a part of wages by being prorated.[21]

Faced with such controversy, the War Labor Board, as so often in the past, again yielded to the employee demand without yielding to the employee concept of vacations. There was little choice but to yield. The Board had already—in the spring of 1944—arrived at its policy of granting vacation plans to workers in highly seasonal industries where the provision of vacation coverage itself required payment for vacations at layoffs.[22] It would have been difficult at such a time to deny the same provision where layoffs were the exception rather than the rule.

The Board began to yield in September 1944 in the RCA Communications case, by approving a voluntary request for vacation pay at layoffs[23] and ordered such payments pro rata for part of a year's service in the Glenn L. Martin Company dispute case decided in March of 1945.[24] Shortly after, the Board issued Field

---

[19]*In re* American Smelting and Refining Co. *and* International Union of Mine, Mill and Smelter Workers, Local 509, CIO. August 22, 1945. *War Lab. Rep.,* vol. 27, p. 168.

[20]*In re* U.S. Cartridge Co., p. 282.

[21]*In re* American Radiator and Standard Sanitary Corp., pp. 751–752.

[22]See Chapter 5.

[23]U.S. Department of Labor, *Termination Report,* p. 349.

[24]*In re* Glenn L. Martin Co. *and* United Automobile Workers, Local 738, CIO. March 13, 1945 (made public April 14, 1945). *War Lab. Rep.,* vol. 23, p. 376.

Memorandum No. 130 permitting the practice in voluntary cases even without submission to the WLB.[25]

In yielding to these demands, however, the Board did not wish to accede to the employees' earned-right view of vacations, particularly when it described vacation pay as wages, after the Board so painstakingly had separated the two to avoid conflict with its wage stabilization responsibilities. Therefore, as it had done in the case of vacation payments at terminations to enter military service, the Board made its policy on an expedient rather than philosophic basis. In saying simply that vacation pay was to be allowed at layoffs in order to ease the impending reconversion to peacetime production,[26] the Board was responding not to the earned-right line of argument but rather to that part of the union agreement based on "the fact that forces may be reduced at any time"[27] and the fact that "layoffs...are completely beyond the workers' control."[28]

The following panel opinion reveals this line of reasoning:

This is a war plant. Numerous layoffs have occurred because of changes in military requirements. Layoffs in great number may occur in the course of the present contract year. Employees when laid off will have worked beyond the date at which they last qualified for vacations as little as one week or as much as eleven months. They are laid off for reasons beyond their control.[29]

[25]U.S. Department of Labor, *Termination Report*, p. 349.
[26]*Ibid.*
[27]*In re* U.S. Cartridge Co., p. 281.
[28]*In re* Bendix Aviation Corp., p. 569.
[29]*In re* U.S. Cartridge Co., p. 281. Although this case is dated October 2, 1945, the panel opinion and recommendation quoted above preceded the Board's Glenn L. Martin decision. The panel noted of that time: "While the majority has found no National Board action directly supporting the recommendation, it has likewise found no action opposed to the recommendation. National Board silence may be evidence that the issue is new." *Ibid.*

With respect to chronology, it should be noted that the purpose of this chapter, as of the last one, is to trace the development of WLB thinking about vacations in both its opinions and its policies as it responded to pressure and counterpressure. The development was roughly chronological as described, but cases used as examples may sometimes appear to be out of order because of the final decision date given. Some WLB cases were handled swiftly, but others were argued many months before the final decision date, as in this case and in the Bendix case above. In this case, for instance, negotiations between U.S. Cartridge Co. and the United Electrical Workers had begun on July 22, 1944; the U.S. Conciliation Service worked with the parties in October 1944; arguments then began before the WLB panel and its

(continued)

This panel, whose recommendations were approved by the National Board, denied the employer charge that such payments would be a bonus or severance payment and took the opportunity to point out that:

...the Board...does not treat vacation allowances as wages. The Board, for reasons arising out of stabilization policy, applies one set of principles to wages, another to vacations. Nothing in Board action, however, indicates that in Board thinking employees do not acquire equities in vacations.[30]

Admitting that employees had an equity in vacations not yet taken was as close as the WLB wished to come to the earned-right concept as long as it had some other justification for yielding to the employee demand—in this case on the issue of layoffs. Use of expedient justifications for both military leave and layoff had thus far enabled the Board to avoid being caught in the head-on collision between the union and the employer views of vacations. Its luck did not hold, however, as the unions pressed one more demand, to be discussed in the subsequent section.

WLB Shifts to Earned-Right Rationale

The issue that routed the Board from its adherence to the employer view of vacations as a means of increasing productivity was the last union demand: accrued vacation pay at terminations caused by voluntary quits and discharges for cause. It was on this issue that vacations as an earned right finally received official acknowledgment.

The basis for the new concept had by now been well laid in Board policies. Ever since their inclusion in contracts, paid vacations had been accepted as "rights," at least for employees still on the payroll at the end of the qualifying year. But they were not generally accepted as "earned" rights accruing day by day or month by month as service was being rendered and therefore due regardless of an employee's subsequent employment status.

report was dated March 9, 1945; the Regional Board issued its decision on June 23; the National Board finally approved the Regional Board's decision on October 2, although not making it public until November 14, 1945. Almost a year and a half had passed since negotiations had begun and a year of that time was consumed as the case worked its way through the WLB.

[30]*Ibid.*, pp. 281–282.

Nevertheless, although unacknowledged and unintended by the Board, this concept was already at the base of several WLB policies even while the Board was paying lip service to another view. The first example was allowance of payment for accrued vacations at termination to workers other than "regular" employees, for whom no vacation coverage could be provided without a terminal vacation pay clause. This provision paying pro rata for vacations based proportionately on service thus made those vacations earned rights even though the Board's announced grounds for granting the plans were that paid vacations were "prevailing practice in American industry generally" and that they would yield benefit to employers in the aggregate.

The earned-right assumption also underlay the Board policy of granting prorated vacations to employees entering military service, although it did so because of the "debt" owed to military personnel and because the practice had general acceptance already. Finally, the earned-right concept was implied when the Board then granted such pay at layoffs with the intention of easing reconversion.

Expedient policies, however, only delayed the day of reckoning. The Board was eventually caught up by the logic of the policies it had allowed to develop.[31] It could not be long before the idea

[31]This situation was unavoidable. Hundreds of thousands of cases came to the WLB during the relatively short war period. For example, over 200,000 voluntary applications and about 6,000 dispute cases on wages came to the twelve Regional Boards in a one-year period from July 1944 to August 1945. On fringe issues, there were almost 40,000 voluntary cases and 3,547 dispute cases approved and ordered in the same one-year period—half being on paid vacations. U.S. Department of Labor, *Termination Report*, vol. 1, pp. 522, 482, 822, and 811.

Of necessity the Board had to grant much autonomy to its subordinate bodies. Thus, even while the National Board was deciding on a policy, a hundred cases on the same issue might be in the process of being argued, decided, and justified at the panel and Regional Board level. Region VII noted with some poignancy in its Termination Report this Board's-eye view: "A Board of twelve (or six) whose membership fluctuated through fifty persons created a serious problem of maintenance of consistency. The unavoidable result was a degree of zig-zag which has a cumulative effect. Earlier 'zigs' contrasted with later 'zags' not infrequently left the parties breathless. As these situations piled one on top of the other we tended to find our action already committed where we did not find that action of any kind was supportable. Our general course in the application of established Board policy showed such wobbling that at times we have thought it well that the agency is being liquidated." *Ibid.*, p. 704; see also n. 1, p. xxiii.

No doubt the National Board could have said the same. At any rate, avoidable or not, the vacation policies had developed and the National Board found itself in the same kind of "action already committed" position.

of vacations as "earned rights" would have to be dealt with more directly than to say, "Nothing in Board action, however, indicates that in Board thinking employees do not acquire equities in vacations." With past policies already treating vacations as if they were an earned right, it took only a handful of cases to bring out the expression of it. This is what now happened.

When it faced the demand for vacation pay at quits and discharges for cause, however, the WLB had no expedient to call upon. No patriotic motive, no reconversion threat could justify granting vacation pay at such terminations. No employer view of vacations as a rest to increase productivity or as a reward for continuous service could justify such a provision. Its only justification could be that vacations had been earned by the service which had already been rendered and that they were therefore due an employee when he left for any reason whatever.

The employees had only to demand vacation pay at quits and discharge for cause, and the Board would have to face up to the conflict the demand posed. It would have to grant the allowance on the basis of the earned-right· view or deny it on the basis of the employer-benefit view, unless it were to cease giving justifications for its policies. This latter was hardly an alternative; as a public body between two protagonists, the Board depended for its success largely upon the acceptability of its policies to the parties and to the public as well.

The Board's Shipbuilding Commission was the first to break with the Board's reliance upon the employer-benefit view. In February of 1944, in an isolated case long before the idea was heard from again, the Commission specifically acknowledged the earned-right concept of paid vacations. Yet, oddly enough, this acknowledgment came not to support the granting of prorated vacation pay, which the logic of the earned-right view would require, but only to justify granting it to those employees who had passed the eligibility date and had thus qualified for full vacations prior to termination. In this case, the union had not asked for vacation pay prorated for partial service in the current year. It requested pay at all terminations, including quits and discharges for cause, only for workers who had completed another full year of service since their last vacations.

In granting the union request, the writer for the majority on the Commission nevertheless spelled out the full earned-right logic of vacations "as a part of the remuneration for employment and, hence, as a right that is gradually built up month by month as employment continues."[32] If he were perhaps overstating his case, one thing was abundantly clear: he was rejecting the employer-benefit view. In preparing the *coup de grace,* the writer of the majority opinion discussed the views of vacations held by the Commissioners and then suggested that "under the first view— that a vacation is granted to maintain efficiency (a view not held by the majority of the Commission)—the assurance of a vacation" for the terminating worker might benefit a future employer. But, he pointed out, vacations in any case were an earned right:

...an employee who has completed the one-year period of service has in a very real sense earned his right to a vacation and should be entitled to receive it if he is subsequently separated before he has had an opportunity to take it. ...payment for the deferred vacation has been earned and is no more to be regarded as severance pay than is the payment of wages earned since the last pay day.[33]

This decision and repudiation of the employer-benefit view in favor of the earned-right concept of vacations stood without having involved the National Board, although the National Board had the right to review on its own motion any decision made by its Regional Boards, Commissions, or panels.[34]

No more was heard of the earned-right view from the WLB until five months later, in mid-1944, when a panel denied a union request for vacation pay for employees who had already passed the qualifying date for a full vacation but who were off the payroll because of discharge for cause before they had taken the vacation. It did so on the ground that such a provision was in conflict with the employer-benefit view of vacations "granted to

[32]*In re* Sullivan Drydock and Repair Corporation *and* Industrial Union of Marine and Shipbuilding Workers of America, Local 13, CIO. Feb. 29, 1944. *War Lab. Rep.,* vol. 14, p. 289.

[33]*Ibid.*

[34]U.S. Department of Labor, *Termination Report,* vol. 1, pp. xxiii–xxiv.

enhance the efficiency of the employee upon returning to work."
Discussing vacations also as a reward for faithful service, the panel
added, "it would be anomalous to require the company to reward
a dishonest or insubordinate employee."[35]

But the Regional Board, to which this case went next, resolved
the conflict in views with a different conclusion. It amended the
panel's recommendation with this opinion:

The majority of the Tenth Regional Board, industry members dissenting, are of the opinion that a vacation is an earned right and that
employees who work the qualifying period are entitled to receive
a vacation or pay in lieu thereof. In adopting the proposal suggested
by the union, the majority of the Board wish to make it clear that
all employees should be entitled to receive vacation benefits regardless of whether they were discharged with or without cause, whether
they quit or whether their employment was terminated.[36]

This decision and its forthright opinion based on the earned-
right view also stood without National Board involvement in the
case.

Thereafter, requests for payment of vacations at both quits and
discharges for cause were approved or ordered where the employees
were qualified by full service during the previous year. Usually
the decisions were rendered without comment, despite the strong
employer opposition, but some of the cases gave added support
to the earned-right view which had now been officially launched.

In July of 1945, the National Board itself gave approval to an
award for the union in a case in which the union, asking vacation
pay for workers discharged for cause after reaching the qualifying date, made one of the strongest arguments for the earned-
right view:

The union looks upon the vacation as a property right in the same
category with wages. A working man is entitled to wages on account
of his satisfactory production and to his vacation on account of
his faithful service. The company cannot deprive him of wages,
nor of vacation, if, after having earned it, he transgresses the company's rules. Contrary to the assertion of the company, a vacation

[35]*In re* Firestone Tire and Rubber Co. of California *and* United Rubber Workers
of America, Local 100, CIO. July 10, 1944. *War Lab. Rep.*, vol. 17, p. 333.
[36]*Ibid.*, vol. 18, pp. 771–772.

is not a gift on the part of the company which it can...make contingent on future behavior....It is unfair for the company to withhold from the workingman his wages or his vacation after he has once earned them.[37]

The company's position expressed the former views of the Board, basing its opposition "on the nature of vacations, the practice in the area, and the policy of the WLB." It explained:

A vacation is granted for two reasons: First, for faithful service during the past year; and, secondly, in the hope of satisfactory service in the future after returning from vacation, refreshed and invigorated.... If an eligible employee is discharged for cause, he does not return to the company but deprives the company of the vacation benefits.[38]

Here was a clear-cut conflict between the earned-right and the employer-benefit views. The panel sided with the union and recommended a clause providing vacation pay for the preceding full year of service at termination "for any cause whatsoever," saying that the vacation "is not a gift of the company that can be withheld from the employee until he fulfills certain conditions or that can be made contingent upon his future behavior."[39] The panel recommendation was approved by the Regional Board and then, in turn, by a unanimous National Board.

The employer-benefit view as the official justification for paid vacations had been given a death blow. Vacations for most employees, who did continue their employment, might still yield a benefit to employers, but this could no longer be considered the primary purpose if vacations or vacation pay were to be granted where no benefit could return to the employer. As one company expressed it:

In the case of employees who are discharged or who resign, the purpose of paying the vacation money is no longer present.[40]

It appeared that the Board had acknowledged that the basic nature of paid vacations was an earned right. But such was not

[37]*In re* U.S. Cartridge Co. *and* International Brotherhood of Teamsters, Local 604, AFL. July 26, 1945 (made public Sept. 12, 1945). *War Lab. Rep.,* vol. 27, p. 149.
[38]*Ibid.*
[39]*Ibid.,* pp. 149–150.
[40]*In re* Bendix Aviation Corp., p. 570.

wholly the case, for the Board now drew the line on full application of that concept.

Full Earned-Right Logic Not Applied

The first acknowledgment of vacations as earned rights had come in cases allowing payment at quits and discharges for cause *only if the employees had worked the full year up through the eligibility date*.[41] If vacations were really earned rights, accruing along with the giving of service month by month, were they not also earned by part of a year's service and due pro rata for the months of service the employee did give? Such prorated vacation allowances for less than the full year's service had been granted at layoffs and at terminations to enter military service, even though, with rare exceptions, they had not been called earned rights in those cases. It was not surprising that having now adopted the earned-right view relative to quits and discharges for cause, the WLB would be faced with the inevitable demand that prorated vacation pay also be granted for these terminations.

The question was decided in the Glenn L. Martin Company case on March 13, 1945, and that decision was adhered to, with one significant exception, for the rest of the war period. The Glenn L. Martin Company's vacation plan already provided pay at all terminations, including quits and discharges for cause, for workers who had worked the full qualifying year, and the union was, in this case, requesting prorated vacations based on each month worked during the current year. The National Board, acting on the recommendation of the National Airframe Panel, specified in its directive order that prorated vacation pay be granted only to employees who had been terminated "through no fault of their own."[42]

Rejection of the full import of the earned-right view, however, did not mean that the Board was returning to the employer-benefit,

[41] It was Board policy to encourage parties to have the qualifying year end as close as possible to the actual vacation or to the beginning of the vacation season. U.S. Department of Labor, *Termination Report*, vol. 1, p. 348. While this reduced the number of those terminating after fully qualifying, it made all or most terminations interruptions of the qualifying year's service, thus increasing the employee demand for prorating.

[42] *In re* Glenn L. Martin Co., p. 376.

142

future-productivity justification of paid vacations. Its policies had carried it too far for that. In fact, the employer-benefit view sounded outdated as argued by the Glenn L. Martin Company, seeking denial of prorated vacation pay at quits and discharges for cause on the grounds that "a vacation is...a recuperative period for someone who is going to continue in employment...."[43] It was also inconsistent. The Company had already negated this view by agreeing to allow vacation pay for such employees if they terminated after the qualifying date. It would have been equally inconsistent if the Board had returned to the employer view. Caught between the two views—unable to use the employer-benefit justification any longer but unwilling to accept more than the language of the earned-right concept—the Board sought an expedient once again as it attempted in successive cases to hold the line with its "through no fault of their own" decision.

To understand why the Board now drew back from extension of the earned-right logic to prorating, it is necessary to take note of the kind of employer arguments the WLB was hearing in cases involving quits and discharges for cause. The Board had yielded to the union pressure demanding that these employees be given terminal vacation pay if they had worked the full qualifying year in part because it had let stand the early and infrequent approvals of this demand by its subordinate bodies—beginning with the February 1944 case in which the Shipbuilding Commission gave official blessing to the earned-right argument the unions had begun to use. The Board now found in prorata cases a chance to yield to the steady counterpressure which had been coming from the employers ever since that case.

The arguments used by the employers touched on strong feelings of the general public relating to individual morality and wartime patriotism. It was argued, for example, that "an employee who is discharged for cause, such as being drunk on the job, smoking and thus endangering life and property, should forfeit vacation rights;"[44] that "employees who voluntarily quit a war plant in these critical times are not entitled to consideration;"[45]

[43] *Ibid.*, p. 392.
[44] *In re* Atlas Powder Co., p. 127.
[45] *Ibid.*

and that allowing such vacation payment "would increase the company's turnover and manpower problem."[46]

The Board had also heard its own dissenting industry representatives caution that any such provision was unwise "at a time when employees are under the extra strain of increasing production in order to assist in winning the war," because it

makes it possible for an employee to work at the company's shipyard...and then quit his job, receive his vacation pay and take a job with another employer without having taken his vacation.

The granting of vacation pay to an employee who voluntarily leaves his employment is unwise in normal times but there is even less justification therefor in an abnormal period such as exists today.[47]

Relative to discharges for cause, employer representatives also protested when the Board allowed terminal pay, saying:

The Board by its action puts a premium on overt acts of employees which cause their discharge by permitting their benefits to the vacation plan notwithstanding their malfeasance.[48]

These were telling arguments to a public body like the Board, charged with responsibility for promoting only those policies which would aid the war effort. There was a general public acceptance of the idea that to quit a job in wartime or to indulge in the kind of misbehavior that would bring discharge were unpatriotic acts and hence to be discouraged or even penalized. The feelings were much more powerful than any theoretical logic of an industrial relations concept, particularly one that affected so few individuals.

But the Board yielded one more time. The Bendix Corporation case, decided by the National Board on October 31, 1945, illustrated both its reaction to pressure and counterpressure and its attitude toward the question of vacation pay as wages. The panel had recommended prorated vacation pay for both quits and discharges for cause.

[46]In re G. F. Richter Manufacturing Co. and United Electrical Workers, Local 1227, CIO. April 11, 1945 (made public August 4, 1945). War Lab. Rep., vol. 26, p. 371.
[47]In re American Car and Foundry Co. and Industrial Union of Marine and Shipbuilding Workers of America, Local 40, CIO. April 21, 1943. War Lab. Rep., vol. 8, p. 268.
[48]In re Texas Pipeline Co. and Oil Workers International Union, Local 367, CIO. March 29, 1945 (made public June 4, 1945). War Lab. Rep., vol. 24, p. 502.

Of quits, it noted first that "It might be argued that employees who quit do so of their own free will and might therefore be expected to forfeit their vacation pay," but then cited a case [unreported] in which the Board had held that such vacation pay should be paid

...because, with cutbacks and layoffs in prospect, it may be desirable for an employee to accept another job several weeks or so before the company plans to lay him off or to discharge him permanently.[49]

The employer representative on the Bendix panel was willing to go along, observing:

The employee who voluntarily quits is guilty of no misconduct but is merely exercising a right and should not be penalized for so doing. Furthermore, during the war emergency, War Manpower Commission employment stabilization rules remove in part the need for any additional control on the employer's part over the worker's freedom of movement.[50]

With industry representative concurrence, allowing prorated vacation pay to those who quit appeared almost the patriotic thing to do. It could be given the same expedient justification that such pay at layoffs had been given: a payment to ease reconversion. The Regional Board and the National Board both approved this unanimous panel recommendation of prorated vacation pay for quits.

Wages Concept Not Accepted

Both Regional and National Boards rejected the Bendix panel's majority recommendation for such pay at discharges for cause, however. The panel, industry representative dissenting, had supported this recommendation only with the wages justification:

...vacation pay must be considered as a part of wages earned and accumulated throughout the year. (It is reasonable to assume that the company has set up an account for this purpose and sets aside a certain amount for this purpose throughout the year.) Thus, it appears that any worker who is laid off or discharged should receive a prorata

[49]*In re* Bendix Aviation Corp., p. 571. The case cited was Fidelity Machine Co., Case No. 111–12229–D (not reported in the *War Labor Reports*).
[50]*Ibid.*, pp. 573–574.

share of the vacation pay. Otherwise. . .the worker would not have received his full earnings at the time of severance.[51]

In rejecting this panel recommendation, the Board held to the end to its distinction between vacation pay and wages. This case, though decided on October 31, 1945, was not made public until December 12, shortly before the War Labor Board went out of existence December 31, 1945. Once it had made its distinction between vacation pay and wages early in the war, the National Board had never thereafter approved a recommendation based on language directly calling vacation pay "wages," and it was not at this point going to yield.

The Board was well-advised not to yield for several reasons. As used in terminal vacation pay cases, the earned-right concept was being mistakenly applied to the vacation pay instead of to the vacation rest. Before the war, the concept had been argued as a justification to win paid annual rest periods, on the grounds that the employer had used the worker's services during the previous year and had an obligation to restore his spent energies by providing paid time off. But during the war, the earned-right view was rarely applied to win vacation plans. Instead, its expression came in the terminal vacation pay cases, where the vacation pay more than the vacation itself took the eye of the worker. As the earned-right concept was used here, it implied that it was the vacation money rather than the time off for a vacation rest that had been earned by the past service.

It was an easy next step in the union argument to say that since vacation pay was *earned* by past service, it was earned "like wages" or "along with wages"—or even directly to call it "wages." Such expressions sought to identify vacation pay so much with wages that the WLB would be constrained to grant it lest "the worker would not have received his full earnings at the time of severance," as the Bendix panel just quoted expressed the constraint it apparently felt.

Although the Board did not approve the wages view, its policies did reinforce the money orientation of the unions when it granted vacation pay at military leave as a bonus and at layoffs as severance

[51]*Ibid.*, p. 571.

pay. It was left to the employers and the WLB industry representatives to point out the essential link to the vacation rest, since without it there could be no employer benefit. Repeatedly they opposed the wages orientation, saying, "Vacation pay is not part of wages but is given to employees for rest and relaxation,"[52] and:

...the union misunderstands the entire purpose of granting vacations. The vacation is not payment for work performed during any past period but is solely a reward for continuous service given in expectation that the employee will continue with the company. The purpose of a vacation is to grant a period of recreation and rest before beginning another year of work.[53]

The question of whether or not vacation pay was wages, however, did not have to depend on the arguments of the interested parties. The Board had been give a broad jurisdiction by Executive Order 9250 and the Economic Stabilization Director's regulations, defining salaries and wages as including "all forms of direct and indirect compensation." The Board held that "A vacation with pay is therefore considered part of an employee's wages or salary." This holding, however, was only for the purpose of determining that the granting or extension of a paid vacation plan required Board approval.[54]

It was, then, within this broad jurisdiction over all issues affecting money payments to workers that the WLB made its distinction between basic wage rates and the "fringe issues," that is, the money payments stemming from the benefits it was increasingly granting in lieu of wage rate increases. The Board, in fact, had invented the term "fringes" precisely to distinguish the wage rate payment for production from these non-production benefits "which did not involve a change in the basic wage rates"[55] and which were social in nature and purpose, as was frequently noted in the

[52]*In re* Atlas Powder Co., p. 127.
[53]*In re* American Radiator and Standard Sanitary Corp., p. 751.
[54]U.S. Department of Labor, *Termination Report,* vol. 2, p. 237.
[55]*Ibid.,* p. 514. Having defined "wages" as all compensation, the term "non-wage" was reserved for such non-money issues as grievance procedure problems, union security, seniority, and the like, which also caused disputes threatening to interrupt wartime production and were also sent to the WLB. Despite the WLB's broad definition of wages, it still made a distinction, as we have noted; it tended to call the basic wage rate "wages" and fringes "not wages."

147

Regional Boards' terminal reports.[56] Thus, when the various branches of the WLB, in their recommendations and awards, called vacation pay "part of compensation" or said that it was earned "like wages," such expressions could be permitted so long as it was not said directly that vacation pay was wages or part of the wage payment for actual productive service.[57]

The wages analogy used by the unions was merely an arguing point. They knew that vacation pay was not really part of the basic wage payment for actual service which was covered by the hourly rate; they knew that it was in fact a "fringe" benefit granted instead of a wage increase. Under pressure from their arguments, however, the whole drift of WLB decisions expressive of the earned-right concept was already misdirecting the theory toward an emphasis on money rather than on rest time. The Board, therefore, was wise in not going further with the concept when it meant endorsing opinions based on the extreme view that the right to vacation pay was an earned right to wages.

The Board was also well-advised to go slow in policies that followed out the full earned-right logic. Both policy and theory at this point had far outrun industry practice. As noted earlier, 70 percent of 1943 vacation plans required that an employee be on the payroll at the vacation season except where the reason for termination was entry into military service. In 1945, no exception to the employment requirement whatever was permitted by employers in half of the companies surveyed by the N.I.C.B. and even these exceptions were made almost entirely for those who had completed the qualifying year but had not yet taken the

[56]U.S. Department of Labor, *Termination Report*, vol. 1, pp. 579–781. Region IX said, for instance, "There is no question but what the granting of fringe adjustments quickened useful, sound and economic advances of a social nature." *Ibid.*, p. 738. In all Regions, paid vacations were the most common of the fringe adjustments granted.

[57]In the very early days, before the Board had ruled that vacation payments were not wages for purposes of stabilization restrictions, expressions of the wages idea were occasionally approved. For example, on Sept. 10, 1942, The Board approved a panel recommendation of terminal vacation pay which said, "While it is true that vacation policies have in part the purpose of encouraging continuity of employment, the vacation allowance is also, as the employer has urged in another connection, a part of the employee's wage, and he should not be required to forfeit it upon termination of his employment. *In re* Phelps Dodge Copper Products Corp. *and* United Electrical, Radio and Machine Workers of America, CIO. Sept. 10, 1942. *War Lab. Rep.*, vol. 3, p. 136.

vacation. Only a quarter of the employers in the survey responded that they might grant vacation pay to those who quit or were discharged for cause. Employer responses in this survey were on the basis of actual discretionary practices rather than vacation plan provisions, and it was apparent that there was a broad area of management discretion in granting vacation pay even to those who had passed the eligibility date. Most plans during the war period and for some time afterwards made no mention of terminations at all, either to provide or deny terminal vacation pay.[58]

The vast majority of workers prior to the war and during this period had not been given and therefore did not expect terminal vacation pay. Vacations were a new and unexpected experience for many of them. They had not struggled to win paid vacation plans before the war, and the new union demand for vacations during the war was granted readily enough. For the most part, workers had simply accepted vacations given them, without protesting when they were not.

The WLB terminal vacation pay directive orders affected few employees, but they were important because they added clauses that were new to vacation plans, as for example from this recommendation: "An employee who has accumulated vacation rights shall be paid his vacation pay whether or not he remains in the employ of the company after the qualifying date."[59] As this indicates, it was generally accepted by both parties and the WLB that specific provision was needed to provide terminal vacation pay even for workers who had worked the full qualifying year and were still on the payroll at the end of it, since it had not been the practice for employers to pay such allowances that were in obvious conflict with the productivity-increase purpose of their plans. Had this not been the understanding by all parties, of course, there would never have been any WLB controversy over terminal vacation pay for workers who were "fully qualified." Although the point seems obvious in this period, it was not at all obvious in the postwar period.

New plans approved and ordered by the WLB were patterned

---

[58]Reynolds, *op. cit.*, p. 7; Chapter 7 contains further discussion of vacation practices.

[59]*In re* Phelps Dodge Copper Products Corp., p. 136.

upon prewar company plans, as noted in the previous chapter, and contained the same qualifying-year requirements that had always limited vacation coverage to continuing or "regular" employees. Even before the WLB period was over, employees came back to the Board to request revision of their WLB plans to permit terminal vacation pay. They knew this required revision of the qualifying requirements or the addition of a terminal vacation pay clause. One panel reported:

The union requests that the present vacation provision be clarified with respect to eligibility. Specifically, they propose that the following clause be added to the contract: "Employees laid off through lack of work or through sickness or through leave of absence shall be considered on the payroll as of December 1 for the purpose of this provision."[60]

The company complained that the union's request would "base eligibility on seniority" and "make payroll and seniority lists synonymous,"[61] but the Tool and Die Commission of the WLB, hearing this case, saw need for revision of its original plan:

The original vacation order of the Board provided that employees on the payroll as of December 1 should receive the various vacation bonus allowances. The parties, however, disagreed as to the meaning of "on the payroll." Both parties, nevertheless, recognized inequities resulting in that an employee might work eleven months of the year and not be on the active payroll as of December 1. On the other hand, another employee might not have worked more than a month during the vacation year and yet have qualified for a full vacation bonus by being on the active payroll on December 1.[62]

The Commission compromised the issue by ordering that a clause be added requiring that an employee must have been on the payroll for at least six months during the preceding year.

The WLB recognized in all cases, as in this one, that workers were not entitled to paid vacations under such plans unless a clause were added qualifying the "on the payroll" requirement or specifically providing for terminal vacation pay. Unlike post-

[60]*In re* Automotive Tool and Die Manufacturers Association *and* United Automobile Workers, Local 155 and 157, CIO. Jan. 11, 1945. *War Lab. Rep.*, vol. 21, p. 468.
[61]*Ibid.*, p. 468.　　　　　　　　　　[62]*Ibid.*, p. 469.

war arbitrators hearing grievance cases on this issue, the WLB did have the power to add such qualifications or terminal vacation pay clauses and thus to change vacation plans from a limited provision of vacations to continuing employees to a broader provision of the vacation allowance.

The extent to which the Board actually added such new clauses, however, was almost insignificant. Out of several thousand vacation dispute cases, no more than a few dozen were reported, with opinions, on the issue of terminal vacation pay. But this handful of cases was significant in two respects. It brought about a shift in the Board's philosophical justification for paid vacations and it introduced the terminal vacation pay idea to workers and their unions. In both these respects, the effect in the postwar period was a startling one.

Summary

The latter part of the War Labor Board period saw a shift in the Board's philosophy of paid vacations: a shift from the employer rationale, under which the vacation was considered to be a means to a future increase in productivity, to an employee rationale, under which vacation was conceived of as an earned right of the worker through the fact of service. Having granted vacation pay at layoffs to irregular employees in seasonal industries (in order to provide them any coverage at all) and to workers entering military service (because it was already granted by 80 percent of employers), the WLB could not deny the allowance for other workers. Since the employer's productivity-increase rationale for vacations provided no justification for granting terminal vacation pay, in granting the further union demands for pay at terminations, the WLB was forced to find a new rationale. It adopted the earned-right concept of vacations being argued by the unions, but did so only when no other expedient reason could be given. First, in rough chronology, it granted prorated vacation pay, as a bonus, to those leaving for military service and then, as severance pay, to those who were laid off. Finally, with no expedient to call upon, the Board granted vacation pay at quits and discharges for cause as an earned right—but only to employees who had worked the full qualifying year and were on the payroll at the close of it. However, prorated vacation pay for less than a full year's service was denied at these terminations even though required by the logic of the concept that vacations were earned month by month with the giving of service.

Inasmuch as the Board was already far ahead of industry practice, both in saying vacations were or should be earned rights and in ordering full or partial vacation pay at all terminations, the caution shown by the Board in denying prorated vacation pay was probably overdue. The majority of plans then in existence did not provide vacations as earned rights but restricted rights— restricted to employees who had not terminated their employment.

Two salient points stand out from the WLB experience with terminal vacation pay demands. Both are highly significant in that both were misunderstood by third parties in the postwar period.

The first point was the successful effort of the Board to maintain to the end, even while adopting the earned-right concept with its money orientation, the clear distinction between wages to pay for actual service and vacation pay, like other fringes, to provide an employee social benefit in lieu of higher wages. Chapter 8 will describe the ignominious end of the Board's careful and clear distinction between wages and vacation pay.

The second salient point was the boost given to the earned-right philosophy by the War Labor Board. Although this philosophy was out of keeping with industry practice, and although the Board itself did not apply the earned-right concept to its full logic, it did have the power to change the nature of vacation plans from employer benefits to earned rights by ordering new contract clauses providing such pay. Postwar arbitrators did not have this power, only rarely dealing with new contract clauses. Yet employees and unions by now had become so imbued with the earned-right concept of vacations that they seemed oblivious to the fact that vacations were earned rights only if the contract made them so.

How the conflict between the workers' attitude toward paid vacations and the actual fact of vacation plan practice was resolved by third parties arbitrating grievance cases is the subject of the next chapter.

152

PART IV

Paid Vacations: Non-Wages to Provide
Social Benefit
_____

The Postwar Years, 1946-1960

CHAPTER 7

The Earned-Right Theory
and Practice

IN THE postwar period, paid vacations continued to be a prominent union demand. Before the war they had rarely been on the bargaining agenda, and during the war they led an unnatural existence for two reasons. First, the War Labor Board had known policies and, in case of dispute, final settlement was out of the hands of the union and management parties to the agreement. Secondly, unions were pushed towards paid vacation demands by the limits on wage increases. With these factors removed, vacation proposals poured liberally onto the bargaining tables.

The "first round" of postwar bargaining in 1946 concentrated understandably on wages, but fringe issues came into their own by the "second round' 'in 1947. The general fear of inflation increased the acceptability and popularity of "package" settlements which included non-wage benefits. Paid vacations, at that time the largest cost item of the fringe issues, clearly led the fringe demands by 1948, the "third round," and held its prominent place in 1949 when holidays, pensions, health and welfare plans, sick leave, and call-in pay were included with the fringes.[1]

Each year, nearly a third of vacation plans were liberalized; some plans were changed annually. By 1949, 93 percent of con-

---

[1] U.S. Chamber of Commerce, *The Hidden Payroll, Non-Wage Labor Costs of Doing Business* (Washington: U.S. Chamber of Commerce, 1949), p. 13. See also the other annual reports on fringe benefit costs issued throughout the postwar period by the Chamber of Commerce.

155

tracts provided paid vacations.[2] Minimum service requirements were lowered to qualify more employees for vacations. Changes came so swiftly at this time that the old War Labor Board standard quickly became obsolete. Reduction of the service requirements to two years for the second week of paid vacation and the addition of a third week after ten years was so common, it was reported, as to "throw the one-for-one, two-for-five pattern into a cocked hat."[3]

Vacations as Employee Social Benefit

The paid vacation, originated by management as an employer benefit to increase productivity, had now become in the eyes of American workers an employee benefit for a social purpose. During the war, vacations to many of them had simply been an employee benefit—a substitute benefit demanded by their unions in lieu of a wage increase. But no longer. The paid vacation in the postwar era was desired for its social effects—rest and recreation with the family and community.

The genuineness of the desire for time off for this purpose was unmistakable. The parties agreed to write into their contracts new prohibitions against both taking pay in lieu of vacation and accumulating vacation time by skipping one year's vacation.[4] A vacation rest period had become a social necessity to American workers—one of the facts of American life. When one's vacation was to be taken and what one was to do during it was a topic of common interest the year around. Magazine articles by the score were written on how to spend a vacation, and whole new industries grew up to accommodate annual vacationers.

No American worker could fail to be influenced by this attitude toward an annual vacation. Even the last-ditch holdouts in building construction were affected by the feeling in the air that paid vacations were a normal and a necessary thing. In less than a

[2]John J. Speed, "Vacation Practices—1949," *The Conference Board Management Record*, vol. 11, 1949, p. 53.

[3]National Foreman's Institute, *Economic Relations Bulletin* (New York: National Foreman's Institute, 1949), p. 8.

[4]U.S. Department of Labor, Bureau of Labor Statistics, *Paid Vacation Provisions in Major Union Contracts, 1957*, Bulletin No. 1233 (Washington: G.P.O., 1958), pp. 28, 30.

decade the whole public attitude toward vacations had changed. Whereas the expression "take your kids to the seashore" had once been a radical's dream of equality with the rich, such an event was now considered almost a necessity of life. The idea of a year without a vacation was to be looked upon with dread. In fact, the accepted view was now that one had to have an annual rest in order to keep going. "What you need is a vacation" came into the language to express one's automatic reaction to the sight of anyone who could not keep his mind on his work or whose enthusiasm about life in general had begun to flag.

Employer Obligation to Rest Employees

In initiating the paid vacation movement, employers had described, often and well, the employee's need for a periodic physical and mental rest. Although they had provided these rests for the benefit of the company and not as an obligation to their individual employees, both workers and the general public came to take management's recognition of the *need* for an annual rest period to be an acknowledgment of an *obligation* to provide one.

The War Labor Board gave the weight of public policy to the idea that there was an industry obligation to provide all employees with annual paid rest periods when it approved vacation plans, and especially when it ordered them in dispute cases, for all American workers without regard to prevailing practice or type of industry.

At the bargaining table, the unions sought, in the "package" settlements, to have management put more money not only into the wage obligation to pay for service but also into the social obligation to rest employees, at an ever-improving standard of what constituted an adequate rest—believing that both obligations were part of an employer's proper cost of doing business.

This feeling that it was management's responsibility was now part of the prevailing public belief, too, shared by third parties representing the public interest in industrial relations. Note, for instance, this expression in an arbitration case awarding a new vacation plan:

In present day labor relations the granting of a vacation period

157

to workers is so widely accepted that no industry or Company can claim to be exempt from the propriety of this practice. The Company which obliges its workers to work 52 weeks the year round and refuses to recognize the principle of vacation lends itself to the open charge of relegating to an inferior position one of the major cost items of good employer-employee relations. . . . The Company claims that it is not financially able to grant vacations with pay. Today, however, common practice decrees, in general, that those who employ workers assume the general obligation of granting them vacations.[5]

Workers had become so accustomed to the annual vacation which they all had that they came to feel it was not only owed them by their employer as a natural right but also as an inalienable right. They readily picked up the idea that the vacation had been "earned" by the past service that had created need for the rest. As distinguished from the management view, the purpose of paid vacations in the employees' eyes was to rest workers from *past* service, not to prepare them for *future* service. This view therefore required that all service in the preceding year be matched by provision of time off, in more or less direct proportion, and for all employees who had given service without regard to whether or not any of them later left their employment.

The very fact that the earned-right concept seemed to be fulfilled for most employees (who continued employment and received their vacations year after year) merely served to draw attention to the cases in which employment was terminated, and the employee received no vacation pay. For the vacation right to be fully received and the employer's obligation fully discharged, a worker had to get vacation or vacation pay prorated for all service rendered to the date of his termination.

Vacations Not Earned Rights in Most Plans

The earned-right concept may have been part of American workers' thinking, but it was not part of the vacation plans most

[5]*In re* J. Zwerdling Bakery, Inc. *and* International Brotherhood of Teamsters Local 145, AFL. Board of Arbitration: Joseph Donnelly, chairman; Samuel Curry, representing employees; and Warren L. Mottram, representing employers. August 20, 1948, clarification dated Oct. 11, 1948. Bureau of National Affairs, *Labor Arbitration Reports* (hereafter referred to as *LA*) (Washington: BNA, 1946 to date), vol. 11, p. 445.

of them worked under; the large majority of plans did not provide terminal vacation pay for all service prior to any termination.

Unless a plan contained a terminal vacation pay clause, the vacations it provided could not be considered earned rights. To illustrate this point, let us take a more familiar and recent example. Pensions are not vested (or earned) rights, no matter how many workers retire and take their pensions, unless the pension plan provides that terminated employees retain the right to collect payments made for them based on past service. Likewise, vacations are not earned (or vested) rights, no matter how many workers get vacations year after year, unless terminated employees are paid the vacation in proportion to their service since the last vacation. The "earned right" expression makes no sense unless applied equally to all workers giving service.

When the War Labor Board called vacations an earned right, it was saying this was how vacations should be treated but were not if there were no terminal vacation pay clause. Although dealing with few cases, the Board changed the nature of vacation plans to the extent that it ordered adoption of terminal vacation pay clauses.

But in the postwar period, arbitrators only rarely dealt with new contract clauses and could not add to, subtract from, or change the nature of any of the plans they dealt with. The terminal vacation pay cases involved *only* plans in which vacations were not earned rights; the terminated workers were bringing these grievance cases to arbitration precisely because the contract contained no terminal vacation pay clause to cover their situation.

Yet, arbitrators held not only that this was the nature of paid vacations in industry plans generally but that vacations under these plans were already earned rights. Why and how the arbitrators made that interpretation is the subject of this chapter. However, a few words need to be said first about the extent to which paid vacations were *not* earned rights in industry generally during the period under study (1945–1960)[6] when arbitrators and

[6]The discussion of arbitrators' interpretations of vacation plans in this chapter as well as in the next one has been based upon an analysis of all arbitration cases involving paid vacations reported in the BNA's *Labor Arbitration Reports* from its first volume in 1946 to volume 35 for 1960. Unless otherwise noted, the views described represented the majority views of arbitrators during this postwar period.

courts were calling them such. Secondly, the specific types of language used in the vacation plans which these arbitrators dealt with will be looked at more closely to see *how* they effected the limited coverage management intended.

As was noted in earlier chapters, the majority of plans historically made no mention whatever of terminations, either to provide or deny vacations. This was true almost until 1949 when the N.I.C.B. reported that 47 percent of contractual plans[7] did not mention termination. Of those that did, 13 percent expressly prohibited vacation pay at termination, 40 percent allowed it at some, and 25.5 percent at all terminations—if an employee had worked the full qualifying year.[8] No figures are available on prorating for service in the current year. Apparently prorated allowances were still too uncommon to merit note by the surveyors of vacation plans, but some of these plans must also have permitted prorating. It is only this number, this prorating part of the 25 percent allowing vacation pay at all terminations, that can be said to have treated vacations consistently and logically as earned rights in 1949.

Little mention of prorating was made until 1956 when the BNA found that 69 percent permitted terminal vacation pay "with certain limitations." But it indicated that not over a fifth of the plans provided vacations as an earned right, prorating the vacation pay at all terminations.[9] By 1960, fifteen years after the wartime government policy of approving and ordering the adoption of clauses prorating vacation pay at most terminations, only about

---

[7]All discussion of postwar vacation plans in this and the next chapter is in reference to contractual plans, unless otherwise noted. There are several reasons for this. First, vacations as an earned right have meaning only within the framework of a contractual agreement and none at all if the employer is always free to grant or deny vacations at termination or any other time, as he is in the absence of a union contract. Secondly, the controversy involving third parties' interpretations of vacations as earned rights came only in reference to arbitration of contractual provisions submitted to them under the terms of a binding arbitration clause. And third, almost all information available on postwar vacation plan practices is to be found in surveys of contractual plans only. Non-union plans may have had fewer terminal vacation pay clauses but, as will be discussed later in this chapter, actual vacation practices quite probably were more liberal in allowing such pay than even contractual vacation plan provisions would indicate.

[8]Speed, *op. cit.*, p. 91.

[9]Bureau of National Affairs, "Vacation Provisions in Union Contracts," *Union Labor Report*, No. 487, 1957, Table II.

one-third of vacation plans did so. Fewer than one-third provided for prorating for *all* terminations.[10]

Clauses Limiting Eligibility

A closer look at the plans themselves shows how vacations, with or without mention of terminal vacation pay, were kept from being earned rights. Prewar plans were company instituted, designed to provide vacations only to employees who most probably would not terminate their employment. The majority of postwar contractual plans were these same company plans simply added to the union contract. The N.I.C.B. reported that in 1946—after the war period's intensive union interest in adoption of paid vacation plans, with vacation coverage over 90 percent and with 88 percent of vacation plans reported to be in union agreements— 60 percent of the existing vacation plans were found to have been originated by the company prior to the establishment of a collective bargaining relationship.[11] Wartime plans (except in irregular-employment industries) had been patterned after the existing company plans, and thus also contained the characteristic clauses limiting vacations to regular workers expected to continue their employment.

To effect limited coverage, management had two requirements for eligibility. First, an employee had to have given a year's continuous service during the preceding year or he was not considered enough in need of a rest to make granting him one worth its cost. This gave rise to the clause setting out a qualifying year of "continuous service" preceding the vacation. Second, no matter how weary an employee was from that year of service, he still had to be an employee after the vacation if the employer were to realize any return from the vacation cost. This in turn gave rise to the clause requiring that an employee be "on the payroll" at vacation time, or at least at the end of the qualifying year, which was usually set close to the start of the vacation season.

[10]Bureau of National Affairs, *Basic Patterns in Union Contracts* (Washington: BNA, 1961), p. 91:8.

[11]National Industrial Conference Board, *Vacation and Holiday Practices,* The Conference Board Reports, Studies in Personnel Policy, No. 75 (New York: N.I.C.B., 1946), pp. 4, 5, and 6. During the year before, the N.I.C.B. had found from a smaller sample that 72 percent of the contractual plans had been established before a collective bargaining unit was recognized.

To fulfill the first requirement, most vacation plans simply specified a qualifying year of "continuous service" or stated that vacations were to be provided all employees who had been "in the continuous employ" of the company during the qualifying year.[12] A minority of plans—a third in 1949 and almost half in 1960[13]—also specified a minimum work requirement during the qualifying year, in terms of a certain number of hours, days, weeks, or months of work, or a percentage of work time or pay periods.

While service requirements underwent considerable liberalization to qualify more employees, they still effectively excluded terminated employees from coverage. Any employee whose employment had terminated was deemed to have interrupted his "continuous service" and was therefore ineligible for any vacation or vacation pay, even if he had fulfilled the minimum service requirement. The service requirement, in short, was not intended as a substitute for "continuous service" to define eligibility to a vacation but as specification of the minimum amount of work to be performed *within* the full year of "continuous service" or "continuous employment."

The second requirement—present employment—was spelled out in half to three-fourths of vacation plans in clauses requiring that employees be "on the payroll" or "in the employ" of the company at their vacation time, or on the day that marked the close of the qualifying year, as, for instance, June 1.[14] Employees not on the payroll at that time, even if they had worked the full year up to that point, were thus made ineligible for any vacation or vacation pay because they would not be returning to yield the benefits of a rest. The BLS reported in 1958:

Over 70% (1,199) of the agreements [surveyed] specified a qualifying date, or a fixed period for determining length of service or vacation eligibility.... Under such provisions, the employee must have been on the payroll and/or must have completed the necessary minimum service by the cutoff date or period in order to qualify for a vacation.[15]

[12]Speed, *op. cit.*, p. 88. This was true of almost two-thirds of plans in 1949.
[13]*Ibid.*; BNA, *Basic Patterns in Union Contracts*, p. 91:6.
[14]BNA, *Basic Patterns in Union Contracts*, p. 91:7; BLS, *Paid Vacation Provisions in Major Union Contracts, 1957*, p. 23.
[15]*Ibid.*

A plan might say, for instance, "All employees who have given one year's continuous service prior to June 1 shall be eligible for a paid vacation of one week..." or it might say, "All employees on the payroll on June 1 shall be entitled to...." Or, in a combination, this might be its language: "All employees on the payroll on June 1 who have given one year's continuous service shall be eligible for a paid vacation...."

Thus, despite the assertions of many arbitrators, most vacation plans throughout this postwar period were not a broad grant of the vacation right to "all employees" but only to "all employees *who*" had given a full year of continuous service and were still on the payroll at the end of it.

The intent of these clauses, by which management limited the provision of vacations, had never been questioned by either party or by third parties since the origin of the movement and even through the war period. Forfeiture clauses were never felt needed and few have ever existed in vacation plans.[16] Management had a more effective way of enforcing its two requirements protecting the return from paid vacations, respected alike by both employees and the wartime third parties: the employers held the initiative and simply did not grant a vacation if employment were terminated before the vacation, even if the employee had worked the full qualifying year and was on the payroll at the end of it, unless his union had negotiated a terminal vacation pay clause.

Union efforts to add terminal vacation pay clauses proceeded slowly, however, for two reasons. First, all other improvements were more popular, affected more employees, and were easier to win from the employers, who remained adamantly opposed to terminal vacation pay clauses. No benefit returned to them from such vacation payments whereas some benefit might from lengthening the vacations of continuing employees. Second, it became obvious as time went on that the allowance could be won from arbitrators' awards in grievance cases without going to the bargaining table for the addition of a terminal vacation pay clause.

[16]As Chapter 4 notes of the prewar period when almost all plans were company plans, forfeiture clauses were rare. Yet employers could easily have written into their plans anything they wished, including forfeiture clauses, if they had expected there would ever be a need for such a prohibition.

Postwar Arbitration Cases

The terminal vacation pay issue arose in grievances initiated by employees who, especially after they had worked most or all of the year, found no vacation pay in their final pay envelope. With a strong belief now that provision of an annual vacation rest was an obligation of the employer and the right of every worker, earned by past service to the date of termination, they pressed their cases with righteous indignation, arguing that employers had denied them a basic right under the contract—and an earned right. The employers pointed to the contractual language providing vacations only to those in "continuous service" or "on the payroll" at vacation time and refused to yield. Unconcerned about the niceties of contractual language or past practice and understanding, the employees pressed their grievances to arbitration. In arbitration, backed up by the courts, the "injustice" could be righted by interpretation. Because of the frequency of the arbitrators' decisions favorable to the unions, the interpretations were almost as effective as if such a clause had been written into the contract. Employers had little alternative but to accept if bound by the contract to arbitrate such disputes and if the employees chose to press each case.

The vast majority of postwar arbitrations on the vacation issue involved grievances over terminal vacation pay, in the absence of an applicable clause in the contract.[17] It is on these cases that the following discussion is based.

In arbitration, the employers insisted upon strict adherence to the wording and the intent of the clauses they had carefully written to provide vacations only to continuing employees. There was no right to vacations, employers argued, beyond what the contract affirmatively specified:

A Paid Vacation is a Contractual Right...a benefit which exists only because of the terms of the agreement, and not otherwise. It is a right

[17]There were relatively few vacation arbitration cases other than grievances over terminal vacation pay. Of these few some involved the rate to be paid or the amount of vacation pay due. Others involved the question of when a vacation was to be scheduled. Only a very small number of cases arose out of new contract negotiations relative either to the adoption of a plan, liberalization of the vacation terms, or the addition of a terminal vacation pay clause.

which flows entirely from the collective bargaining agreement and such right is, therefore, limited and prescribed by the terms of the contract.[18]

Why, and then how, did the postwar arbitrators find vacations under these plans to be earned rights requiring terminal vacation pay without specific provision for it in the contract?

Arbitrators approached the cases with an *a priori* judgment that vacations were the basic right of every employee—an employee benefit, not an employer benefit. They looked at the vacation plan in question and interpreted its provisions in that light, finding that the plan was a broad, not limited, grant of the vacation right, that the right had been "earned," and that it must therefore be due at termination of employment.

Always sensitive barometers of prevailing winds, the arbitrators reflected the postwar view of vacations as an earned right to a social benefit and made their awards and wrote their opinions as if no other view of the purpose or justification of vacation plans had ever existed—as if, in fact, vacation plans had arisen first at the bargaining table, written by the unions and acknowledged as earned rights by the employer's signature to the labor agreement. Arbitrations involving vacations having been uncommon before the war, the first experience with vacation plans for most arbitrators came with the War Labor Board. Here they saw the strong union demand, heard the union argument for vacations as an earned right, and read the awards of a few of their colleagues giving WLB approval to that view. The Board's reliance upon the employer-benefit view for almost all of its wartime vacation policies was largely erased by the earned-right controversy in its last months, in a handful of cases. Relative to these cases, arbitrators had seen the war end with official renunciation of the employer-benefit view.

Arbitrators without War Labor Board experience had only to look up WLB decisions on terminal vacation pay cases to learn what the official view was. Those who did so would have no hint of the WLB's long reliance upon the employer-benefit view since this was expressed in vacation plan adoption or liberalization cases

[18]*In re* Rockwell Spring and Axle Co., Ohio Axle and Gear Division *and* United Automobile Workers, Local 1037, CIO. Arbitrator: Harry J. Dworkin. Oct. 29, 1954 (hearing date). *LA,* vol. 23, p. 483.

but not at all in the terminal vacation pay cases. They would have seen only the employers arguing for the employer-benefit view with the Board holding otherwise. The history of vacation plans prior to the war which, under the management view, had brought coverage to the 50 percent mark, was neither so easily consulted nor so "authoritative" as this.

In the postwar period there was little to indicate to arbitrators that on philosophical grounds vacations were anything other than earned rights, except the employers' self-interest argument. In fact, the psychology that prevailed in the postwar period in regard to the justification for paid vacation plans was so pervasive that it is difficult to realize the hold that the employer-benefit view had once had on management, on third parties, particularly the WLB for most of the war, and presumably on the public at large—not to mention on the unions and workers themselves. But the general public, including arbitrators, had a short memory. The assertion of a few years earlier that vacations were to be justified primarily as a means of increasing employee productivity was now matched by an equally positive assertion that this was not their primary purpose. Only a year after the end of the war, an arbitrator said:

The theory of the company that vacation pay is given merely to enable the employee to rest up for another year of service is out of harmony with the practice and the apparent thinking of management and labor in most of industry today.[19]

"Most arbitrators agree," said an arbitration board in 1954, that vacations are "not unilaterally awarded by management purely as an investment in the future productive efficiency of the employee."[20]

Vacations were for the benefit of employees because, as this arbitrator explained:

...inherent in the definition of "vacations" and their justification is

[19]*In re* Automatic Electric Co. *and* International Brotherhood of Electrical Workers, Local B-713, AFL. Arbitrator: Alex Elson. August 3, 1946. *LA,* vol. 4, p. 120.

[20]*In re* Allied Drum Service, Inc. *and* United Mine Workers of America, District 50, Local 13778. Board of Arbitration: Carl A. Warns, Jr., chairman; Irwin G. Waterman, employer-appointed arbitrator; and Richard C. Snider, union-appointed arbitrator. Nov. 16, 1954. *LA,* vol. 23, p. 677.

the thought that they are rest and relaxation periods required by the employees because of the modern tempo of production.[21]

Industry therefore owed employees this "required" rest period, and it became an employee's right upon the giving of service.

This was a subjective judgment, of course, and not one based on contractual provision. Since the vacation plans in these arbitration cases did not specifically provide vacations for terminated employees, the "right" to vacation pay had to be supported by abstract considerations such as "equity" and "justice." This was frequently evident in the language of the opinions, as, for instance, in the following, with its strong employee-benefit orientation:

To hold that an employee who is laid-off due to no fault of his own shall lose his vacation with pay, is in my opinion inequitable. Particularly is this true where an employee has worked for the better part of a year and given his employer the benefits of his labor. To lose the much sought for rest period with compensation would work an injustice on all concerned.[22]

The courts were found to back up arbitrators in their use of abstract and subjective criteria. In one case, a New Hampshire board of arbitration had given weight to the employees' argument that, although admittedly nothing in the contract provided terminal vacation pay, " 'many of the people had worked for the Company a long time and morally were entitled to vacation pay.' "[23] The New Hampshire Supreme Court review ruled the argument to be equitable grounds for a favorable decision by the board of arbitration, saying that it was proper for the board to "make a ruling based on simple justice."[24] The Tennessee Supreme Court,

[21]*In re* St. Louis Smelting and Refining Company *and* International Union of Mine, Mill and Smelter Workers, Local 809, CIO. Arbitrator: Clarence M. Updegraff. June 5, 1947. *LA,* vol. 8, p. 221.

[22]*In re* Style Metal Specialties Co., Inc. *and* Playthings, Jewelry and Novelty Workers International Union, Watch and Jewelry Workers Union, Local 147, CIO. Arbitrator: Morton Singer. Sept. 23, 1947. *LA,* vol. 8, p. 447.

[23]*In re* Franklin Needle Co. *and* American Federation of Hosiery Workers, Local 173-A, etc. New Hampshire Supreme Court. May 27, 1954. *LA,* vol. 22, p. 511. The contract said, "Each employee who is on the payroll of the Employer during the vacation period of June to August inclusive, and who has been employed by the Employer for at least six months out of twelve months ending June first of any year is eligible that year for the vacation week and vacation pay." *Ibid.,* p. 509.

[24]*Ibid.,* p. 511. The North Carolina Supreme Court in a similar case referred to "homespun honesty and simple justice." *In re* Calvine Cotton Mills, Inc. v. Textile

in another case in which the contract contained no terminal vacation pay clause, said:

...where there is room for construction, as we think there is in this case, the contract should be construed so as to meet the justice and equities of the circumstances of the parties to the contract.... We are, therefore, of the opinion that fair dealing and common justice require that we affirm the decree of the Chancellor in holding that these complainants are entitled to vacation pay.[25]

Third parties were grafting a welfare concept onto the bargaining agreement; what normally could be accomplished only by collective bargaining negotiations, or by legislation, was effectively being achieved in these cases by the spirit of the times. Reflecting and expressing this spirit, third parties assumed vacations to be every worker's right even if not so specified in the contract. Starting with this assumption, the arbitrators had little trouble finding that the vacation plans before them were a broad grant of vacations to all employees.

Arbitrators Discard Employers' Eligibility Requirements

Without doubt, the contractual plans fixed a management responsibility to provide vacations, but only to the extent of the specific provisions in the plan. Nevertheless, arbitrators found that the "continuous service" and "on the payroll" clauses were not limitations on vacation eligibility. They interpreted these management clauses to refer only to seniority. As measures of seniority, these clauses determined *when* an employee had sufficient length of service to receive his second or third week of vacation, but not *whether* he was eligible each year for whatever that amount was. In other words, "continuous service," arbitrators were saying, did not refer to the qualifying service in the preceding year but to the total length of service since first being hired, or seniority.

If under the contract an employee retained his seniority during

---

Workers Union of America, CIO, Local No. 677, *et al.* North Carolina Supreme Court. Dec. 2, 1953. *LA,* vol. 21, p. 572.

[25]Textile Workers Union of America, Local No. 513, *et al.* v. Brookside Mills, Inc. Tennessee Supreme Court. Dec. 6, 1957. Bureau of National Affairs, *Labor Relations Reference Manual* (hereafter referred to as *LRRM*) (Washington: BNA, 1937 to date), vol. 41, p. 2297.

a temporary layoff, then he was still an employee in "continuous service" and due a vacation or vacation pay. An arbitration board explained, "The phrase 'in the continuous service of the company' does not mean 'at work continuously.' "[26] Similarly, if employees retained seniority rights, they were held to be still "on the payroll" or "in the employ" of the company even if on layoff on the specified date:

...a person employed by another remains on the payroll of the employer until his employment has been finally and definitely terminated.... The provision contained in the contract relating to the seniority of employees...indicates clearly that all of these employees who were laid-off because of lack of work, sickness or injury remain in the employ of the employer and it is my conclusion remain on the payroll of the employer.[27]

Arbitrators were defining employment termination to mean the point at which seniority for rehire ceased. This kept workers "on the payroll" longer and thus eligible for vacation or vacation pay. An arbitrator said, for example:

The accumulation of service is broken only after eighteen consecutive months of layoffs. It follows therefore that the phrase "in the employ of the employer" does not mean "on the active payroll continuously" or "at work continuously." It follows, too, that the date June 1st constitutes a day for the measurement of service rather than a date for the inclusion or exclusion of employees for vacation purposes.... [28]

Employers objected to such an interpretation, of course, arguing, for example:

Vacation rights, like seniority and other similar rights, are purely and solely contractual, and do not exist otherwise.... What the Union seeks is to have the arbitrator write into the Agreement a modification of the express language of Article XI, which is in terms of "employees"

[26]*In re* Rib Mountain Granite Co. *and* Alvin Bucholz. Wisconsin Employment Relations Board: L. E. Gooding, chairman; J. E. Fitzgibbon and Morris Slavney, commissioners. Sept. 14, 1953. *LA*, vol. 21, p. 220.

[27]*In re* Dunphy Boat Corp. *and* Upholsterers' International Union of North America, Local 352, AFL. Arbitrator: L. E. Gooding. Jan. 3, 1950. *LA*, vol. 13, p. 883.

[28]*In re* L. Hyman Co., Inc. *and* Textile Workers Union of America, Allentown District Joint Board, CIO. Arbitrator: Robert P. Brecht. Sept. 29, 1949. *LA*, vol. 13, p. 803.

who have been and "are employed by the Company on June 15" so as to add to that language somewhat as follows: "or such other date prior thereto as the Union may desire or the arbitrator may determine to be proper." This is clearly beyond the scope of the arbitrator's authority.... The contract specifies but one eligibility date, a condition precedent to vacation pay,...[29]

But arbitrators did not see it this way. Some spoke as if the employer were requiring presence at work on only a single day out of the year. In one case, for example, in which the contract required employees to be in the "active employ" of the company on June 1, the arbitrator said it was "absurd and untenable" to require that an employee be at work on one certain day; an employee might be sick or on other valid leave on that day and would lose his vacation, he said.[30] Another said it was "inconceivable" that the language, "each employee in the employ of the employer on June 1st," required presence at work in the plant on that day and held that the employee who was on layoff on June 1 was still to be considered an employee because he remained on the company's roster of employees.[31] Other arbitrators simply dismissed the requirement as being, in the words of one, "too harsh."[32]

Postwar arbitrators lived in a different world from the one that had once thought of vacations as a management device to increase the productivity of employees at work *after* the vacation. In 1959, an arbitrator looked suspiciously at the employer view of the requirement that an employee be "on the service rolls" at the end of the qualifying year (December 31), and said, "Here it would seem the Company is adding a further condition or criteria— [vacations] to those who will be consistently employed in the immediate foreseeable future." Seeing only the employee-benefit side, this arbitrator held that vacations were due all employees

---

[29]*In re* Brookford Mills *and* Textile Workers Union of America. Arbitrator: Samuel H. Jaffee. June 17, 1957. *LA,* vol. 28, p. 840.

[30]*In re* Rockwell Spring and Axle Co., p. 486.

[31]*In re* Amory Mills, Inc., Amoskeag Mills, Inc., and Amoskeag-Lawrence Mills, Inc. *and* Textile Workers Union of America, Locals 560, 864, and 897, CIO. Arbitrator: Maxwell Copelof. Sept. 7, 1948. *LA,* vol. 11, p. 244.

[32]*In re* Style Metal Specialties Co., p. 447. This arbitrator commented, "It is my considered opinion that these employees may still be part of the working staff even though they are not doing productive work." *Ibid.*

who had met the service requirement, including the twelve in this grievance who were laid off before December 31. Since they continued to accumulate seniority for rehire, he said, they were still to be considered "on the service rolls of the Company" on December 31.[33]

Throughout the postwar period, the seniority interpretation of these management clauses ruled the day. It reflected the arbitrators' subjective judgment—more or less openly expressed—that vacations were every worker's right. As the foregoing arbitrator said, "any other interpretation would be unfair and unreasonable."[34]

Just as firm in their belief, the employers continued to protest the arbitrators' definition of "employees" to mean, for vacation purposes, all those who retained seniority rights with a company. Anxious to preserve their limited coverage, they urged arbitrators to stick to the contract language "without any forced interpretations based upon theories...of employees who remain 'employees' indefinitely after having been permanently terminated. ...."[35] They argued that terminated workers were no longer employees and if on temporary layoff had to return to get their vacations: "Continuous service only becomes an established fact for a laid off employee upon his return to work after layoff."[36]

Under attack for exceeding their authority in departing from a literal interpretation of contractual language, arbitrators felt the necessity to defend their awards granting terminal vacation pay where the contract made no express provision for it. Some suggested that the very fact that a plan was in the contract made it a broad grant of vacations to all employees, apparently without recognizing that it was not the contractual nature of the vacation arrangement but the actual language which determined how broad

[33]*In re* Penn-Dixie Cement Corp. *and* United Steelworkers of America, Local Union No. 2738. Arbitrator: B. Meredith Reid. July 15, 1959. *LA,* vol. 33, p. 319.
[34]*Ibid.*
[35]*In re* Kleene-Fibre Corp. *and* Textile Workers Union of America, CIO. Arbitrator: Henry Parkman. Sept. 11, 1953. *LA,* vol. 21, p. 236. Nevertheless, the arbitrator in this case held that July 1 was only a cut-off date for measuring length of service and not an "eligibility date on which employees must be on the payroll to acquire right to vacation pay as contended by the Company." *Ibid.*
[36]*In re* Central Packing Co. *and* United Packinghouse Workers of America, Local No. 36, CIO. Sept. 20, 1948. *LA,* vol. 11, pp. 374–375.

the vacation grant was.[37] But this was precisely the attitude toward vacation plans the employers were protesting.

Other justifications occasionally used were equally unconvincing to the employers. The most common of these was the citation of the many similar rulings:

Over the past ten years a long line of decisions by arbitrators and Courts of law have uniformly held that the eligibility date cannot be used as a reason for denying seniority rights to vacation pay on grounds that the employees have been "permanently separated" and are no longer "employees of the employer"....[38]

A few arbitrators held that it was industry's obligation to provide all workers with rest periods, but this opinion also failed to satisfy the employers who objected that it was for the unions in collective bargaining and not arbitrators to impose any such obligation by extending vacations or vacation pay to terminated workers.

But almost to a man, the arbitrators placed their major reliance upon the earned-right justification for their awards, in answer to the employers' protests. The real reason that all employees were entitled to vacations, they said, was that the vacation or vacation pay was *earned* by the worker's past service, and having once earned it, no employee could later be denied it solely because his employment terminated—whether or not the contract provided for this possible event. In keeping with the earned-right concept, arbitrators emphasized the service basis of paid vacations.

[37]See Monument Mills, Inc. *and* Textile Workers Union of America. Arbitrator: Robert L. Stutz. Oct. 2, 1957. *LA,* vol. 29, p. 403. In this case, the contract required that employees be in the employ of the employer on June 1 "hereinafter called the 'eligibility date'" and to be employed in at least the preceding three months, but provided for no terminal vacation pay. The arbitrator said, "It seems to the writer that the Company's argument on the issue really begs the question, and ignores completely the rights guaranteed to employees by the contract." *Ibid.*

See also McQuay-Norris Manufacturing Co., St. Louis, Connersville and Indianapolis Divisions *and* United Automobile Workers, Locals 226, 231, and 315, CIO. Arbitrator: Verner E. Wardlaw. May 27, 1947. *LA,* vol. 7, p. 672. The arbitrator here said, "The parties have provided for certain vacation rights in the agreement, such rights thereby become a matter of contract and cease to be a privilege over which the Company exercises exclusive control." The "exclusive control" which the company sought in this case was the right to exclude from coverage employees permanently laid off before June 1 as not having fulfilled the contract's requirement that employees be "on the payroll continuously." The arbitrator made the customary seniority interpretation of the clause. *Ibid.*

[38]*In re* Wamsutta Mills, Inc. (New Bedford, Mass.) *and* Textile Workers Union of America. Arbitrator: John A. Hogan. Sept. 5, 1959. *LA,* vol. 34, p. 165.

172

Vacations Due Because Earned by Service

In holding, by means of the seniority interpretation, that the actual presence of an employee at work at vacation time was an extraneous consideration, arbitrators were eliminating the "continuous service" and "on the payroll" clauses as requirements for vacation eligibility. In place of them, they substituted an eligibility criterion of their own. Past actual service, arbitrators said, was the proper criterion for eligibility. By that service, employees had "earned" and were due their vacations.

As was noted earlier, specific work requirements existed in less than half of vacation plans during the postwar years, but *where such a work requirement existed* and the employee had fulfilled it, he got his vacation whether the preceding or qualifying year's service had been "continuous" or had been broken by layoff or permanent termination. If he did not fulfill it, of course, he did not get a vacation, even though his seniority continued and he was still by that definition an employee—although he might be awarded a partial vacation based upon the proportionate amount of the service requirement that he had fulfilled.

Unless the contract specified otherwise, arbitrators generally did not permit non-work time, even when paid for, to count as part of the work requirement. For instance, time spent on union business, sick leave, or holidays, although it was paid time and seniority accumulated and employee status was maintained, could not be counted since it did not represent working time. One of the arbitrators who held that paid holidays could not be counted in the work requirement as days worked said:

A vacation is intended to serve as a period of rest and relaxation earned through service to the Company. Measuring eligibility on the basis of time spent on the job during the preceding year clearly conforms to this objective. The inclusion of paid time off the job would seem on its face to be unrelated to this purpose.[39]

In the absence of a specific work requirement arbitrators might

[39]*In re* International Harvester Co., West Pullman Works *and* United Electrical Workers, United Farm Equipment and Metal Workers Council, Local 107. Arbitrator: Ralph T. Seward. Nov. 24, 1950. *LA*, vol. 15, p. 644.

173

hold that seniority alone qualified an employee,[40] but even here, they often prorated the full vacation on the basis of actual time worked.[41] In some cases, arbitrary limits were placed on the amount of layoff time that could be excepted from the preceding year's otherwise "continuous service." In one case, for example, the arbitrator permitted seniority to qualify an employee, in the absence of a work requirement, for a period not exceeding six months, although seniority continued for a full year. Out of fairness, he said, the major part of the year must have been spent at actual work.[42]

This emphasis upon actual service as the only proper eligibility requirement would not alone have offended the employers. They had themselves based vacations on actual service as a means of determining both an employee's need for rest (and hence the profitability of providing one) and whether he was a sufficiently "regular" employee to be likely to continue employment. Employers were offended, however, when arbitrators, after discarding management's eligibility clauses protecting its return, then used this service basis to prove that vacations were due at employment termination, even without specific provision for it in the contract. Although none of the contracts before these arbitrators provided for terminal vacation pay for the employees in question, arbitrators nevertheless found ample evidence that vacations under them were intended to be earned rights.

Arbitrators pointed to clues in the vacation plan to prove that the contract itself—and hence the parties—recognized that since vacations were based on service, they accrued with the giving of service and therefore were "earned." Any evidence of the "accrual principle" was taken as acknowledgment by the parties that vacations were earned and due. Even work requirements themselves

[40]See, for example, Des Moines Railway Co. and International Association of Machinists, Local Lodge 479, AFL. Board of Arbitration: Judson E. Piper, chairman; J. P. O'Connell, union-appointed arbitrator; and M. F. Reeder, employer-appointed arbitrator. April 10, 1952. LA, vol. 18, p. 823.

[41]See Ardee Plastics Co., Inc. and United Gas, Coke and Chemical Workers of America, Local 121, CIO. Arbitrator: Arthur T. Jacobs. Sept. 21, 1947. LA, vol. 8, p. 445.

[42]In re Wilmington Welding and Boiler Works and Independent Union of Marine and Shipbuilding Workers of America, Local 9, CIO. Arbitrator: Paul A. Dodd. Nov. 4, 1946. LA, vol. 5, p. 485.

might provide such a clue, as an arbitrator said of a plan requiring that an employee work in 60 percent of the pay periods in the preceding year:

In the first place, the 60% requirement acknowledges the accrual principle in vacations, i.e., a man earns his vacation as he works on the job.[43]

Where a contract contained no work requirement and required only that employees be "on the payroll," the question of whether vacations were an earned right due workers at termination, said an arbitrator, "would depend on other clues, e.g., is the accrual principle inherent in the vacation computation?"[44] If vacation pay were calculated as a percentage of the previous year's earnings, this might be taken as proof that vacations accrued with service rendered and were therefore due at termination.

In the following case, both the work-time requirement and the pay method were cited. The contract provided that employees with over four months but less than twelve months of service were to receive 2 percent of the previous year's earnings. The arbitrator commented:

Vacation pay, within the context of this specific contract, is an accrued right. . . . The amount of vacation pay due the employees is based on the amount of time they have worked. For example, less is accrued by those who have worked six months than by those who have worked one year. The detailed breakdown of the vacation clause in this particular contract indicates that vacation pay was intended to be an earned right with the amount of pay depending on the amount of work performed and the length of service. . . . This breakdown in terms of time worked supports the Union's view of

---

"Fairness" undoubtedly did play an important part in arbitrators' adherence to the actual-service basis for vacations. They were confronted repeatedly with expression of employers' fears that vacations would be allowed for no service. In one case, for instance, in which the arbitrator granted a full vacation to an employee not "in the employ" of the company on June 1 due to layoff, the employer had argued that, although this particular employee had worked much of the year, "If the Union position is sustained, it would result in workers getting vacation pay who had worked a negligible amount of time during the year." In re Amory Mills, Inc., p. 244.

[43]In re Springfield Foundry Co. and United Steelworkers of America, Local 3650, CIO. Arbitrator: James J. Healy. Nov. 17, 1949. LA, vol. 14, p. 1019.

[44]In re Whittet-Higgins Co. and International Association of Machinists, Lodge 1597. Arbitrator: James J. Healy. Dec. 1, 1949. LA, vol. 15, p. 15.

intent—that vacation pay was intended to be considered as an earned right accrued on the basis of time worked and length of service. . . . [45]

As an earned right, terminal vacation pay could be permitted even without a terminal pay clause in the contract, but any provision for it in the contract was a firm clue. Provision for vacation pay at certain terminations, such as layoffs, instead of being proof that other terminations (where it had not yet been won) were meant to be excluded, was sometimes taken as evidence that vacations were considered earned rights and, with this justification, were to be extended to other terminations such as quits or deaths.[46] Or, if terminal vacation pay were provided for those who left their employ *after* the eligibility date (a clause unions usually demanded and won before prorating, as was indicated in Chapter 6), this might be held a sufficient clue to prove vacations were earned rights and to justify granting prorata pay to those terminated before that date.[47] Or sometimes, even the words "earned" or "accumulated" were clues:

Furthermore, section 10 (1) refers to "vacation pay and other earned and/or accumulated benefits***." This clearly indicates that vacation pay is thought of as being "earned."[48]

The employers were fighting a losing battle before arbitrators who picked clues that supported their view that contractual plans were a broad grant of vacations, and who ignored or discounted the clues which management insisted were proof that their plans were a limited provision of vacations.

In one case, for example, the arbitrator stated, "There is no language supporting the 'Future Investment' concept," which the employer insisted was the basis of his plan. Yet that contract stated that those who quit before June 1 were not entitled to receive

[45]*In re* Bachmann Uxbridge Worsted Corp., Andrews Mill *and* Textile Workers Union, CIO. Arbitrator: John A. Hogan. Dec. 7, 1954. *LA,* vol. 23, pp. 601–602.

[46]See, for example, National Casket Co., Inc. *and* Metal Polishers, Buffers, Platers and Helpers International Union, Local 177, AFL. Arbitrator: Jacob J. Blair. Sept. 11, 1951. *LA,* vol. 17, pp. 571–572.

[47]*In re* Wauregan Mills, Inc. *and* Textile Workers Union of America, Local 757. Arbitrator: Albert J. Hogan. Sept. 27, 1958. *LA,* vol. 31, p. 522.

[48]*In re* Texas Textile Mills *and* Textile Workers Union of America, CIO. Board of Arbitration: Clyde Emery, chairman; J. M. Rabun, union-appointed arbitrator; and Arthur J. Riggs, employer-appointed arbitrator. Dec. 20, 1950. *LA,* vol. 15, p. 778.

176

vacation pay; it required forfeiture of vacation pay in the case of those discharged for cause before or after June 1; and it prohibited any employee from taking pay in lieu of the time off. This arbitrator observed, however, that the fact that the contract permitted those who quit *after* June 1 to receive vacation pay "would clearly negative the 'Future Investment' concept."[49]

One employer appealed to the courts to vacate the award of an arbitrator who, in the absence of provision for prorated terminal vacation pay, had nonetheless granted it on the grounds that certain provisions of the contract indicated that prorated pay was contemplated even though there were other contract provisions which would warrant a contrary construction. The North Carolina Supreme Court, affirming the ruling of a lower court, held that the arbitrator had a right to choose his clues. This court also saw vacation plans as a broad grant of the vacation right which could be limited only by the addition of forfeiture clauses and did not see as limiting provisions the clauses which management had written to restrict vacation coverage to those still on the payroll at the end of the qualifying year of continuous service. The Court commented:

The parties could have—but did not—write into the contract any limiting provision such as the one plaintiff now contends should be implied from the other language used.[50]

Apparently unaware that until the postwar period almost no employers had ever granted terminal vacation pay and that employees had not expected it, many arbitrators discounted the evidence of this past practice, as for example:

It is true that apparently the Company has heretofore interpreted the agreements in that manner but such interpretation appears to have been a unilateral one and likely applied to but few individuals

[49]*In re* Globe Corp., Aircraft Division *and* Independent Aircraft Workers Union. Arbitrator: Peter M. Kelliher. August 10, 1954. *LA*, vol. 23, p. 301.

[50]*In re* Calvine Cotton Mills, p. 572. This contract provided that those whose employment terminated after June 1 should receive their vacation pay. Yet the court, upholding the lower court and arbitrator, held this to be "nothing more than a declaration that if an employee continued with the Company up until 1 June...the Company had no defense...." *Ibid.* The Court then said that the provision for new employees to become eligible for annual vacations after six months of service, to be paid for at 2 percent of annual earnings, "clearly permits and requires" prorata vacation pay at terminations.

during the years preceding this agreement due to the high level of employment during that time.[51]

If, on the other hand, any past practice of granting terminal vacation pay were to be found at all, even if only to a selected few employees, this might be considered "an admission that... employees have earned the vacation allowance and are entitled to claim it."[52]

Many arbitrators did not feel called upon to point to any clues either in the contract or in practice, so pervasive was the earned-right concept. One arbitrator in 1947, for example, found that terminal vacation pay was to be granted despite the absence of provision for it in the contract, and even despite past practice to the contrary, because:

It has been generally held and appears to be a well-established principle of labor relations that where vacations are a matter of collective bargaining covered by the agreement that they are considered as an earned right....[53]

Another, in 1950, apparently felt that evidence of even a trend toward negotiation of such clauses elsewhere was relevant to his decision to permit the practice under the contract before him into which the parties had not negotiated such a clause. He said:

There is little question but what the trend in collective bargaining

[51]*In re* McQuay-Norris Manufacturing Co., p. 672.

[52]*In re* Campbell Soup Co. *and* Retail, Wholesale and Department Store Union, Local 194. Board of Arbitration: John Day Larkin, chairman; John Gallagher, union-appointed member; E. N. Davis, company-appointed arbitrator, dissenting with opinion. Nov. 15, 1956. *LA*, vol. 28, p. 219. The employer had in the past granted vacations to some employees who had retired and the board of arbitrators held this to be admission that the survivors of those who died were also entitled to it.

Employers defended the occasional times when they had granted such pay not required by the contract. In one case, for instance, the arbitrator reported, "The Company asserts that such payments were gratuities within the discretion of the employer and were made without any consultation with the union and only to persons who died leaving dependents." Two arbitrators in this case agreed with the employer and denied the union request for full or prorated payments to relatives of the deceased employee who had fulfilled the work requirement but was not on the payroll June 1. *In re* Albert Trostel and Sons Co. *and* Leather Workers Union, Local 47, Amalgamated Meat Cutters and Butcher Workmen of North America. Board of Arbitration: Arvid Anderson, chairman; Owen G. Brown, company-appointed arbitrator; and John Churka, union-appointed arbitrator, dissenting. Dec. 4, 1956. *LA*, vol. 27, p. 645.

[53]*In re* McQuay-Norris Manufacturing Co., p. 672.

agreements is to treat vacation pay as an earned right....Vacation pay being thus considered to be an earned right...it is one which cannot be taken from the employee once he has qualified by the unilateral action of the employer.[54]

Employers, in companies where the union had not negotiated a terminal vacation pay clause, strongly objected to what must have appeared to be the final effrontery, but usually without avail. In a case, for instance, in which the arbitrator had justified his award of terminal vacation pay with the opinion that, among other things, vacation pay was an accrued benefit "for such is the general accepted practice in industry...,"[55] the employer appealed to the courts with the objection that arbitrators could not properly substitute industry practice for what the contract itself said. But the New Hampshire Supreme Court ruled that it was proper for the arbitrators to base their decision on simple justice "even if it meant going outside the scope of the bargaining contract, considering the general accepted practice in industry...."[56]

Employers Sent to Bargaining Table

Under the arbitrators' view that the vacation plans they dealt with were a broad grant of the vacation right to all employees who gave service, it was now the employers who were required to take their case to the bargaining table. Instead of the unions having to extend the management obligation to provide a rest period by winning coverage for terminated employees, the employers had to negotiate forfeiture clauses to affirm the limited extent of the vacation provision they had intended. The requirement of forfeiture clauses was imposed by the many arbitrators who spoke in such language as this:

There is ample evidence by way of arbitrators' decisions and court decisions that vacation pay where earned is due and payable employees as a matter of right *unless specifically limited by the contract.*[57]

[54]*In re* Dunphy Boat Corp., p. 883. The omission in this quote was the arbitrator's effort in a few sentences to liken vacation pay to wages. This is discussed in the next chapter.

[55]*In re* Franklin Needle Co., p. 511.

[56]*Ibid.*

[57]*In re* Garfield Box Co. *and* Textile Workers Union of America, Passaic Joint Board, CIO. Arbitrator: Joseph F. Wildebush. Sept. 29, 1949. *LA*, vol. 13, p. 378, italics added. This case involved exceptions to service in the qualifying year.

Eligibility to vacations was automatically vested with the giving of service, arbitrators were saying, and there had to be a specific "divesting" of that right before an employee could be denied terminal vacation pay. One who noted:

The time when the vacation is to be taken bears no relationship to the vesting of vacation benefits and rights. Once the employee has complied with the eligibility requirement, his vacation allowances must be paid to him.[58]

also commented on vacation plans generally and on the plan before him:

Under various vacation plans, vacation rights become partially or wholly vested and under certain agreements may be divested. The agreement in effect between the parties makes no provision for divesting an employee of vacation credits earned during a calendar year.[59]

An appeal from the interpretation that vacations were a broad grant to which the employer must negotiate specific exception was likely to meet the same requirement from the courts. A California court, for instance, had approved an award of terminal vacation pay to workers who had almost completed the full year's service, despite the absence of specific provision for it in the contract, on the grounds that the required service had been substantially performed. It commented on the employer's idea that terminated employees were not entitled to vacation pay, as follows:

...if the proposition contended for had been in the minds of the parties, it is difficult to believe that they would not have found clearer language in which to express it....The parties must be supposed to have made the contract in the belief that its terms would be fulfilled, that the payments would be made....[60]

But it was too late for employers to secure the "clearer language" that arbitrators and courts were requiring. In giving wide public

[58]*In re* Allied Mills, Inc. *and* American Federation of Grain Millers, Local 110, AFL. Arbitrator: Bert L. Luskin. Sept. 1, 1954. *LA,* vol. 23, p. 184.

[59]*Ibid.,* p. 183. This arbitrator granted terminal vacation pay to retired employees not included in the clause providing it for all other terminations but also not specifically excluded by a forfeiture clause.

[60]Division of Labor Law Enforcement, Department of Industrial Relations v. Ryan Aeronautical Company. California Superior Court, Appellate Department, San Diego County. Sept. 28, 1951. *LRRM,* vol. 29, p. 2029. The judge was applying here the thinking of an earlier case.

expression to the employees' earned-right view, third parties had far-reaching effects not only upon vacation practice but upon the vacation plans themselves.

For employers to go into negotiations and try to win forfeiture clauses would have been a difficult assignment. They could do so only at the risk of appearing to be mean and petty. The employers' opposition in grievance cases had already been made to appear so under the arbitrators' opinions denying the justice of their argument, reducing it to a "selfish purpose,"[61] and making it appear as if they were cheating employees out of their basic rights. Although settlements in collective bargaining are based on economic strength and are not won or lost by moral or theoretical arguments, the arbitrators' public expression of the earned-right view in subjective terms had spread a feeling of righteousness that strengthened employees' will to resist forfeiture clauses. As the arbitrators built up a store of decisions to support the "well-established principle of labor relations" that vacations were earned rights and due at terminations without specific provision in the contract, the argument that vacations were only for employees who continued with the company began to sound antedeluvian or worse. "The time is past when a vacation should be considered anything other than an earned right," it was said in an arbitration case involving a union proposal for a new contract clause providing terminal vacation pay.[62]

The old rationale that vacations were to increase employee productivity had lost out, and there was no hope of winning any recognition of it in either arbitration or negotiation. Certainly forfeiture clauses to cover specific terminations were not the way to do it, even if employers could win them. Any specification of exceptions seemed merely to confirm the arbitrators' view that vacations were inherently earned rights. Some arbitrators saw for-

[61]*In re* Consolidated Vultee Aircraft Corp. *and* International Association of Machinists, Aero Lodge 735. Arbitrator: Whitley P. McCoy. Dec. 14, 1945. *LA*, vol. 4, p. 28.

[62]*In re* California Street Cable Railway Co. *and* Amalgamated Association of Street Electric Railway and Motor Coach Employees of America, Division 1380, AFL. Board of Arbitration: Hubert C. Wyckoff, chairman; S. Waldo Coleman, employer-appointed arbitrator; and Wendell Phillips, union-appointed arbitrator. April 7, 1947. *LA*, vol. 7, p. 97.

feiture clauses simply as limited exceptions agreed to by the unions presumably for reasons only of bargaining strength and having no wider implications of their own relative to the justification for a particular paid vacation plan. It was pointed out that employees did have the right to surrender a part of their basic vacation right. Vacations were due, said one arbitrator, unless "the parties negotiated away that compensation." He went on to explain, "Technically speaking, the parties can agree to most anything provided their agreement is not contrary to public policy."[63] But workers were not about to negotiate away a basic right they had just discovered they had.

Arbitrators' Awards Inconsistent with Theory

The arbitrators' efforts to read the earned-right concept into plans clearly not based on it led the arbitrators into theoretical inconsistencies. For instance, the seniority interpretation of "continuous service" and "on the payroll" permitted vacation pay at layoffs but prohibited it at quits, deaths, or discharges for cause because seniority ended with these terminations. One arbitrator, in fact, commented, "The June 1 eligibility date is a cut-off date for purposes of...determining who is ineligible by virtue of having lost seniority because he quit or was discharged...."[64] Sometimes the distinction was made in one and the same case, as, for example, the one in which laid-off employees were granted terminal vacation pay on the grounds that they retained their seniority, and two employees in the same case who had quit were denied it because seniority ended at quits.[65]

Arbitrators were merely substituting a different criterion for eligibility in place of the one the employers already had set up: seniority replaced actual employment. The employers had meant their criterion to exclude all terminated employees. The arbi-

---

[63]*In re* Wabash Corp. *and* International Brotherhood of Electrical Workers, Local 3, AFL. Arbitrator: Sidney L. Cahn. July 12, 1949. *LA*, vol. 12, p. 1041. The arbitrator here was speaking in general terms. The vacation plan in the Wabash contract did not have a forfeiture clause.

[64]*In re* Wamsutta Mills, Inc., p. 165. A first point, omitted in the above quote, referred to vacation pay and read as follows: "(1) calculating the amount of vacation pay earned by the employees over the year...."

[65]*In re* Dunphy Boat Corp.

trators' seniority criterion included some and excluded others, even though their opinions concurrently held that vacations were inherently earned rights for all workers equally, terminated or continuing, and that any forfeiture of these rights had to be an express one.

Where there was a service requirement or the arbitrator set one himself instead of relying on seniority alone, it was even less logical to exclude certain terminations. If vacations really were earned solely by past service, then denial of such pay at terminations due to quits and discharges for cause could not be justified. Yet many arbitrators tried to do just that when they faced an express forfeiture clause which, of course, had to be respected. In one case, the arbitrator justified a forfeiture clause for discharged employees as follows:

The Parties have provided that employees who are discharged shall not receive vacation pay and this is in accord with the general understanding that an employee who is discharged for proper cause *forfeits his earned vacation rights*. The language of other provisions of this contract as well as the general Labor Relations understanding is that a discharge grows out of actions attributable to an employee.[66]

In short, the worker who did not guard his own conduct would find that his service had not earned him a vacation after all, even though "the general theory that vacations are earned has been established."[67]

Although arbitrators did not desert the earned-right view of vacations as a social benefit and although they almost invariably rejected the idea that vacations were primarily measures to increase productivity for the employer's benefit, it was difficult to avoid making some concession to the employers' view. The excep-

[66]*In re* Globe Corp., p. 301, italics added.

[67]*In re* National Casket Co., Inc., p. 752. The arbitrator who made this statement ruled that terminal vacation pay was due the survivors of an employee who died because death, like layoffs, was beyond the control of the worker, which, of course, was not an earned-right reason. Nor was he thinking in earned-right terms when he granted terminal vacation pay to those who quit, saying, "The logic rests squarely upon the question of whether an employee should be penalized for taking an action which he believes to be of benefit." Then, still ignoring the earned-right reasoning, he denied terminal vacation pay to employees who were discharged for cause because this was the practice in 75 percent of that union's other contracts. *Ibid.*

tion made for terminations which were due to some fault of the worker implied that the employer was not to be penalized for a termination that was not the employer's fault. To this extent, the vacation right appeared to be not an inherent right of the worker for his own benefit but a right based upon behavior which benefited the employer.

But arbitrators in the postwar period were rarely deterred by such inconsistencies with their own theory.

Few Arbitrators See Limited Vacation Right

So pervasive was the earned-right view during the postwar period that few arbitrators could resist the appeal of its apparent logic and, if one did not look too closely, justice. Even those who recognized that paid vacations were limited rights in the plans before them sometimes tried to hold both views at once. "I find myself in complete accord with the... many courts and arbitrators" holding vacations to be earned rights, said one arbitrator.[68] He would like to rule that way himself, he added, but could not because vacations in this case were not earned rights. In previous negotiations the employer had refused to yield to the union demand for a terminal vacation pay clause that would have covered the aggrieved workers:

When the Employer rejected this proposal, it gave the Union notice that it was not prepared to agree to pay vacation to employees not in the employ of the company....[69]

A few other arbitrators acknowledged that, although in principle vacations might be earned rights, past practice under the contract in question indicated they were not. If this had been the first contract, one said, he would agree with the union. However, since workers had not previously been paid for any vacation at termination, he said, "the parties have clearly followed certain past practices that have given meaning to Article 11 that cannot be ignored."[70]

[68]*In re* Illinois Powder Manufacturing Co. *and* United Steelworkers of America, Local 4255, CIO. Arbitrator: Sanford H. Kadish. Jan. 25, 1956. *LA,* vol. 26, p. 40.
[69]*Ibid.,* p. 41.
[70]*In re* Baugh and Sons Co., Philadelphia Plant, *and* International Chemical Workers Union, Local 128, AFL. Board of Arbitration: G. Allen Dash, Jr., chairman;

An occasional arbitrator threw up his hands at the controversy and even denied that the rationale for paid vacations was relevant to whether or not terminal vacation pay was due. One board of arbitrators, for instance, held that the absence of a terminal pay clause meant the parties had not intended to provide such pay, and said:

The Union in this dispute puts forth the contention that vacations are rights earned by employees, while the Company subscribes to the contention that vacations are necessary rests from the tedium of work to foster efficiency in the work force. It would serve no purpose for the Board to endeavor to resolve this difference of opinion, since it has no direct bearing in light of the contract terms.[71]

It was a rare arbitrator who directly denied that paid vacations were inherently earned rights, as did the following (although, significantly, in a case not involving terminal vacation pay):

Perhaps it should be pointed out at this point that Employees' vacation and the rights incidental thereto are not, even as many of us, including the Arbitrator, would like them to be, vested rights; they are in fact and basically contractual rights which can be increased or diminished according to the terms of the agreement entered into between the Company and the Union.[72]

In another case, the employer position was reported as follows:

The Company states that regardless of the theories that may exist about the nature of vacation pay being an earned right, the ultimate right to such pay exists only to the extent that it is granted by the labor contract. In the absence of an agreement on vacation pay, the Company states that no inherent right to vacation pay exists.[73]

This opinion was stated:

The Arbitrator finds no quarrel with the Union's position that vacations are generally considered to be an earned right. . . . However . . .

J. E. Weer, employer-appointed arbitrator; and G. P. Raber, union-appointed arbitrator, dissenting. August 16, 1945. *LA,* vol. 23, p. 181.

[71]*In re* Jenkins Brothers *and* International Union of Mine and Smelter Workers, Local 623, CIO. Board of Arbitration: Robert L. Stutz, W. Stewart Clark, and Mitchell Sviridoff, dissenting. July 19, 1949. *LA,* vol. 12, p. 1154.

[72]*In re* Canada Dry Ginger Ale, Inc. *and* International Brotherhood of Teamsters, Local 118, AFL. Arbitrator: V. Sumner Carrol. March 16, 1955. *LA,* vol. 24, p. 223.

[73]*In re* Albert Trostel and Sons, Co., p. 645.

the right to vacations and vacation pay *are not inherent rights* existing apart from the terms of the collective bargaining agreement.[74]

The writer of this opinion was quite right. Throughout the postwar period, no one could deny that vacations were "generally considered" to be earned rights, but it was equally true that this was not their nature in the majority of vacation plans and certainly it was not the nature of vacations in the particular plans being interpreted by the arbitrators in these postwar grievance cases, even though it was out of these cases that the earned-right theory won its general acceptance.

Summary

At the close of World War II, paid vacations and their liberalizations became a major union demand, desired for the first time as an employee social benefit: to provide rest and recreation with the family and community. As if no other rationale had ever existed, employees and the general public, including third parties in industrial relations, thought vacations to be every worker's basic right, an obligation due him by the employer who had used his services and thereby created the need for a rest.

However, management had written its plans to provide vacation coverage not to every worker but only to those who were most likely to continue their employment to yield an increased productivity after the vacation, and these eligibility clauses remained, unchanged, in postwar vacation plans.

The large majority of postwar arbitrators, hearing employee grievance claims for terminal vacation pay and sharing the current thinking about the vacation right, interpreted the management clauses as intended only to measure length of service, or seniority, and not to determine vacation eligibility. Although vacations were not earned rights in the majority of plans throughout this period, as the arbitrators often claimed they were, and certainly were not in the plans before them, most arbitrators nevertheless held that even without a terminal vacation pay clause, vacations were due terminated workers because they had been "earned" by the preceding year's service.

[74]*Ibid.*, italics added.

186

Thus interpreting contractual vacation plans to be a broad grant of the vacation right to all employees, terminated and continuing, these arbitrators said it was the employers who had to go to the bargaining table, if they intended vacations to be a limited right, and negotiate forfeiture clauses. Because of the uniformity of the arbitrators' rulings, unions with contractual provision for arbitration did not have to win terminal vacation pay clauses. By taking grievances to arbitration, they could and did win the practice through the new interpretation of existing language.

The initiative for further progress in the vacation movement had shifted; it now lay in union hands. The change in the rationale for paid vacations had come about with the postwar period's positive employee interest in vacations as a social benefit. However much employers may find their vacation plans of benefit as an investment to increase productivity, this was no longer their primary purpose. The labor cost for vacations, once voluntarily incurred by management, had now become a management obligation which the unions sought to extend.

The story does not end here, however. In the course of justifying their terminal vacation pay awards, arbitrators expounded another, and wholly fallacious, theory along with and as a part of the earned-right concept. This fallacious theory, misreading the intent of both parties, held that what had been earned was not the time off for rest from past service but wages in payment for that service. These third parties held that the purpose of paid vacations was neither to provide a social benefit nor to increase productivity, but to compensate a worker for his actual service.

Because of the serious confusion the wage notion has left, affecting many fringe benefits other than vacations, it is necessary to examine it separately from the earned-right concept discussed in this chapter, although in practice both concepts were often advanced in the same grievance case opinions. The next chapter analyzes the "deferred wage" part of these postwar opinions to discover how and why the theory arose and what its errors are.

⊹ CHAPTER 8 ⊹

The Deferred Wage Fallacy

THE social significance of labor's demand for paid vacations in the postwar period was not just ignored; it was denied with a very special effort. That effort was the deferred wage theory.

Only a monumental effort could obscure what had happened to the one fringe benefit to span almost half a century, from employer origin to employee "ownership." After decades of employee disinterest in paid vacations (while management brought vacation coverage to 50 percent of American wage earners by 1940), and after the transitional wartime interest in vacation plans as little more than a benefit that workers could get when wages were frozen (raising coverage to 90 percent in five years), employees suddenly claimed paid vacations as their own. An annual vacation became so thoroughly a part of workers' lives that they needed to be "reminded" of the glorious story of how the unions in many bloody battles had wrung the recognition of management's social obligation to workers from reluctant employers, as this mid-1962 editorial in a union newspaper did:

As all employees prepare for their vacations at the end of this month, we want to remind you....A quarter of a century ago, paid vacations were almost unheard of, but today, because of unions, they are taken for granted and are almost universal. *But many a worker lost his job and some their lives to make paid vacations become a reality.* As you enjoy your vacation, you should contemplate what you might be doing if it were not for the sacrifices made by the working men and women who preceded you.[1]

[1] *Local 320 IUE-AFL-CIO News* (Liverpool, New York), July 1962, p. 1, col. 1, italics added.

188

The change in employee attitude toward vacations was remarkable but unmistakable. During the postwar years, unions negotiated longer periods of time off—even though it would not increase the employee's total income as the negotiation of a wage increase would do—to liberalize an industry social obligation that was separate and distinct from the employer's obligation to pay wages for actual service. Vacations were related to past service only to the extent necessary to fulfill the purpose of providing workers an adequate rest from that service, free from financial anxieties. The freedom from financial worries in turn required that the worker be "made whole" for whatever loss of income he might suffer as a result of taking the vacation rest. The "make-whole" principle had governed the amount of vacation pay due a worker since the origin of paid vacation plans. Unlike wages, which are directly related to actual work time, vacation pay had always been a more or less arbitrary amount calculated by whatever method would most closely approximate normal income to keep the worker's bills paid while he relaxed and recuperated.

Historically, as we have seen, vacation pay had never been considered part of the wage payment for actual service given. Employers had considered it an investment in future productivity and employees had accepted it as such. During the war period, the government had made a special effort to keep the purpose of vacation pay separate from the purpose of hourly wages.

Nevertheless, we saw the unions argue that vacation pay was wages to support their demands for terminal vacation pay clauses in cases before the War Labor Board. We saw some of the WLB panels pick up the argument to justify recommending such clauses. We also noted the money orientation which characterized the Board's attitude toward these cases even though most of its experience with vacation plans involved adoptions or liberalizations for the express purpose of providing time off for rest, not a money benefit.

In the postwar period, the situation was more extreme in all these respects. Arbitrators rarely had a case involving a plan adoption or liberalization but dealt almost entirely with grievance cases over terminal vacation pay, all of which had one common characteristic: they involved only vacation *pay,* unattached to any scheduled time off. Even more than the WLB, arbitrators tended to see vacations only as a money benefit and to lose sight of the basic rest purpose for which the plan as a whole and its liberalizations had been negotiated.

This more extreme money orientation left the postwar arbitrators more open to the union argument that vacation pay was wages. The position that unions took could have been predicted. They naturally spoke in terms of money since it was money they were seeking in lieu of a scheduled vacation. In looking for convincing points to win their cases, the unions turned to the "part of wages" argument that had found favor with some parts of the War Labor Board and which, it quickly became apparent, would work even greater magic with postwar arbitrators who, unable to add to a contract as the WLB could do, had the more difficult task of granting terminal vacation pay where the contract did not provide it. With little regard to more than winning each case, the unions pushed the wages argument for all it was worth.[2]

In response, the majority of arbitrators picked up this idea more readily and embraced it more thoroughly than any of the WLB panels had done.[3] They did so in many of the same cases discussed in the last chapter, but for the purpose of analyzing and tracing the extent of the earned-right thinking, the wage aspect

[2]An example of the kind of argument arbitrators heard from the employees is reported as follows: "In support of its position the Union asserts that vacation pay is a collectively negotiated economic benefit that constitutes part of the remuneration for which an employee performs his services. Therefore when the services have been performed, payment must be made." *In re* Albert Trostel and Sons Co. *and* Leather Workers Union, Local 47, Amalgamated Meat Cutters and Butcher Workmen of North America. Board of Arbitration: Arvid Anderson, chairman; Owen G. Brown, company-appointed arbitrator; and John Churka, union-appointed arbitrator, dissenting. Dec. 4, 1956. Bureau of National Affairs, *Labor Arbitration Reports* (hereafter referred to as *LA*) (Washington: BNA, 1946 to date), vol. 27, p. 644. See also Wamsutta Mills, Inc. (New Bedford, Mass.) *and* Textile Workers Union of America. Arbitrator: John A. Hogan. Sept. 5, 1959. *LA*, vol. 34, p. 161.

[3]A few arbitrators attributed the wages idea to what they apparently thought, however mistakenly, was the official WLB view, as for example: "Influenced by War Labor Board decisions on wage increases, it has now become the accepted view that vacations are a collateral form of wages...." *In re* Goodyear Tire and Rubber Co. of Alabama *and* United Rubber, Cork, Linoleum and Plastic Workers of America, Local 12, CIO. Arbitrator: Whitley P. McCoy. May 15, 1946. *LA*, vol. 3, p. 258.

190

was omitted from the opinions discussed there. Furthermore, not all arbitrators who said that vacations were an earned right also expounded the wages idea. There is still another and more important reason for giving separate treatment to the two ideas. The concept of vacations as an earned right is a legitimate concept which in truth underlies many, if not yet most, current vacation plans, through contractual provision for terminal vacation pay. But the wages idea applied to vacation plans is a fallacious concept under almost any circumstance and requires separate analysis. The story of the arbitrators' response to the wages argument the unions were pushing is the subject of this chapter.

Arbitrators Describe Vacations as Deferred Wages

As is noted above, paid vacations had not been considered by either party or by third parties as any part of, or supplement to, the hourly wage rate in payment for actual service, prior to the postwar period. Yet many arbitrators throughout this period said it was exactly that: a part of back wages for service already given, no different from the hourly rate except in the form and time of payment. Their idea was that as an employee worked each hour, he earned (1) a given rate per hour in cash, and (2) an additional amount per hour which he did not receive at once, but which instead was deferred in payment. The purpose of both payments was the same: to compensate for actual service. Note, for instance, this expression of the deferred wage idea:

For each day that an employee is operating his job, he earns not only the take-home pay which he received within the week, but also a fractional share of the total vacation pay which he will receive upon the occasion of his vacation. *This vacation pay represents a deferred wage due for work actually performed,* and payable not as the work is performed, but when the vacation is taken.[4]

Sometimes the only difference appeared to be the time of payment. As another arbitrator explained it:

[4]*In re* Calvine Cotton Mills, Inc. *and* Textile Workers Union of America, Local 677, CIO. Arbitrator: Gerald A. Barrett. April 4, 1952. Quoted in Brookford Mills *and* Textile Union of America. Arbitrator: Samuel H. Jaffee. June 17, 1957. *LA,* vol. 28, p. 842, italics added.

This is not to say that there are not some differences between this form of wage payment and the form that reflects itself in the payment of wage scales that provide so many cents per hour of work. Thus, payment in the latter case is not long deferred; the payment in the former case is normally deferred for a much longer period in the very nature of the situation,....[5]

In opinions such as these, vacation pay was to be considered as part of the hourly rate of pay. Thus, for an employee paid $1.00 an hour, the hourly rate was really $1.02, if he was entitled to a one-week vacation. But he got $1.00 an hour immediately and accumulated the other 2 percent or 2 cents per hour to be collected after a year's service. It was said that

...vacation pay is considered in all respects in the same manner as would be the actual earned rate per hour or per week.[6]

Not all arbitrators were so explicit. Many did not feel any necessity to relate vacation pay to or describe it as a part of the hourly rate of pay. They felt it enough merely to assert that it was wages, as the following pages will amply illustrate.

How did the deferred wage theory, and other such descriptions of vacations as pay for service,[7] arise?

"Legal" Justification

As described in the preceding chapter, most arbitrators were convinced that all workers had a right to an annual paid vacation and interpreted vacation plans as being such a broad grant of vacations. Furthermore, they said, this right to a vacation had been earned by past service and could not be denied a worker if he subsequently terminated his employment. But the employers were

[5]*In re* Brookford Mills, p. 841.

[6]*In re* National Casket Co., Inc. *and* Metal Polishers, Buffers, Platers and Helpers International Union, Local 177, AFL. Arbitrator: Jacob J. Blair. Sept. 11, 1951. *LA,* vol. 17, p. 571.

[7]Since arbitrators did not make clear what their definition of "wages" was in many cases, and it appeared to range from rate per hour to all employee compensation, we must deal with their opinions more directly in terms of whether or not they saw vacation pay as pay for actual service, regardless of what they chose to call it. Those who called it "wages" meant pay for service, they usually made plain. But others also meant this when they called it "compensation" by defining all compensation or employee income as pay for service. These other concepts will be discussed in succeeding pages.

192

singularly unimpressed with the earned-right argument. Their opposition to granting terminal vacation pay where the contract had made no provision for it was so strong that arbitrators felt the need for a more compelling justification for their terminal vacation pay awards than simply to argue that vacations were an earned right. Describing vacations as part of wages due for past service would supply this added justification, they believed. To their earned-right view, most arbitrators simply added the wages idea:

I regard such provisions...as constituting an earned right in the nature of wages,...[8]

Since back wages for actual service rendered are legally due a worker at employment termination for any cause, arbitrators sought to bring terminal vacation pay under this same umbrella:

We consider vacation pay an earned right in the form of deferred compensation and as such, cannot be taken away from the employee once he has qualified....[9]

Their belief in the quasi-legal necessity of granting vacation pay at terminations was evident from the way arbitrators expressed the deferred wage argument:

If vacation pay in this contract constitutes a portion of the total wage earned each day by each employee, as the Arbitrator is compelled to hold, then it follows that the grievants were entitled to their pro-rata vacation pay at the time of their termination,...[10]

As this quote indicates, the wages idea was of special value to arbitrators over the more vague earned-right concept because it would particularly justify the granting of prorata vacation pay in the absence of contractual provision for it. Even where the minimum work requirement had not been met, vacations were due for the amount of it that had been worked. Arbitrators' emphasis on actual service as the only proper eligibility requirement for vacations made it an easy step to the view of vacation pay as com-

[8]*In re* Brookford Mills, p. 841.
[9]*In re* Rib Mountain Granite Co. *and* Alvin Bucholz. Wisconsin Employment Relations Board: L. E. Gooding, chairman; J. E. Fitzgibbon and Morris Slavney, commissioners. Sept. 14, 1953. *LA*, vol. 21, p. 220.
[10]*In re* Calvine Cotton Mills, Inc., Arbitrator Barrett, pp. 842–843.

pensation for that service. Right to the vacation pay was thus automatically a vested right. A board of arbitrators stated that:

...vacation pay...represents an additional form of wages paid to the employees, that employees earn a pro-rata amount of their vacation pay in addition to their cash take-home pay as they perform their daily work, and that the right to this vacation pay *vests as it is earned* with the time for payment being deferred.[11]

How could the employer oppose such payments? As one arbitrator said, "The only burden placed on the Employer is to pay its employees for something which they have already earned."[12]

The Deferred Wage Theory Spreads

With arbitrators quoting and requoting each other, the notion grew by feeding upon itself. Negotiations are rarely made public but arbitration awards and opinions almost always are. As a result, the errors of the earlier opinions, without corrective effects, were compounded. With such comments as "the substantially universal prevalence of this rule would support a similar finding in the instant case,"[13] the wages idea was carried to the point of "universal acceptance." Postwar terminal vacation pay opinions were introduced by imposing prefixes such as these:

It is a well established rule that vacation pay is in the nature of wages....[14]

It has been held again and again that vacation pay...is considered to be a direct part of wages.[15]

From arbitrators the idea spread to the courts reviewing their awards on appeal. For example, the Mississippi Supreme Court

[11]*In re* Mary-Leila Cotton Mills, Inc. *and* Textile Workers Union, Local 384, AFL-CIO. Board of Arbitrators: Gerald A. Barrett, chairman; Charles Auslander, union-appointed arbitrator; and Hugh M. Dorsey, Jr., employer-appointed arbitrator, dissenting. March 31, 1956. *LA,* vol. 26, p. 542, italics added.

[12]*In re* Wabash Corp. *and* International Brotherhood of Electrical Workers, Local 3, AFL. Arbitrator: Sidney L. Cahn. July 12, 1949. *LA,* vol. 12, p. 1044.

[13]*In re* Calvine Cotton Mills, Inc., Arbitrator Barrett, p. 842. "This theory is now well supported with precedents permitting a precise determination of the issues," said another arbitrator. *In re* National Casket Co., p. 571.

[14]*In re* Catoir Silk Co. *and* Textile Workers Union of America, CIO. Arbitrator: Maurice S. Trotta. Sept. 16, 1949. *LA,* vol. 13, p. 368.

[15]*In re* American Window Glass Co. *and* Window Glass Cutters League of America, AFL. Arbitrator: Clair V. Duff. Jan. 11, 1956. *LA,* vol. 26, p. 107.

affirmed the granting of prorated vacation pay at termination in the absence of provision for it with this expression of the wages idea:

...and when it is recognized also, as it is generally recognized, that vacation pay constitutes extra wages or compensation, it must necessarily follow that the employee is entitled to the wages earned to the date of the termination of his employment and if vacation pay is a part of such wages, as we hold it to be, then he is necessarily entitled to his pro-rata share of such vacation pay for the period from June 1, 1951, to February 29, 1952. Certainly it could not be successfully maintained that appellee could terminate the employment under similar circumstances and thereby escape liability for the regular wages of its employees earned to date of such termination. We can perceive no difference in the result to follow where the wages claimed consist of vacation pay.[16]

The courts also applied the wages idea in deciding the question of the arbitrability of vacation disputes. "...vacation pay is included in the term wages and therefore arbitrable," said the New Hampshire Supreme Court.[17]

In bankruptcy proceedings, where the federal law provided priority up to six hundred dollars for "wages," vacation pay was held by the courts to be part of the "wages" due workers in two cases, one in 1902 and another in 1939,[18] which were frequently cited by arbitrators as evidence that terminal vacation pay was due as a legal "wage" obligation. Despite this early appearance of the idea, it did not become widespread among the courts until the

[16]Livestock Feeds, Inc. v. Local Union No. 1634, CIO. Mississippi Supreme Court. June 14, 1954. Bureau of National Affairs, *Labor Relations Reference Manual* (hereafter referred to as *LRRM*) (Washington: BNA, 1937 to date), vol. 34, p. 2433.

[17]*In re* Brampton Woolen Co. v. Local Union 112, etc. New Hampshire Supreme Court. Nov. 3, 1948. *LA*, vol. 11, p. 487. The North Carolina Supreme Court had also said that vacations were arbitrable as wages. *In re* Calvine Cotton Mills, Inc. v. Textile Workers of America, CIO, Local 677, *et al.* North Carolina Supreme Court. *LA*, vol. 21, p. 571.

[18]With the Federal Bankruptcy Act giving priority to workers' "wages" for over a hundred years and with vacations preceding all other fringe benefits, it was natural that the question would have arisen early as to whether vacation payments were to be considered as "wages" under the law. In 1902, they were held to be part of "wages." Gladding Co., 120 Fed. 709. In 1939, another court said that "vacation with pay is in effect additional wages...the week's vacation pay had been completely earned and only the time of receiving it postponed." Wil-Low Cafeterias Inc., 111 Fed. 2d 429.

arbitrators had popularized the idea of vacation pay as wages in their awards and opinions in the postwar period. From that point on, however, federal courts in bankruptcy cases felt little need to press the point that vacation pay was "wages," saying, as in one case, simply that "Vacation pay is, by all the decisions, regarded as wages."[19]

The deferred wage idea was now taken up by all third parties and in all questions relating to paid vacations whether they involved terminal vacation pay or not. Various government agencies, such as state unemployment compensation boards, also found that the nature of paid vacations was wages to compensate for service, with the courts upholding their decisions based on this concept. Finally, from all these sources came application of the idea to other fringe issues. Partly because it has become so widespread, the deferred wage theory requires examination at its origin—the arbitrators' opinions in terminal vacation pay grievances.

Evidence of the Parties' Intent

At least among third parties in this postwar period, there seemed little question but that the deferred wage idea had become the "universal understanding." But, in using the idea to justify their awards, arbitrators had to and did attribute it to the parties as well. What evidence did they have to prove that this was intended by the parties to the contract containing paid vacations?

From an examination of the opinions of all arbitrators who enunciated the deferred wage doctrine during this postwar period, we find that they adduced evidence of such intent in three ways.

First, to avoid the appearance that they were merely substituting outside precedents for the intent of the parties, many arbitrators claimed that since the "general understanding in industry" was that vacations were wages, the parties must have had this same understanding in mind when they negotiated on vacations.

The doctrine that vacation pay represents a form of wages, payment of which is deferred, is now accepted everywhere. It was certainly accepted in the textile industry when the parties negotiated this

[19]U.S. v. Munro-Van Helms Co. Inc. U.S. Court of Appeals, Fifth Circuit (New Orleans). March 21, 1957. *LRRM*, vol. 39, p. 2599. One judge dissented.

agreement and there is nothing in the language of the agreement to indicate that they were departing from the general understanding.[20]

In another similar case:

It is inconceivable to suggest that the Company and the Union negotiators who wrote this vacation clause were not aware of the effect of the considerable body of arbitration awards and court decisions on the very question that is under consideration here, and which were decided prior to the signing of this contract in 1954. Nothing in this contract suggests any different intent on the part of these parties as to the nature of vacation pay or as to the entitlement on the part of laid off employees...vacation pay under this contract is a deferred wage payment based on earnings in the year prior to March 31,...[21]

Although the unions were making the most of the deferred wage idea in these cases, having found the justification to which third parties, from the WLB on, were most receptive, the employers strongly objected to it. Arbitrators must stick to the contract, they said, "without any forced interpretations based upon theories of 'accrued wages....' "[22] Yet the arbitrators, with the courts backing them up, insisted that even the employers must have shared the "wages" concept of vacations as, for example, in this New Hampshire Supreme Court opinion:

We believe that ordinary men in the position of these individual defendants would have thought of vacation pay as part of their pay or wages and no reason appears why the same meaning should not have been equally clear to their employer.[23]

Secondly, having made the assumption that the deferred wage idea was the understanding of both parties, the arbitrators turned to the contract itself for proof of that understanding. They used the same "clues" which arbitrators had found to prove that vacations were "earned rights." Recognition of the "accrual principle" was also recognition that vacations were wages. Note, for instance, this opinion:

[20]*In re* Wauregan Mills, Inc. *and* Textile Workers Union of America, Local 757. Arbitrator: Albert J. Hogan. Sept. 27, 1958. *LA*, vol. 31, p. 522.

[21]*In re* Monument Mills, Inc. *and* Textile Workers Union of America. Arbitrator: Robert L. Stutz. Oct. 2, 1957. *LA*, vol. 29, p. 403.

[22]*In re* Kleene-Fibre Corp. *and* Textile Workers Union of America, CIO. Arbitrator: Henry Parkman. Sept. 11, 1953. *LA*, vol. 21, p. 236.

[23]*In re* Brampton Woolen Co., p. 487.

Once the employee had "worked" in the specified number of pay periods he has accrued vacation credit. The Arbitrator must, therefore, find the Parties contemplated that vacation payments should be considered as additional wages. As well as being supported by Contract language, this is almost universal understanding today in Collective Bargaining.[24]

Where the percentage pay calculation method was used, as in seasonal industries of irregular earnings, this was taken to prove that vacations were wages, just as it had also been cited to prove that vacations were earned. For instance:

A clear provision in advance for a fixed percentage of earnings already made, certainly sounds like the "vested rights" or "deferred wage" theory which the vast majority of cases seem to follow.[25]

But arbitrators found evidence of a "wages" intent whatever pay calculation method was used. If the contract provided that "regular wages" or "full pay" be allowed for the vacation period, even this indicated to some that the parties saw the vacation pay as wages.

Thirdly, arbitrators used their own reasoning to determine the intent of the parties. One said:

...it is not the long line of previous decisions that is determinative. It is the validity of the reasoning behind the principle that vacation pay is part of wages that is determinative.[26]

But an examination of the reasoning of the deferred wage theorists reveals it was little more substantial than that of the arbitrator who found in the proximity of the section on vacations to the one on wages a shred of evidence of the intent of the parties to consider vacation pay as wages.[27]

[24] *In re* Globe Corp., Aircraft Division *and* Independent Aircraft Workers Union. Arbitrator: Peter M. Kelliher. August 10, 1954. *LA,* vol. 23, p. 300. Prorata terminal vacation pay was denied in this case, for other reasons, however.

[25] *In re* Texas Textile Mills *and* Textile Workers Union of America, CIO. Board of Arbitration: Clyde Emery, chairman; J. M. Rabun, union-appointed arbitrator; and Arthur J. Riggs, employer-appointed arbitrator. Dec. 20, 1950. *LA,* vol. 15, p. 778.

[26] *In re* Bachmann Uxbridge Worsted Corp., Andrews Mill *and* Textile Workers Union, CIO. Arbitrator: John A Hogan. Dec. 7, 1954. *LA,* vol. 23, p. 602.

[27] "The Company brief (page 3) argues that the vacation bonus can't be a form of wage, because it is a separate section, apart from the wage section. On the contrary, the arrangement of the sections implies, if anything, that the vacation

Arbitrators' Reasoning

A close look at the "validity of the reasoning behind the principle that vacation pay is part of wages" reveals four points which were generally made:

One, the fact that vacations were negotiated made them wages: The primary reason for this conclusion is that vacations are negotiated as part of the contract,....[28]

It is earned pay in the form of deferred wages. To deny [it] would improperly withhold money due them as part of the bargain which settled the contract when vacation pay was bargained into it.[29]

Second, the fact that the vacation pay was money income to the employee proved it was wages:

A dollar bargained is still a dollar whether it is paid as wages for work performed or in lieu of wages during the vacation period.[30]

It was pointed out that vacation pay was taxable earnings to the employee and thus "considered as 'wages' under applicable Federal Law."[31]

Third was the fact that paid vacations were a cost to the employer, spelled out in terms of cents per hour:

In the negotiation of labor agreements the cost of vacations is always considered, both by employer and union representatives, as part of the labor cost. During the negotiations whenever vacation pay is discussed both parties are constantly computing the per hour cost to the employer and per hour benefit to the employees.[32]

---

bonus is akin to wages; its section (section 20) immediately precedes the one on wages (section 21) and immediately follows the one on premium pay (section 18) and reporting time pay (section 19)." *In re* Texas Textile Mills, p. 778.

[28]*In re* Allied Drum Service, Inc. *and* United Mine Workers of America, District 50, Local 13778. Board of Arbitration: Carl A. Warns, Jr., chairman; Irwin G. Waterman, employer-appointed arbitrator; and Richard C. Snider, union-appointed arbitrator. Nov. 16, 1954. *LA*, vol. 23, p. 677. While the "conclusion" referred to was that "eligibility to vacation is earned," the arbitrator granted terminal vacation pay because to do otherwise would be to deny the employee "part of his negotiated wages." *Ibid.*

[29]*In re* Bachmann Uxbridge Worsted Corp., p. 601.

[30]*Ibid.*, p. 602.

[31]*In re* Allied Drum Service, Inc., p. 677.

[32]*In re* Dunphy Boat Corp. *and* Upholsterers' International Union of North America, Local 352, AFL. Arbitrator: L. E. Gooding. Jan. 3, 1950. *LA*, vol. 13, p. 883.

And the fourth proof that vacation pay was wages was the fact that vacations appeared to have been negotiated in lieu of a wage increase:

Very frequently an increase in wages is traded for a vacation program or vice-versa. Vacation pay being thus considered to be an earned right in the form of deferred compensation,....[33]

Wages may be traded for "fringes," "fringes" for wages. Vacation pay or holiday pay is often negotiated instead of a wage increase of greater amount.[34]

The prima facie nature of the "evidence" is immediately apparent. Obviously, not the fact that vacations are negotiated, nor the fact that vacation pay represents income—even taxable as "wages"—nor the fact that vacations represent a cost to the employer makes vacation pay wages, either by intent of the parties or otherwise. Mere incorporation of a vacation plan into a labor agreement could not make the vacation pay compensation for service if it had not been so before. The fact that the cost to the employer and benefit to the employees were spelled out in terms of cents per hour was merely the use of a convenient common denominator for comparing the cost of this employee benefit to the major labor cost item or source of income, the hourly wage rate.

But what of the idea that vacations were wages because they were negotiated in lieu of "wages" or of a wage increase? It would appear that here the arbitrators were reasoning that vacation pay was wages because it was not wages. But a closer look reveals the fact that two definitions for the word "wages" are being used. When an arbitrator said that vacation pay "is earned pay in the form of deferred *wages*...negotiated instead of a *wage* increase...,"[35] his second reference was to the hourly rate and the first one comprehended "wages" to be all compensation or all income from an employer. But a closer look also reveals that both uses of the word "wage" or "wages" meant pay for service.

In holding all income to be "wages," some used the expression "total wages," as the arbitrator who commented that "...vacation

[33]*Ibid.*
[34]*In re* Bachmann Uxbridge Worsted Corp., p. 602.
[35]*Ibid.*, p. 601, italics added.

200

pay is part of the total wage earned by the employee."[36] Some were more specific:

There can be little doubt that workers generally consider the money which comes to them as a result of their labors, whether it be regular pay, overtime or vacation pay, as part of their wages and courts have recognized this fact.[37]

Still others suggested that the total wage package was at least a hidden "wage" increase, increasing still more—as the supplied emphasis indicates—our store of definitions:

Vacation pay is normally a form of accrued *wages* payable to the worker at the time of vacation. It is bargained for by collective bargaining and usually is part and parcel of a *"wage package"* including *wages,* vacations, holidays and other fringes, if any. Present day collective bargaining has dispelled any illusions as to whether vacation pay is considered nothing more or less than a *hidden wage increase.*[38]

Now it must be said, before we lose ourselves in total confusion, that the definition of "wages" in certain situations might well be used to comprehend all income or certain forms of income. The Bureau of Internal Revenue, for instance, is properly concerned with all employee income, by whatever name it chooses to call that income.[39] In bankruptcy cases the question is what money due workers should be given priority to fulfill the law's purpose. And receipt of employee income affects eligibility to unemployment compensation by the various "wage" definitions set up in the state laws. The National Labor Relations Act defines "wages" for the purpose of determining what is proper subject for collective bargaining. It is the use of the word "wages" in these and other laws that requires the administrators of those laws to call certain

[36]*In re* Calvine Cotton Mills, Inc., Arbitrator Barrett, p. 842.

[37]*In re* Brampton Woolen Co., pp. 487–488. This expression came not from an arbitrator but from the New Hampshire Supreme Court.

[38]*In re* Garfield Box Co. *and* Textile Workers Union of America, Passaic Joint Board, CIO. Arbitrator: Joseph F. Wildebush. Sept. 29, 1949. *LA,* vol. 13, p. 378, italics added.

[39]While the Bureau of Internal Revenue uses the term "wages" loosely to be somewhat synonymous with "income," exclusion of some sick leave payments from taxability would indicate that all employee income is not necessarily "taxable as wages." It is conceivable that vacation pay could have been considered exempt income as a health measure.

income payments "wages." In each case, the word has a legal meaning.

But in cases involving grievances over whether terminal vacation pay was due, the use of the word "wages" to describe all income was unnecessary and made no sense unless there was some magic in the word "wages." Arbitrators, of course, felt that there was. They did not say "vacation pay is a part of income," because this would have provided no special justification for allowing terminal vacation pay where the agreement didn't specifically provide it. The connotation of the word "income" does not necessarily mean pay for actual service; the connotation of "wages" does, and it is pay for actual service that is the employer's legal obligation. Arbitrators could not say that vacation pay was the same as the hourly rate, however much they could liken it to the hourly rate or find it somehow an undefined part of it. The best they could say was that vacation pay was "wages" in the same sense as the hourly rate, that is, in performing the same function: pay for service. And this is what they did say.

It was, in fact, to get this idea across that arbitrators drew together all the sophistry at their command as if the mere weight of superficial arguments would supply what the soundness of each did not. Contemplate, for instance, this opinion which arrayed the complete battery of arguments used by arbitrators to prove intent, the prevalence of the wages concept, private deductions, and contractual "evidence":

It is well established under existing precedents that vacations are deferred earnings. This is evidenced by, first, the manner in which vacations are negotiated. In negotiations, vacations with pay are frequently granted in lieu of the equivalent cost in a cents-per-hour increase in wages. Second, there is no question but what vacations are payroll costs to the employer, fully deductible as expense items. Finally, there is no question but what vacation pay is taxed under the Income Tax Laws as earned. In this sense, too, *such vacation pay is considered in all respects in the same manner as would be the actual earned rate per hour or per week.* For these reasons, the general position taken by the Union with reference to the employee being entitled to receive vacation pay is sound. This is even recognized by the employer who had pro-rated vacation pay earned by employees whose services

202

are terminated as a result of lay-offs or other conditions beyond their control. By this acknowledgment of Company policy....[40]

The Basic Fallacy

But despite such marshaling of prima facie evidence into a logical-sounding structure, it was a house of cards built upon a single fallacious assumption. The parties had *not* negotiated vacations as pay for service but rather for the purpose of providing a rest period.

When arbitrators cited the fact that vacations were negotiated in lieu of a wage increase, they were giving evidence of the very reason why vacations were *not* wages in payment for service. Take, for example, this arbitrator's expression of the idea:

The parties have collectively bargained on the subject. What they agreed to is in their Agreement, the fruit of that bargaining. Obviously, too, when an employer negotiates with a union he includes vacation pay when calculating his wage and related costs. And correspondingly it would not be unfair to assume that had a vacation pay provision not resulted from the bargaining, the union would have sought a corresponding increase in the general wage scales. Collectively bargained paid vacations are thus a form of, or in the nature of wages. The fact that the parties have chosen to apply some of this money "in the pot" for vacation pay makes it no less so; indeed, this reinforces the conclusion that vacation pay provisions in collectively bargained contracts are a form of or in the nature of wages.[41]

But, indeed, this reinforced the opposite conclusion. Why, if vacation pay were no different from wages, should the union not have "sought a corresponding increase in the general wage scales?"

The answer was simple: in declining an increase in their wage rates in preference for more time off, the employees were indicating as clearly as it could possibly have been indicated that their intent in negotiating vacations was not to receive more pay for

[40]*In re* National Casket Co., pp. 571–572, italics added. In the absence of an express contractual provision for it, the employees in this case were seeking an interpretation which would allow terminal vacation pay, pro rata, for those who died, quit, or were discharged for cause.
[41]*In re* Brookford Mills, Inc., p. 841.

service but for a distinctly different purpose: to secure more time off, without loss of normal income, in which to rest and relax. They were declining pay for service in favor of a social benefit.

The employers, too, when the initiative was theirs, had made the choice of putting the cost into vacations instead of into wages— for reasons of their own. To the extent that it made any difference to them now, the preference was still for paid vacations rather than a wage increase of equal cost. And this preference was based upon the beneficial effects they might still realize from the physical rest for employees. In short, however different their view of vacations, as a management social obligation or an investment in increased work force efficiency, both parties agreed that vacations were being negotiated as rest periods.

Arbitrators Discard Rest Purpose

Arbitrators, however, denied that the purpose of vacations was to provide a rest, either as an employee social benefit *or* as a means of increasing the efficiency of the work force.

Consistent with their conviction that every employee had a right to a paid vacation superseding management's interest in a benefit to itself, arbitrators were not buying the employers' view which would have required denial of vacations to terminated employees. In place of it, they picked up the employees' view which gave terminal vacation pay the appearance of a legally-required payment, as for instance in the following case. The arbitrator reported of the company position that

It...appears that the sole reason for the refusal to pay the two weeks' vacation pay of the aggrieved employee is the opinion of the company that vacation pay is not a form of additional compensation but is intended to provide a period of rest....[42]

The union takes the position that vacation provisions are a form of additional compensation and even though an employee is not in

[42]*In re* Indiana Gas and Chemical Corp. *and* United Mine Workers of America, District 50, Local 12009, AFL. Arbitrator: Alex Elson. Jan. 15, 1947. *LA*, vol. 6, p. 451. This quote continues as follows: "and that an employee who quits the employ of the Company foregoes his vacation...because he is no longer an employee of the Company."

the employ of the company at the time the vacations are normally taken, he is entitled to it.[43]

In throwing out the employer's view that vacations were rests for the purpose of increasing productivity, arbitrators tended to discard with it the idea that they were for a rest. Note this language:

...vacations with pay are in the nature of additional wages earned, and not a benefit granted by the employer to enable the employee to refresh himself and recoup his strength for the work ahead.[44]

Another arbitrator stated his agreement with the view of

...vacations not primarily as periods of rest before another year of service but rather as additional compensation which an employee earns by working a specified period....[45]

As in the above language, some arbitrators did not actually use the word "wages" but called vacation pay "extra" or "additional" compensation, but the purpose they had in mind was the same: to pay for actual service rather than to provide a social benefit. A payment could not be both.

If the purpose of this money were not to finance a rest period, then it had to be considered as an increase in the compensation for

[43]*Ibid.* The arbitrator agreed with the union, commenting that under "the prevalent view in industry today...vacation pay is additional compensation," *ibid.*

[44]*In re* Kleene-Fibre Corp., p. 237. Another arbitrator remarked the view's wide acceptance: "There was a time when vacations were given by the employer on the theory that it was to refresh the employee for his next year of service. It was even treated as something of a gratuity, allowed by the employer, after a stated period of service. This is no longer the prevailing theory. Among those acquainted with the industrial relations picture today, vacation allowances are earned....It is wages earned." *In re* Campbell Soup Co. *and* Retail, Wholesale and Department Store Union, Local 194. Board of Arbitration: John Day Larkin, chairman; John Gallagher, union-appointed member; E. N. Davis, company-appointed arbitrator, dissenting with opinion. Nov. 15, 1956. *LA,* vol. 28, p. 218.

Still another arbitrator had a different explanation: "Vacation clauses are now a standard feature of collective bargaining agreements. Although originally predicated on the worker's need for rest and relaxation, the practice among many companies of paying a bonus in lieu of vacations—born of the wartime needs for uninterrupted production—has somewhat changed the concept of a vacation benefit from a gratuity to a right to additional compensation based on prior service." *In re* Penberthy Injector Co. *and* United Steelworkers of America, Local 2395, CIO. Arbitrator: Harry H. Platt. *LA,* vol. 15, p. 714.

[45]*In re* Grocers Wholesale Outlet, Inc. *and* International Brotherhood of Teamsters, Local 443, AFL. Board of Arbitration: Joseph F. Donnelly, Samuel F. Curry, and W. Stewart Clark, dissenting. July 17, 1951. *LA,* vol. 16, pp. 914–915.

work done in the rest of the year. But additional time off, even though paid for, did *not* add to an employee's total income. It could be considered as "extra" or "additional" compensation only in the sense of increasing his effective rate of pay, as the following arbitrator said:

The theory of vacation pay is extra compensation for work done in the other weeks of the year.... [46]

Yet this arbitrator went on to say, "so that the worker may be secure while building up strength for the balance of the year." And many other arbitrators, too, claimed that the vacation provision had both the wages purpose and the rest purpose, as, for instance, in this opinion:

Vacation pay is regarded as additional compensation for work *already* performed in order to enable the employees to take a rest period.[47]

What was wrong with the idea that vacations were to pay for the actual service already performed *and* to provide a rest period?

To begin with, whatever incidental advantages it might have for either party, initially the payment could be made only for one purpose. If, as the arbitrators said, the purpose of this money was to compensate for service, then any other "purpose" attributed to it merely referred to its subsequent expenditure. Saying that vacation pay was wages to provide a rest period is like saying that wages are paid an employee for the purpose of feeding and clothing himself and his family. A worker's wages for his actual service

---

[46] *In re* Art Chrome Co. of America *and* United Furniture Workers of America, Local 136-B, CIO. Arbitrator: A. Howard Myers. Dec. 3, 1948. *LA,* vol. 11, p. 937. This case involved the amount of vacation pay due for a scheduled vacation and the arbitrator was speaking of the actual vacation.

[47] *In re* Bendix Aviation Corp., Keyport Plant, Radio Division, *and* United Electrical Workers, Local 417, CIO. Arbitrator: Sidney L. Cahn. April 4, 1949. *LA,* vol. 12, p. 332, italics in original. Vacations were sometimes held to be both wages and a reward, as in the case where a court held vacations to be "a supplement to the employment agreement which in effect constitutes an offer of reward or additional wages for constant and continuous service." Division of Labor Law Enforcement Department of Industrial Relations v. Ryan Aeronautical Company. California Superior Court, Appellate Department, San Diego County. Sept. 28, 1951. *LRRM,* vol. 29, p. 2027.

In another case where prorated vacations accrued at a given rate per month, the court commented that vacations were seen as extra compensation per month for not quitting each month. The court believed and said that the employer kept the accumulated vacation pay as the year went on as his guarantee against the employee's quitting. Haag v. Rogers 9 Ga.App. 650, 72 S.E. 46.

belong to him to spend as he sees fit. It it true, of course, that he may decide or agree to have his employer spend it for him on a certain commodity, service, or benefit, particularly if there were some convenience or other saving to be gained, but the payment was still made to him for the service rendered and not for the subsequent purchase.

This was precisely how the arbitrators saw the vacation pay, however. The employer, they were saying, owed the employee only payment for actual service. Out of these wages for service, the employee then bought his own vacation. Under such a scheme, the employee was negotiating annual periods of unpaid leave, convenient to production schedules, and the employer was kindly agreeing to withhold some of his wages for him until the time when he wished to spend it on a rest to recover from the ill effects of continuous employment.

But this was not the sense in which either party had dealt with paid vacations.

The idea was reminiscent of the early days when a few employers had vacation savings clubs for their employees, withholding some of their wages for a "vacation," or permitting employees to work twelve minutes a day overtime, the pay for which went into a vacation fund to be collected by the employee annually. As will be recalled from Chapter 3, such "contributory" plans did not last. The *paid* vacation movement grew up instead, with the employer taking upon himself, though for his own benefit, the cost of the rest time off. To the extent that employers still found benefit in annual rest periods for their employees, their intent in negotiating on paid vacations was to provide such rests at their own cost and not the employees', directly or indirectly. They were, in fact, still very much concerned with whether the employee actually took the rest. Requirements that employees eligible for vacations actually take the time off are commonly to be found in vacation plans today as they were in management plans of the early days.

Nor did the employees negotiate on vacations with the notion that they would pay for their own vacations. While they may have mistaken the management interest in paid vacations for acknowledgment of an obligation to provide them, the employees' own view was never anything other than that. They were not negotiating on vacations with the idea that the loss of vigor through service was simply one of the hazards of life which employees had to cope with themselves out of their pay for actual service, employers having no direct or indirect responsibility for it. Rather, they were declining wage increases in favor of vacations, or improved vacations, specifically to fix upon management the social obligation to pay for employees' restoration as a proper cost of doing business, in keeping with a rising standard of what constituted an adequate rest.

Third parties, in their deferred wage theory, had misinterpreted the nature of the right which employees had negotiated. The idea that an employee's vacation pay was wages for past service out of which he bought himself a vacation reduced the vacation right to nothing more than a "right" to back pay. It eliminated all recognition of an industry obligation to pay the cost of restoring employee's vigor which had been the source of this right.[48]

Conflicts with Practice

Since the parties had not negotiated vacations with pay for the purpose of compensating a worker for his actual service, the deferred wage theory was bound to conflict with actual vacation plan practices in many respects.

First, if vacations were pay for service, as legally due, vacation pay would have to be exactly proportionate to service in the preceding year.[49] In actual practice, however, this was not the

[48] It was ironic that third parties should do this when the deferred wage theory itself arose out of their conviction that all employees had a basic right to paid vacations superseding management's interest in a benefit from the plan.

[49] In describing how paid vacations were wages, arbitrators were often vague as to the exactness of the relationship. However, where an arbitrator said "A paid vacation, like an hourly, weekly or monthly wage, is granted to an employee for services rendered," the assumption had to be that, if not exact to the last hour of work, it certainly had a very direct relationship. This arbitrator remarked a "reasonable" relationship. He continued, "Usually paid vacations are earned and are paid for in a fixed relationship to the employee's hourly or weekly earnings. They are a function of the wage, a collateral form of wage payment associated with the fulfilling of reasonable requirements in terms of actual job performance. *In re* Westinghouse Airbrake Co. and Union Switch and Signal Co. *and* United

208

case. Paid vacations were a concomitant of the employment relationship, not "for" but "because of" employment, and were based on service only to the extent that it was necessary to fulfill their purpose of providing a rest from past service. While the need for rest accrued with the giving of service, the providing of that rest required only a roughly proportionate relationship between time off and past service. Provision of vacations for "all employees who have worked in two-thirds of the pay periods in the year preceding June 1," and other such minimum work requirements existed in many plans. Yet, if vacations were wages, how could one account for the fact that an employee who had only met the required minimum of, say, 1000 hours received the same vacation "wages" as one, paid at the same rate, who had worked 2000 hours?

Under a graduated type plan, allowing one week's vacation after one year of service and two weeks after five years, how could a five-year employee abruptly double his vacation "wages" over what he had received for the same amount of service in his fourth year of employment? And did a ten-year man eligible for three weeks of vacation earn one-third more "deferred wages" than a nine-year employee eligible for two weeks? How could the deferred wage theory account for the fact that a new employee who had given five, or eleven, months of service received no vacation at all in his first year?

Many vacation plans also permitted short periods of non-work time to count toward vacation eligibility in such clauses as this: "Time out for bona fide sickness or accident shall be considered as time worked for purposes of vacation eligibility." But vacation "wages" could not accrue for time, however short, when no work was done. The deferred wage idea would have required this kind of ruling:

It is generally recognized that paid vacations are a deferred form of wages and are an integral part of the wage structure....During a period of layoff the employee renders no services for the Company, and he cannot claim that the vacation was earned during that period.[50]

Electrical Workers, Local 610, CIO. Arbitrator: Saul Wallen, Sept. 26, 1946. *LA*, vol. 5, p. 348.

[50]*In re* Hancock Steel Co., Inc. *and* United Automobile Workers, Local 174, CIO.

(continued)

But very few arbitrators adhered to the logic of the deferred wage theory this closely. They awarded terminal vacation pay only very roughly proportionate to past service both where the contract permitted non-work time to count and where, in the absence of such contractual permission, an employee would not qualify for a vacation. Holding the qualifying requirement to be seniority alone, the arbitrators who believed vacation pay to be wages sometimes found themselves having to give assent to such strange concepts as "wages based on accumulated seniority." In the following case, for instance, the board of arbiters granted the union request for full vacations for employees on layoff part of the year saying:

Specifically, we must decide then, whether or not an employee has "earned" his vacation while on involuntary layoff for any period of time. The thought behind the Union's argument is that an employee laid off because work is not available is in a kind of suspended animation state—he receives no pay but is available for work and accumulates his seniority. To place him in the same position as a new man as far as his vacation is concerned, upon recall, is to deny the older worker a part of his negotiated wages based upon his accumulated seniority.[51]

The deferred wage theory also conflicted with the actual practice of limiting vacations to continuing employees or permitting only certain terminated employees to receive vacation pay. Yet, if they were truly wages for past service, vacations would be due at all terminations regardless of the cause for the termination, just as any other back wages were due. Forfeiture clauses would be an anomaly, and employers were quick to point out this inconsistency with the wages idea:

Arbitrator: Hyman Parker. June 29, 1954 (hearing date). *LA,* vol. 23, p. 47. See also Waldes Koh-I-Noor, Inc., *and* United Electrical Workers, Local 1227, CIO. Arbitrator: I. Robert Feinberg. Oct. 16, 1947. *LA,* vol. 8, p. 876.

[51]*In re* Allied Drum Service, Inc., p. 677. In this case the contract simply required "continuous service."

"Wages based on accumulated seniority" was no worse a concept than "wages accruing according to length of service" in the following opinion: "It is a well established rule that vacation pay is in the nature of wages and accrues to the benefit of the employee in accordance with his length of service." *In re* Catoir Silk Co., p. 368.

...vacation pay is not a collateral form of wages, for the vacation clause contains a forfeiture provision which would be meaningless....[52]

Yet some arbitrators tried to combine an expression of the wage theory with the contractual refutation of it, as one who regarded vacation pay to be

in the nature of wages, the scope of earnings increasing with the time worked, and subject to defeasance or forfeiture in the nature of a condition subsequent, only by certain conduct on the part of the employee such as an early, voluntary quitting by him of his employment, or the commission of some employment dereliction resulting in a discharge for just and proper cause.[53]

If vacations were wages for past service, in fact, the whole concept that retaining seniority preserved an employee's employment status, and therefore his eligibility to vacations, was unnecessary. There would be no need to explain away the management clauses limiting vacation coverage. An employee would be eligible for his back vacation "wages" regardless of his seniority status.

More important, however, was the deferred wage theory's misinterpretation of the purpose of the vacation pay. It was here that conflict with actual practice was the sharpest. From the origin of the movement to the present day, vacation pay has always been set down in vacation plans in such a way as to approximate what an employee would have earned had he not gone on vacation, in order to make him whole for the period of rest time off. Different types of work situations, with varying degrees of irregularity, required different methods of calculating the vacation pay which would make the employee whole. For most employees, this was simply the "regular rate" in effect at the start of the vacation period, times the regular weekly hours in effect at that time. For those whose earnings were irregular, it might be average weekly earnings as calculated from an immediately preceding period, or a percentage of the preceding year's earnings, where work schedules were so irregular that no one period would be representative of normal earnings.

Although the purpose was to approximate an employee's normal

[52]*In re* L. Hyman Co., Inc. *and* Textile Workers Union of America, Allentown District Joint Board, CIO. Arbitrator: Robert P. Brecht. Sept. 29, 1949. *LA,* vol. 13, p. 802.
[53]*In re* Brookford Mills, p. 841.

earnings to assure no loss for taking the rest, some arbitrators missed that purpose completely when they tried to prove that vacation pay was wages, as the following arbitrator's comment reveals:

...the parties in Section X have plainly stated that vacation pay in their contract constitutes deferred wages by providing that it shall be a "percentage amount of each individual employee's total earnings."[54]

Vacation pay calculated by the percentage or average earnings method would necessarily include earnings from non-work time, such as sick leave, holidays, and so on. Ignoring this inconsistency with the wages concept, however, arbitrators usually ruled that all earnings in the base period were to be counted, including overtime, sick leave, shift differentials, and holiday pay so that the vacation pay, they said, would more accurately reflect normal earnings.

For workers in regular employment industries, the "make-whole" principle required that vacation pay be allowed at the current rate in effect at the time of the vacation. If vacation pay were wages for the service given in the preceding year upon which the vacation was based, it would have to be paid at the rate in effect during the period in which the service was given. But arbitrators here, too, adhered to actual practice and made no attempt to conform to the logic of the deferred wage theory when grievances came to them involving the amount of vacation pay due an employee.

Usually vacation plans were specific in indicating that the current rate was to be used, but where a contract only specified the "regular rate," employers occasionally took a turn at arguing an expedient line and pressed for the lower rate in effect during the preceding year. In one case, revealing a neat reversal of the usual roles, a board of arbitrators reported that it was

...the Company's theory that vacations are earned by service performed in the pervious year and hence should be paid for according to the wages paid in that year.[55]

[54]*In re* Calvine Cotton Mills, Inc., Arbitrator Barret, p. 842.

[55]*In re* K. Krasberg and Sons Manufacturing Co. *and* International Association of Machinists, Die and Tool Makers Lodge 112, AFL. Board of Arbitrators: Horace

This, of course, was the deferred wage theory's logic, but few arbitrators followed it. In this particular case, the arbitrator held the new wage scale to be controlling and said:

Such a conclusion is in accord with the basic purpose of vacation pay which is to compensate employees for loss of pay while on vacation, so that they might receive while not working the same wages they would have received had they worked.[56]

This did not mean, however, that arbitrators recognized the error of the deferred wage idea. Some simply avoided the theoretical controversy which posed a conflict between the make-whole principle and deferred wage idea. In a case, for example, where the hours of work had been forty-eight per week during the preceding year and had been reduced to forty at the time of the vacation, the employer argued that vacation pay was to be based on the current forty-hour work week, saying:

...employees given vacations for the purpose of rest and recreation should be compensated in a manner which would most nearly approximate the amount which the employee would earn if he had worked during the period he actually took his vacation.[57]

The employees in this case argued that vacations were wages for service in the preceding year and therefore should be paid on the basis of the forty-eight hour week then in effect. But the arbitrator, making a special point of avoiding any necessity of agreeing with either party, held that the words "regular scheduled work week" meant the work week in effect at the time of the vacation.

Others tried to hold to the deferred wage idea while ruling in favor of the current rate on the make-whole principle. For instance, in one case cited earlier, where the arbitrator held that

A. Ruckel, chairman; Leon Despres, union-appointed arbitrator; and Bruce Krasberg, employer-appointed arbitrator. Sept. 1, 1954. *LA*, vol. 23, p. 529. See also Canada Dry Ginger Ale, Inc. *and* International Brotherhood of Teamsters, Local 118, AFL. Arbitrator: V. Sumner Carrol. March 16, 1955. *LA*, vol. 24, p. 222.

[56]*In re* K. Krasberg and Sons Manufacturing Co., p. 528.

[57]*In re* Proctor and Gamble Manufacturing Co. *and* Proctor and Gamble Employees' Association. Board of Arbitration: Benjamin Aaron, chairman; Homer I. Mitchell, employer-appointed arbitrator; and James L. Daugherty, union-appointed arbitrator, dissenting. Feb. 28, 1947. *LA*, vol. 6, pp. 888–889.

vacation pay was pay for work previously done, he also held that vacation pay should be allowed on the make-whole principle:

The theory of vacation pay is extra compensation for work done in the other weeks of the year so that the worker may be secure while he is building up strength for the balance of the year. This requires at least continuance of normal income.[58]

The prevalence of the wage concept of vacations succeeded in clouding the issue so thoroughly that some arbitrators did not appear to know why vacations were paid on the make-whole principle.[59] Where the purpose of vacations and of vacation pay was lost in the confusion, there appeared also the idea that the year's wages were merely being spread out to provide regularity of income.[60] Note the language of the following opinion:

The generally accepted purpose of vacation clauses in agreements is to provide compensation for a period when no work is performed, or in other words to hold back some of the pay for work previously performed until the vacation period.[61]

There were very few postwar arbitrators, perhaps because most arbitrators did not look back at what vacations had been, who perceived the purpose of paid vacations or described it as accurately as the one who stated:

Historically, the motive for granting vacations with pay was to dissipate fatigue, produced by long periods of uninterrupted labor which

[58]*In re* Art Chrome Co. of America, p. 937.

[59]In one opinion, for instance, the current rate was held to be the correct one for this reason: "...since the time for vacations is fixed by the Company, the vacation pay must be computed in terms of the rate paid the employee at the time he takes his vacation." *In re* Ohio Malleable Iron Company *and* United Steelworkers of America, Local 2654, CIO. Board of Arbitration: Paul N. Lehoczky, impartial member; David Clayman, union-appointed arbitrator; and William E. Taylor, employer-appointed arbitrator. Nov. 19, 1947. *LA,* vol. 9, p. 451.

[60]This was suggested by an economist who named vacations as an "income-protective device." He said, "Since 1940 unions have diverted much money from potential increases in basic rates to fringes such as health insurance and sick pay, longer paid vacations, retirement plans, and supplemental unemployment benefits. The main purpose here is to stabilize income when work is interrupted...." George H. Hildebrand, "Wage Policy and Business Activity," *Proceedings of the 11th Annual Meeting, Industrial Relations Research Association, Papers Presented at Chicago* (Madison, Wisconsin: Industrial Relations Research Association, 1959), p. 174.

[61]*In re* Monty Cleaners *and* Amalgamated Clothing Workers of America, Cleaners and Dyers, Local 183, CIO. Arbitrator: A. Howard Myers. Dec. 13, 1947. *LA,* vol. 9, p. 604.

diminished the employee's productivity, and consequently his value to his employer. Vacations with pay were originally initiated, not as a bonus or additional salary for satisfactory service, but rather to enable an employee who has worked a considerable number of months or years, to secure the mental and physical relaxation which a change in surroundings usually produces, while one is free from concern over income and expenses, and resulting in a restorative and recuperative effect on his mental and physical vigor.[62]

If any final refutation of the deferred wage theory is needed, it lies in the practice under vacation plans of prohibiting employees from continuing to work and taking, in addition to their regular wages, vacation pay in lieu of the vacation. Furthermore, rarely in actual practice are workers allowed to accumulate their vacations; if they do not take them in one year, the vacation right is lost.[63] Many plans, in fact, specify that employees are "entitled to and shall take" vacations annually. Such provisions have existed in plans from the origin of the movement. The fact that they were now negotiated by both parties clearly expressed the view of both parties that vacations are to provide a rest period, not to pay for past service. There could have been no reason for thus limiting management's obligation fully to compensate for a worker's past service, although some arbitrators denied or failed to see the conflict between the theory and actual practice.[64]

[62]*In re* American Smelting and Refining Co., Selby Plant *and* International Union of Mine, Mill and Smelter Workers, Carquinez Local 51. Arbitrator: George Cheney. Oct. 9, 1950. *LA,* vol. 15, p. 360. The arbitrator was dealing with actual vacations, not just with vacation pay in this case. It involved the rights of employees, who had qualified under a previous contract, to a vacation under the new contract. He said the need for vacation arose out of the period of work performed under the old contract.

[63]Although about half of the plans studied by the BLS in 1957 were silent on both questions, 40 percent prohibited pay in lieu of time off or permitted it only under special circumstances, and 37 percent specifically prohibited accumulation of vacations compared to only 3 percent specifically permitting such accumulation. The BLS observed of the pay-in-lieu-of-vacation practices, "The concept of a paid vacation as time off for rest and relaxation is reflected in the number of agreements which did not permit the worker to claim vacation pay in lieu of all or part of his vacation period." U.S. Department of Labor, Bureau of Labor Statistics, *Paid Vacation Provisions in Major Union Contracts, 1957,* Bulletin No. 1233 (Washington: G.P.O., 1958), pp. 28, 30.

[64]One arbitrator said of a contractual requirement that all vacations be taken within the calendar year, "even if it should be construed to mean also that an employee normally cannot receive payment in lieu of taking a vacation, this would

Summary

Third parties in the postwar period developed out of the earned-right concept a new doctrine: namely, that what was being earned was not the right to a paid rest period but the right to back pay for the service performed. They developed this theory by directly adopting the union argument for terminal vacation pay where no provision for it existed in the contract. They adopted the argument because it seemed to provide a "legal" claim to a payment they felt was due.

The notion grew and spread as arbitrators and courts quoted each other until it could truly be said that the deferred wage doctrine was "universally accepted" by third parties. A more accurate way of putting the matter was that the basis of paid vacations was by now "universally misunderstood."

By superficial reasoning, arbitrators misread the intent of the parties and contended that they had negotiated vacations as another means of compensating for service. Ignoring the fact that unions sought vacations instead of wage increases, arbitrators in the main saw only the money in these terminal vacation pay cases and translated this payment into pay for service performed in the rest of the year.

The purpose of providing a rest period was completely lost in the process. Furthermore, this theory conflicted with actual practice in other ways, most conspicuously in the case of denial of vacation pay to those who quit or were discharged.

There seemed to be no end to the mischief which this fallacious concept caused. As the next chapter will show, it also created difficulties for state unemployment insurance boards attempting to determine laid-off workers' eligibility to unemployment compensation under laws providing that any payment of "wages" disqualified workers from receiving benefits. The decisions made by these boards affected many thousands of workers.

But the most serious mischief caused by this notion that vacations were wages for past service was its distortion of the real

---

merely express the agreement of the Parties that an employee should take the rest provided and would not serve to negative the concept of vacations as additional wages." *In re* Globe Corp., p. 300.

216

significance of the paid vacation movement, particularly in the postwar period. In other countries, provision for annual rest periods had been achieved by legislation. In the United States, the same universal coverage was reached privately. Yet, although privately imposed, it represents the same kind of general public feeling that it is an industry obligation to provide for this social need of workers.

Surely no one can dispute the statement that "a dollar bargained is still a dollar whether it is paid as wages for work performed or in lieu of wages during the vacation period." But such tautology as this, engendered by the deferred wage notion, not only contributes nothing to our understanding of why workers took their dollars in the form of fringes rather than wage rates, but tends to deprecate the whole social movement for this fringe benefit and, in turn, of all fringe benefits, which has been one of the most significant developments in the history of industrial relations and of social history generally: the successful imposition of social costs upon industry by private rather than public means. There seems to be little likelihood of reversal of this process, even if some of the gains are made uniform by government intervention with standards or financial aid. It is therefore important to understand the full significance of what is happening before the day we awaken to discover already accomplished a social phenomenon which has never before occurred in an industrial society outside of government auspices.

This was the fuller measure of the significance of the employees' efforts when, by negotiating some of the available dollars into vacations rather than wage rates, workers secured their employers' recognition of an obligation to do more for employees than simply compensate them for their actual service. The real error of the deferred wage theory was that it lost sight of the social significance of the employee bargaining first on paid vacations, and then in larger context on all fringes.

PART V

Understanding Fringe Benefits

CHAPTER 9

The Practical Effects of the Wage Concept

IF THE "wages" idea had remained only a third party's way of justifying terminal vacation pay in grievance cases, it might have gone down in history as a curiosity in industrial relations. But it did not. The theory was a Pandora's Box. Once opened, it spread its mischief widely. It played havoc with all fringe benefits, obscuring both the nature and the significance of the fringe benefit movement. In practical terms, the result has often been the loss of these benefits. Failure to consider the social purpose of a fringe benefit, in fact, may frustrate both the purpose of laws dealing with such payments and the purpose for which the parties negotiated the fringe benefit. It has done violence to the concept of wages as payment for service as well. In this chapter, we shall consider in practical terms the effects of the wage theory when extended to other fringe benefits and shall see the importance of keeping their social purpose in mind.

Chapter 2 discussed the social nature and non-wage purposes for which employers and unions took action on fringe benefits. It was seen in the intervening chapters that consulting the purpose for a fringe benefit sheds light on its nature. It was seen that paid vacations were originated by the employers for the non-wage purpose of increasing productivity and became an employee non-wage demand for provision of social benefit. Then these purposes were ignored and denied when vacations were called "deferred wages" in payment for past service.

Other fringe benefits have had a similar experience. The non-wage purpose of each one, whether negotiated as a social benefit or voluntarily adopted to increase productivity, has also been ignored and then denied as they, too, were called "wages" in payment for actual service.

But application of the wage concept of fringe benefits had more serious effects than simply a theoretical confusion with the purpose of wages. This chapter will show what happened, for example, when fringe benefit payments were called "wages" by state administrators and courts in determining laid-off workers' eligibility to unemployment compensation.

The "Wages" Test of Eligibility

The state unemployment insurance laws have three categories of worker status for determining eligibility to benefits. A worker may be 1) employed, 2) voluntarily unemployed (as, for a given period of time, an employee who quits), or 3) involuntarily unemployed. The first two conditions make him ineligible for benefits and the third, eligible. Of course, a worker who is laid off is no longer employed. He is unemployed and (unless voluntarily out of the labor market) eligible for unemployment compensation.

However, the laws do not define the term "employed," but only the term "unemployed." Whether a worker is eligible for unemployment compensation, then, has come to turn upon the question not of whether he is employed but upon whether or not he is "unemployed." In practice, therefore, another category, "not unemployed," has been added. The idea that once a worker has been laid off and is no longer employed, he may still not be "unemployed" was urged upon unemployment insurance agencies by employers seeking to disqualify former employees for unemployment compensation.

Experience-rating plans, provided for in all state unemployment insurance laws in one form or another,[1] gave the employers

[1]U.S. Department of Labor, Bureau of Employment Security, *Comparison of State Unemployment Insurance Laws as of January 1, 1962*, pp. 20–21. The Bureau notes, "In spite of significant differences, all systems have certain common characteristics. All formulas are devised to establish the relative experience of individual employers with unemployment or with benefit costs." *Ibid.*, p. 21.

a direct and tangible incentive to avoid the loss of credits that would result from too many claims being lodged against their accounts. For example, if an employer could persuade the state unemployment compensation agency to count a twenty-week severance payment as twenty weeks during which the employee was "not unemployed" after layoff and therefore not eligible for unemployment benefits, he could realize a considerable tax saving in contributions to the unemployment insurance fund of the state. Or if all terminal vacation payments to laid-off workers could be held to disqualify them from unemployment compensation for the number of weeks of vacation provided for, this, too, could reduce the employer's obligation to pay into the fund. Even holiday pay during a layoff week might be sufficient in amount to disqualify or partially disqualify the workers from unemployment benefits for that week. Or, the employer could eliminate all future charges against his experience-rating account for workers who were retired under a compulsory retirement pension plan, even though they did not want to stop work and were actively seeking work elsewhere, if those workers could be held to be "not unemployed" as long as they were receiving the pension.

Shortly after World War II, employers began regularly to protest the claims for unemployment compensation made by laid-off workers who had been paid terminal fringe benefit payments, on the grounds that fringe benefits were "wages" and that, the employers said, receipt of "wages" disqualifies a worker under the laws' definition of the "unemployed" status. They pointed to the clause defining the "unemployed" status, which is typically worded in state unemployment insurance laws as follows:

An individual shall be deemed "totally unemployed" in any week during which he performs no services and with respect to which no wages are payable to him.[2]

Of course, the laid-off worker performs no services following the layoff, even if he is paid a terminal fringe benefit payment. But employers insisted that the "and" in this clause intended two

[2]Commerce Clearing House, *Topical Law Reports, Unemployment Insurance Reporter* (hereafter referred to as CCH, *op. cit.*), vol. 2, Colorado, P 4013.

separate requirements and that even a worker who was giving no service was still not "unemployed" if he received "wages."[3]

State unemployment compensation agencies and the courts agreed with the employer view that payments and service could be separated and that one *or* the other might be held to indicate whether a worker were unemployed and eligible for unemployment compensation. The separation was expressed by the Attorney General in one state as follows:

It is observed that the conjunctive form "and" is employed in this definition between phrases containing the key words "services" and "wages"; and it therefore appears that even if a worker performed no services he conceivably still might have wages payable to him during a certain week, thus eliminating him from the ranks of the unemployed.[4]

This interpretation of the law, of course, was essential to the success of the employers' argument that fringe benefit payments were disqualifying "wages"; no service being given after layoff in any of these cases, the worker would otherwise have been eligible for unemployment compensation. Under this interpretation, the relevance of a payment to eligibility now depended only upon whether it could be called "wages."

[3]Although the laws do not define the employed status as such, it may be derived from this clause as being the state of giving paid service. What the employers proposed here, of course, was to separate that paid service into pay *or* service. Such a separation would raise the question of why the legislators would have included the words "during which he performs no services" if receipt of pay alone, without service, could have indicated employment. No state considers a worker employed if he is giving service but receiving no pay for it. Yet the obverse, that he was employed (or not "unemployed") if he were receiving pay but was giving no service, was considered an acceptable notion. It was, in fact, the basis for the "wages" test of eligibility.

[4]Utah Attorney General Opinion, April 22, 1957, *Supplementation of Unemployment Benefits, Federal and State Rulings, Statutes and Cases in Full Text*, 2nd ed. (hereafter referred to as *SUB*) (Washington: Industrial Union Department, AFL-CIO, 1957), p. 185. State courts have upheld this interpretation of the clause. The Washington Supreme Court, for instance, stated: "It is clear from the language of the statute that, before an individual can be deemed unemployed for the week, two conditions must be met...even though the claimant has not performed services, if he has received [wages]...he is not totally unemployed for the week." In the matter of the Employees of the Weyerhaeuser Timber Company. Washington Supreme Court. Dec. 4, 1958. Bureau of National Affairs, *Labor Relations Reference Manual* (hereafter referred to as *LRRM*) (Washington, BNA, 1935 to date), vol. 43, p. 98.

Fringe Benefits Held to Be "Wages"

The fringe benefit movement had arisen quite suddenly, adding new types of payments in rapid succession. Having previously dealt largely with payments that were more easily distinguishable as wages, to pay for actual service, or gratuities, the unemployment insurance boards were not prepared to cope with the abundance of new types of employee income that were not clearly one or the other. It seemed obvious to the state administrators that fringe benefits won in or added to union contracts, as most of these were, could not be considered gratuities. But, if not gratuities, were they then "wages" as the employers were arguing?

The necessity for an answer to this question, lagging slightly behind the fringe benefit movement itself as more and more of the applicants for unemployment compensation had such payments in their final pay envelopes and as the employers increasingly protested the claims, came shortly after World War II when the deferred wage theory of paid vacations was reaching its peak of popularity. Vacation pay, furthermore, was the first fringe benefit to present itself to the state unemployment agencies in a significant number of cases. As the agencies looked about for some guide as to the nature of vacation pay, they quickly found that there was no need to make an independent inquiry of their own into the nature, or purpose, of this fringe benefit. Arbitrators, and even the courts in many states, had already discovered its nature. In fact, for several years after 1945, the only significant discussion of fringe benefit payments was the controversy over terminal vacation pay. As early as mid-1946, the unemployment law administrators could read such findings as this arbitrator's opinion had expressed:

The theory of the company that vacation pay is given merely to enable the employee to rest up for another year of service is out of harmony with the practice and the apparent thinking of management and labor in most of industry today. In general, vacation pay is regarded as an additional compensation for work performed....[5]

[5]*In re* Automatic Electric Co. *and* International Brotherhood of Electrical Workers, Local B-713, AFL. Arbitrator: Alex Elson. August 3, 1946. Bureau of National Affairs, *Labor Arbitration Reports* (hereafter referred to as *LA*) (Washington: BNA, 1946 to date), vol. 4, p. 120.

225

Or even, more specifically, this—also in 1946:

A paid vacation, like an hourly, weekly, or monthly wage, is granted to an employee for services rendered...a collateral form of wage payment associated with the fulfilling of reasonable requirements in terms of actual job performance.[6]

By 1949, when most state unemployment agencies had received claims relative to all the fringes and had heard the employers argue that all such payments were "wages," this was being said of the foremost fringe benefit:

It is almost universally accepted that paid vacations must be considered...as additional compensation for work *already* performed....[7]

It is not surprising that the administrators of the unemployment insurance laws accepted these pronouncements. The view described almost exactly the definition of "wages" contained in most of the unemployment insurance laws they were administering: "...all remuneration for personal services...."

State agencies applied the wage idea first to paid vacations[8] and then, to a varying extent in different states, to all terminal fringe benefit payments. By 1951, the Minnesota Supreme Court (though not itself agreeing) noted that severance pay was held to be "wages" in 13 states.[9] In reference to another fringe benefit, the Kansas Supreme Court said, for example, that a claimant's holiday pay

...was a condition of his employment, and he had to work to get it, and he got it as part of his compensation. If that be not true then the employee received something to which he was not strictly entitled, a

[6]*In re* Westinghouse Airbrake Co. and Union Switch and Signal Co. *and* United Electrical Workers, Local 610, CIO. Arbitrator: Saul Wallen. Sept. 26, 1946. *LA*, vol. 5, p. 348.

[7]*In re* Bendix Aviation Corp., Keyport Plant, Radio Division, *and* United Electrical Workers, Local 417, CIO. Arbitrator: Sidney L. Cahn. April 4, 1949. *LA*, vol. 12, p. 332.

[8]Although we are speaking here of terminal vacation payments, even the vacation pay of employed workers on their regular vacations was held to be "wages." By 1954, it was reported, "Pay for such a vacation...is held universally to be remuneration for services. It is construed to be taxable, to form the basis for wage credits, and to render the recipients ineligible for benefits." U.S. Department of Labor, Bureau of Employment Security, "Guaranteed Wage and Related Payments— How Treated under State Unemployment Insurance Systems," *Labor Market and Employment Security*. (Washington: G.P.O., April 1954), p. 38.

[9]Ackerson and Hendrichs v. Western Union Telegraph Co., Minnesota Supreme Court. June 1, 1951. *LRRM*, vol. 28, p. 89.

thing ordinarily called a bonus and if it was a bonus, it was still wages under the statutory definition of wages.[10]

With terminal vacation pay leading the list, fringe benefits also began to find their way into state laws; the amendments specified that one or another fringe benefit was to be included in the term "wages."

But simply to assert that a fringe benefit was wages did not make it so, and the substitution of another purpose for the real purpose of these fringe benefits only led to difficulties when unemployment compensation boards attempted to apply the "wages" test of eligibility. If fringe benefit payments were pay for service, where was the service?

It will be recalled that the typical clause defining the unemployed status in state laws read:

An individual shall be deemed "totally unemployed" in any week during which he performs no services and with respect to which no wages are payable to him.

Since, as has been shown, the words "during which he performs no services" were largely ignored, the "wages" test was contained in the remaining words of the clause defining the unemployed status:

An individual shall be deemed "totally unemployed" in any week... with respect to which no wages are payable to him.

By this test, then, "with respect to" what week or weeks did the states say the fringe benefit "wages" were payable? Were these "wages" to be allocated to the layoff period of no service or to the preceding period during which service had been given? This was the question the state unemployment compensation boards now had to answer.

Fringe Benefit "Wages" Not Allocable to Past Service

The deferred wage theory as expressed by arbitrators and courts in terminal vacation pay cases had made quite clear that vacation pay was compensation for service already performed. By this logic, a fringe benefit payment would be allocable to the period of

[10]Clinton Erickson, *et al.* Kansas Supreme Court. Nov. 13, 1954. *LRRM*, vol. 35, p. 126.

service prior to termination and not to the period of unemployment; laid-off workers would be "totally unemployed" and eligible for unemployment benefits.

New York, for example, commented as follows in one early ruling relative principally to pooled vacation fund plans common in seasonal industries where vacations were to be taken some time during the slack season:

...certain kinds of so-called "vacation pay" provided for in management-labor contracts, or as a matter of employer policy, are actually bonuses for past services to which the worker is entitled whether he is granted vacation time off or not; whether he is still working for the employer or not. Such payments are not considered vacation pay, and...affected workers are unemployed and may be entitled to [unemployment compensation] benefits.[11]

Relative to severance pay received by an employee at layoff, a Texas court commented:

Having performed no services during such period no wages could be payable to her with respect to such period. If the agreement that such sums are wages be accurate, then the wages must be applicable to some period with respect to which and during which she did perform personal services for the company.[12]

Despite this logic, however, few states held fringe benefit payments to be deferred wages allocable to the past period of service. The trouble with that position was that it made laid-off workers eligible for unemployment compensation and did not meet the persistent arguments of the employers who sought to minimize their tax liability under the unemployment insurance laws. If the amount of layoff time chargeable to their accounts were to be reduced, the fringe payment had to be allocated to the layoff period. In case after case, the employers directly expressed their concern for tax savings. For instance, one court noted:

A final argument of the employer...was that failure to allocate the severance pay to the period after discharge would impose a double

[11]Industrial Commissioner of New York, Policy Statement, April 27, 1956. *LRRM*, vol. 38, p. 132.

[12]Western Union Telegraph Co. v. Texas Employment Commission, *et al.*, 243 S.W. 2d 217 (1951).

burden on it by permitting employees to receive jobless benefits chargeable to its account.[13]

The "double burden" argument was one frequently heard in reference to fringe benefit payments.[14] In another case, involving SUB, the Illinois Supreme Court reported this employer position:

Petitioners state that such private benefits constitute wages...and that, therefore, the recipients of said benefits are ineligible for State unemployment compensation;...that the total payments from the State fund would be greater if such unlawful disbursements were made; and that this would adversely affect the State experience factor and ultimately result in a higher tax rate for the petitioners.[15]

Although this Court denied the employer's charge, state courts and unemployment agencies were generally receptive to the employer argument. The Arkansas Supreme Court, for example, disqualified an employee who had been granted a lump sum termination payment, saying:

The employee is protected against the economic burdens of unemployment, while the employer is not penalized for having provided the funds for the dismissal payments.[16]

As employers pressed their cases against adverse state rulings to the highest courts, the question of allocability became a settled one in many states and for many payments.[17]

All that was left was to explain *how* fringe benefit "wages," under the legal definition of wages as pay for *service,* could be allocated to a period of no service.

Fringe Benefit "Wages" Allocated to a Period of No Service

In allocating the fringe benefit "wages" to the period after layoff, the administrators had to face directly the problem they had

[13]Bradshaw v. California Employment Stabilization Commission. August 3, 1955. *LRRM,* vol. 36, p. 227.

[14]For example, see Ackerson and Hendrichs, p. 88.

[15]Barco Manufacturing Co., *et al.* v. Treasurer of Illinois, 139 N.E. 2d 227 (1956).

[16]Thornbrough, Commissioner v. Gage. Arkansas Supreme Court. Oct. 23, 1961. *LRRM,* vol. 49, p. 107.

[17]Many of the state supreme court rulings described in these and the following pages were reversals of the original position taken by the state unemployment compensation boards. For example, see Weyerhaeuser Timber Co., p. 97.

created for themselves first by ignoring the purpose of fringe benefits and ostensibly substituting the "pay for service" purpose of wage payments, and second, by then ignoring even the "pay for service" purpose of wages. The word "wages," as one state had said, "anticipates employment during the period for which 'wages' are paid."[18]

Since no service was given after layoff, the fringe benefit payment could not be held to be wages *for service* during that period. But, with "wages" defined in the laws as "remuneration for personal services," how did the administrators manage to detach a "wage" payment from service?

The explanations were in great variety. Sometimes a fringe benefit payment was allocated to the period of unemployment simply because the payment was *for* a time of no service. For example, the Washington Supreme Court noted that the understanding of the parties as provided in their agreement was that holiday pay was for the holiday. "It is only by a strained construction of the contract," said the Court, ". . . that it can be said that holiday pay is payable with respect to some other day than the holiday."[19]

But others managed to find that some "service" *was* being performed during the layoff. The Attorney General of Oregon suggested that dismissal, separation, guaranteed wage, vacation, and retirement payments were pay for "merely standing-by." The worker receiving these payments of "wages" could therefore not be unemployed whether or not he was seeking work.[20] The Connecticut Supreme Court of Errors found holiday pay to be remuneration for services rendered during the week in which the holiday fell. It mentioned the service rendered in order to qualify for the holiday pay, namely, the service on the day before and the day after the holiday helping to maintain continuity of production on those days; the 90 days' continuous service required of one employee for eligibility to paid holidays; and the worker's holding himself in readiness to work on the holiday if asked to, which the contract

[18]Arizona Attorney General Opinion. Sept. 26, 1956. *SUB*, p. 30.
[19]Weyerhaeuser Timber Co., p. 98.
[20]Oregon Attorney General Opinion. May 2, 1957. CCH, *op. cit.*, vol. 8, Oregon, P 8109.

permitted the employer to require if necessary. But then the Court, almost admitting that in fact *no* work was performed, contended that "wages are no less earned when the employee holds himself in readiness to perform than when he actually performs." Holiday pay, it said, is therefore "wages" in the same category as regular pay for productive service.[21] The Michigan Supreme Court spoke similarly:

It is not essential that actual personal service should be rendered by the employee to justify the conclusion that "holiday pay" is an emolument earned during that holiday week.[22]

In another justification for allocating a fringe payment to the layoff period, the Oklahoma Supreme Court found that sick leave paid at termination was allocable to the period of unemployment following the layoff because it was a form of reimbursement for loss of time due to sickness in the future, not for time lost in the past year.[23] The fact that an individual had to work a full year to become eligible for sick leave pay indicated that the services rendered in the previous year simply lay the basis for sick leave eligibility in each following year. It was in other cases, too, this "prospective nature" of sick leave that justified allocating the sick leave "wages" to the layoff weeks.[24]

In most states, it was only necessary to note of a fringe benefit "when it was payable" to allocate it to the layoff period. In Maryland, for example, the Court of Appeals ruled that receipt of terminal vacation pay disqualified employees for unemployment benefits and explained:

The appellants, of course, are right when they say that the vacation is earned during the preceding year, but from this does not follow that it is allocable to any part of the preceding year or is payable "with respect to" any part of the preceding year. Under the statute, *the*

[21] Anthony Geremia v. Administrator, Unemployment Compensation Act, *et al.*; Philip Popple, *et al.* v. Administrator. February Term, 1959. Connecticut Supreme Court of Errors. *CCH, op. cit.*, vol. 3, Connecticut, P 8435.

[22] General Motors Corporation v. Michigan Unemployment Compensation Commission. Michigan Supreme Court. Oct. 1, 1951. *LRRM*, vol. 28, p. 89.

[23] Carter *et al* v. Board of Review Under Oklahoma Security Act *et al.* Oklahoma Supreme Court. March 18, 1958. *LRRM*, vol. 41, p. 119.

[24] Barrett *et al.* v. California Unemployment Insurance Appeals Board *et al.* California District Court of Appeals, 2nd District, Division 1. April 6, 1961. *LRRM*, vol. 48, p. 114.

decisive question is not when was the vacation earned, but when is it payable...

The great weight of authority is that vacation pay is to be considered referable to so long a time following its payment as it would have taken to earn it.[25]

Some state laws were amended to specify this allocation to the period of unemployment. In the Missouri law, for example, vacation and holiday pay are defined as "wages for the week with respect to which it is payable."[26] The Nebraska law provides even more directly that certain disqualifying terminal fringe benefit payments "shall be prorated by weeks on the basis of the most recent weekly wage of the individual."[27]

"Wages" Test Defeats Fringe Benefit Purpose

Use of the "wages" test applied to fringe benefits to disqualify workers for unemployment compensation frustrated the purpose for which the fringe benefit had been negotiated and often resulted in a partial loss of the benefit to the worker. Had the administrators and courts looked at the purpose of these fringe benefits, they would have seen what even the man on the street knew, that the union had not negotiated vacations and dismissal pay as wages for "merely standing by," nor holidays as wages for service on the day before and the day after the holiday. Nor had they negotiated any of the fringe benefits as a private substitute for unemployment compensation.

The employer has also had a non-wage purpose in adopting fringe benefits voluntarily and in yielding to the union demands for them, including "certain intangibles which are of very real worth and value to the employer who desires a stable labor force..." the Maine Supreme Court said. It added, "Such plans... tend to foster good will and sound employer-employee relations. The construction put upon the Act by the Commission would tend to destroy their efficacy..."[28] For many fringe benefits the em-

[25]Allen v. Maryland Employment Security Board. Maryland Court of Appeals. Feb. 18, 1955. *LRRM*, vol. 35, p. 123, italics added.

[26]CCH, *op. cit.*, vol. 6, Missouri, P 4034.

[27]*Ibid.*, Nebraska, P 4053.

[28]Dubois v. Maine Employment Security Commission. April 25, 1955. CCH, *op. cit.*, vol. 5, Maine, P 8119.

ployer received a specific *quid pro quo*. The provision for in-lieu-of-notice payments enabled the employer to keep a worker to the point when he no longer needed his services. A pension plan provided him an orderly way of retiring older workers from the work force. Dismissal payments relieved the employer of all further responsibility to the worker after layoff. The Minnesota Supreme Court observed of dismissal payments that the company had

undoubtedly considered the desirability of retaining its trained personnel until the job of mechanization could be completed. It is reasonable to assume that in arriving at a contract by collective bargaining, under which [the company] became obligated to make such payments, it did so with full knowledge of the advantages to be gained by it in making such payments, without any strings tied to it, in return for the continued service of its employees until the time arrived when such services could be dispensed with.[29]

Disqualification of a worker for unemployment compensation if he had been paid any of these payments at layoff thus represented a "double saving" for the employer. The employer received his "quid" and, in addition, a tax saving. But the employee often lost his "quo," or part of it.

In-lieu-of-notice payments were negotiated as compensation for the loss of advance notice during which an employee might begin his search for another job. Speaking of such a payment, Massachusetts noted that it is

payment in addition to any back wages due where an employee is given a contractual or customary notice of the date of termination of his employment, but instead of being required to work between the date of the notice and the termination, he has been given the amount of wages which he would have earned had he been permitted to continue working.[30]

Yet the worker who is paid two weeks' pay in lieu of notice, for example, and then is disqualified for unemployment compensation for two weeks, loses part of the premium payment intended to compensate him for lack of advance notice. He has to live on

[29]Ackerson v. Hendrichs, p. 88.
[30]Board of Review Decision No. H-24334-A, *et al.* May 27, 1958. CCH, *op. cit.*, vol. 5, Massachusetts, P8221.42.

his pay in lieu of notice as a *substitute* for unemployment compensation and regains the part lost (equal to the weekly benefit) only if, and after, he subsequently exhausts the unemployment compensation allowed in his state.

The purpose of severance pay was described by a California court as having been a

consideration of the employee's willingness in the past to continue on the job and his loss, by reason of the discharge, of the opportunity to further continue his equity in the job toward enjoyment of other agreed rights.[31]

In another case, it was described as compensation for loss of seniority rights and as compensation for retraining and acquiring new skills.[32] Yet, a worker who had received twenty-four weeks of severance pay, as in one case, and was disqualified for unemployment compensation for twenty-four weeks following the layoff, was denied part of the fringe benefit negotiated to compensate for the loss of those valuable rights he had built up over many years. The worker could recoup it only if the unemployment continued beyond the twenty-four weeks and then also beyond the duration of benefits the state provided. In this case, one judge dissented, pointing out that the purpose of severance pay was to compensate for the loss of rights and credits, including seniority and pension rights, and that its purpose was

not to relieve the employer indirectly, for loss that would accrue to it in contributions to the unemployment compensation fund if benefits were allowed her under the unemployment compensation law.[33]

Although the unemployment insurance laws contain no "means test," one was, in effect, being added. The practice of disqualifying these laid-off workers, in fact, made fringe benefit "wages" even more disqualifying than regular wages. A worker might have a bank full of back wages which did not disqualify him, but his nonwages (even though they might be called "wages" for the same

[31] Robert Hand v. California Employment Stabilization Commission. California Superior Court. April 30, 1952. *LRRM,* vol. 30, p. 120.
[32] Ackerson and Hendrichs, p. 88.
[33] Krupka v. Western Union Telegraph Co. Ohio Court of Appeals. March 26, 1951. *LRRM,* vol. 29, p. 47.

past service) did disqualify him. The California court mentioned above, after noting the purpose of severance pay, commented on this effect:

The fact that the employee's pockets may be bulging with funds accumulated as a result of employment does not render him ineligible...if he becomes unemployed.[34]

But it was a rare state agency or court that recognized that the "wages" test was basing eligibility not upon the availability and desire of an individual for other work but upon receipt of an irrelevant payment.

Thus, use of the "wages" test for eligibility to disqualify laid-off workers for unemployment compensation ignored fringe benefit purpose, substituted other purposes not intended by either party in negotiating it or by the employer where fringe benefits were voluntarily adopted, and often denied the worker part or all of the benefit he had negotiated. Furthermore, use of the "wages" test violated the concept of wages set down in the laws as pay for personal service by separating "wages" from the service it was intended to compensate. The "wages" test, in short, frustrated fulfillment of both the purpose of the fringe benefits and in several respects the purpose of the unemployment insurance laws.

Involuntary Vacations Defeat Purpose

Failure to look at the purpose of a fringe benefit had much the same effect even in some cases where it appeared the state was deciding eligibility not on the "wages" test but on the grounds of availability for other work; that is, by considering whether the worker was voluntarily or involuntarily unemployed. Such a situation existed particularly in reference to terminal vacation pay where it was often held that the worker was ineligible because he was on his vacation after layoff and thus voluntarily unemployed and ineligible for unemployment compensation. It was sometimes held that the worker was in some way also "not unemployed."

In one case, the employees with terminal vacation pay protested their disqualification as an "unconstitutional impairment" of the contract because it substituted the contractual right to vacation pay

---

[34]Robert Hand, p. 120.

for unemployment benefits. But, on appeal, the court held that there was no substitution because the applicants were not unemployed in the sense of the statute but were on vacation. The court noted that, since the contract provided only for "vacation with pay," the workers could not take the pay without taking the vacation and therefore the laid-off workers receiving terminal vacation pay must be on their vacation after layoff.[35]

It had been recognized in an early case (1939) that

...a vacation is an absence from work and can exist only while the relationship of employer and employee exists. It is impossible to impress upon the period which immediately follows detachment from service or upon any other period thereafter, the status of a vacation period.[36]

But in the postwar period, unemployment compensation boards scheduled the vacations for laid-off workers during the period thereafter by denying them unemployment compensation for as many weeks as they had vacation pay, saying the workers were on their vacation at that time.

The administrators were assuming, of course, that the workers could take their vacation at such a time. But could a laid-off worker take a vacation in the week or two immediately following a layoff?

Employers had recognized from the start, in making the vacation movement a paid one, that a worker could not get a proper rest without freedom from financial worries. The War Labor Board also had recognized this and had frequently expressed it when extending paid vacation plans to seasonal industries, saying, "...a vacation or a layoff without pay is not a vacation; the purpose of a vacation is to give an employee a feeling of freedom and relaxation."[37]

Failing to see this conflict between a vacation and layoff time,

[35]Shand v. California Employment Stabilization Commission. California Court of Appeals. First District, Division Two. March 23, 1954. *LRRM*, vol. 34, p. 99.
[36]New Jersey Chief Counsel Opinion. April 26, 1939. CCH, *op. cit.*, vol. 7, New Jersey, P 1220.01.
[37]*In re* Burlington Dyeing and Finishing Co., Inc. *and* Textile Workers Union of America, Local 297, CIO. Dec. 31, 1942. Bureau of National Affairs, *War Labor Reports, Wage and Salary Stabilization Reports of Decisions and Orders of the National War Labor Board and Subsidiary Agencies* (hereafter referred to as *War Lab. Rep.*) (Washington: BNA, 1942–1946), vol. 5, p. 521.

because they did not look carefully at the purpose of paid vacations, unemployment compensation boards were, in effect, telling the laid-off worker to say to himself on the day he lost his job: "Now I will take the next two weeks to get a good rest and to enjoy relaxation and recreation with my family. Then I will begin to worry about finding another job."

If, for some reason of the worker's own financial status, he was able to take a vacation then, well and good. He was, by that decision, voluntarily unemployed, neither seeking work nor available for it. But this was a decision which only the individual worker could make. If the purpose of the vacation provision were to be fulfilled for terminated as well as continuing employees, as the states were implying that it should be by holding laid-off workers to be on vacation,[38] the maximum individual choice as to when vacations would be taken was essential.

The scheduling of vacations for continuing employees recognized the need for such choice. While an employer might require that employees *take* the vacation, he knew that the question of *when* it was taken had to involve some individual choice. In contractual plans, the parties arranged for a mutually-agreeable scheduling of vacations. In some cases, it was provided that the individual could select his vacation period; in others the employees agreed to let the employer do the scheduling, with or sometimes without the individual's approval. Even a certain amount of arbitrariness in scheduling did not prevent the purpose of paid vacations from being fulfilled. Employees took their vacations secure in the knowledge that they had a job waiting for them at the end of the period. The financial anxieties of a layoff were not present.

But for employees who were laid off, either temporarily or permanently, the matter was quite a different story. This was noted in reference to a temporary layoff by arbitrator who re-

---

[38]The administrators could have held the terminal vacation pay to be a premium payment *in lieu* of the vacation. In that case, of course, the worker would still have lost his premium if he had to live on it as a substitute for unemployment compensation. But in holding workers to be on vacation after layoff and therefore voluntarily unemployed, the states were rejecting the pay-in-lieu concept.

ported the union position on the question of whether a vacation could be scheduled during a layoff as follows:

The union urges that this cannot properly be done, not only because of the possible effects on the employees' entitlement to unemployment compensation but also because, during a layoff, an employee is not in an emotional or financial condition suitable for vacationing. It urges that such scheduling of vacations is in conflict with the underlying theories of vacation allowances and unemployment compensation.[39]

Then, in a subsequent opinion in this case, the arbitrator distinguished between a vacation and a layoff as follows:

A vacation is a period of rest between periods of work. A layoff is a period of anxiety and hardship between periods of work. The tremendous difference lies in the assurance of the vacationer that he will return to work at the end of his vacation and the equal assurance of the employee on layoff that he does not know when he will return to work. The basic difference, with its financial, emotional and psychological implications, is not obliterated by the form of words or by the receipt of income for a part of the indefinite period of layoff.[40]

It did not matter, in fact, whether the employer or the union could be held responsible for the scheduling during layoffs; the effect was the same. In seasonal industries it was particularly common for the unions to agree to the scheduling of vacations during layoffs. They, too, like their employers, were concerned about interruptions during the busy season. But, despite the union's assent to this practice, many individual workers found that protecting maximum income was incompatible with getting a proper rest. They registered their protests by individually making application for unemployment compensation for the whole period of layoff. In many states, the unemployment compensation agencies ignored the individual worker's status and, finding that the union had spoken for their status collectively, held them to be voluntarily unemployed.[41]

[39]*In re* Ford Motor Company *and* United Automobile Workers, CIO. Arbitrator: Harry Shulman, impartial umpire under the contract. Dec. 10, 1945. *LA,* vol. 3, p. 828.

[40]*In re* Ford Motor Company *and* United Automobile Workers, CIO. Arbitrator: Harry Shulman. May 9, 1946. *LA,* vol. 3, p. 830.

[41]There was particularly strong employer insistence that workers whose vaca-

For the worker permanently laid off, there was no question that he was involuntarily unemployed. The state could not make him voluntarily unemployed by virtue of an administrative ruling or by legislation. The condition existed in fact only as the employee saw it. A Missouri Appeals Referee, in a case occurring before that state amended its law to disqualify workers in receipt of terminal vacation pay, spoke clearly:

...an individual who is given an indefinite layoff, even though he may be told that it is for vacation purposes, cannot be considered on vacation unless the individual by some act on his part has shown that he intends to consider it as a period of rest and relaxation with no thought of work.[42]

If an employee did not find that the first week or two after the layoff was a possible rest time, the denial of unemployment compensation for that period forced him to live on his vacation pay in substitute for the public benefits while he looked for work. The vacation pay became not the provision of a rest period but compensation for loss of wages during a period of unemployment, which was the purpose of the unemployment benefits.

---

tions were scheduled during a temporary layoff be held ineligible. For companies expecting to have some layoff time during the year, a considerable tax saving would result if a week or two of that layoff time could be designated as a vacation period of the shutdown type and the workers held to be on vacation rather than on layoff. The position of the companies that so scheduled their layoffs and vacations can be illustrated by this protest of the General Electric Company against a state referee's decision to consider certain of these laid-off workers eligible for unemployment compensation: "...the referee's decision is contrary to the intent of the unemployment insurance law. The law was created, and rightly so, to provide a form of income to people who become unemployed through no fault of their own. But people on paid vacations are not unemployed. That's so obvious, it shouldn't even have to be stated." *Schenectady Gazette*, Jan. 3, 1958. In a number of states even workers who had not qualified for any vacation at the time of the layoff shutdown were held to be on "vacation," voluntarily unemployed and ineligible for unemployment compensation. For example, see Appeals Tribunal v. Texas Unemployment Commission, Appeal No. 57, 917–A7–57, Nov. 4, 1957. *LRRM*, vol. 42, pp. 139–140.

Similar to the vacations-during-temporary-layoffs situation, workers retired under a compulsory retirement plan providing pensions were also held in many cases to be voluntarily unemployed on the reasoning that the union had spoken for them in negotiating the retirement, with no consideration given to the status of the individual worker. See, for example, Lamont *et al.* v. Director of Division of Employment Security. Supreme Judicial Court of Massachusetts. April 9, 1958. *LRRM*, vol. 42, pp. 128–129.

[42]Appeals Referee Decision, Oct. 11, 1949. CCH, *op. cit.*, vol. 6, Missouri, P 1901.25.

This was quite the way several of the states saw it. Connecticut's highest court found that:

payments provided for in a contract...and intended to be compensation for vacation periods are payments "by way of compensation for loss of wages."[43]

Under Connecticut's law, this described a disqualifying payment. Ignoring the fact that the contract intended vacation pay to provide a rest period, the court was denying this to be the purpose of the payment. California was even more specific when it commented that the purpose of an SUB plan was to supplement state unemployment insurance benefits and "not to replace or duplicate them, which is the nature of vacation pay...."[44]

If, indeed, the purpose of vacation pay and unemployment compensation were the same, the vacation pay should not have been a disqualification, according to the logic used in SUB cases. Employees receiving SUB were held eligible for unemployment compensation because, said most states, SUB and unemployment compensation had the same purpose. New Jersey, for instance, said that SUB "constitutes a voluntary effort to further the purposes" of the state's unemployment compensation law.[45]

But, of course, the purpose of unemployment compensation and vacation pay are not the same. The purpose of unemployment compensation is to provide income for a period of unemployment and the purpose of vacation pay is to provide workers an annual rest. Neither purpose is properly fulfilled where either the "wages" test or a finding of voluntary unemployment without consulting the individual is used to disqualify the recipient of this or any other fringe benefit.

But if disqualification of a worker from unemployment compensation required denial of the purpose for which the parties had negotiated a fringe benefit, the absence of such a disqualification permitted, and even called for, an affirmation of fringe benefit purpose. Without employer pressure to disqualify, or when it was

[43]Kelly v. Administrator, 136 Conn. 482, 72 A. 2d 54 (1950).

[44]California Unemployment Insurance Appeals Board, Benefit Decision No. 6540. Oct. 18, 1957. *LRRM*, vol. 40, p. 18.

[45]New Jersey Attorney General Formal Opinion, No. 39–1955. Nov. 10, 1955. *LRRM*, vol. 36, p. 223.

resisted, quite a different result followed. The non-wage, social purpose of a fringe benefit suddenly became apparent. This situation, although occurring in occasional cases relative to all terminal fringe payments, as we have noted, existed when SUB came to the states for a decision all at once in the mid-1950's. With a somewhat unexpected realignment of political forces,[46] both the unions and employers appealed jointly for a ruling that SUB was not "wages." It was desired by the unions who wished to qualify workers for unemployment compensation and by the employers who would then not have to pay contributions to the state funds on their SUB payments.[47] Along with the occasional state administrators and courts who saw the social purpose of one fringe benefit or another in scattered cases before them, now suddenly almost every state found that SUB was a fringe benefit with an important social purpose which must not be frustrated, denied, or defeated.

SUB Not "Wages" but a Social Benefit

The unions had sought SUB out of a desire to accomplish a very specific social purpose. They were not seeking to increase wage payment for service by this unique form, the effects of which were so unevenly distributed among the employees in the bargaining unit, nor to have the employer pay privately and directly to them a substitute for the public unemployment compensation. They sought to assist laid-off workers in the industries which were suffering technological displacement with the problem of more adequately meeting the economic hazard of periods of unemployment.

[46]In the summer of 1953, a group of state unemployment security officers surveyed some of the problems they expected relative to the impending SUB payments then in the course of negotiations. Although reporting the proposal even at that early point to be "protection against layoffs...afforded through employer financed supplementation of state unemployment compensation," they likened it to a guaranteed annual wage and noted that in a few cases in which such plans have been reviewed, "payments have been universally regarded as wages and therefore constitute a bar to the receipt of benefits." *LRRM*, vol. 32, p. 22.

[47]Most of the opinions discussed here were given in reference to the Ford Plan. The same reasoning was used in reference to all SUB plans, however, except those of the glass industry type which are not here considered. The employer-union requests for a ruling from the states typically asked two questions: whether SUB would be considered as "wages" or as an otherwise disqualifying payment, and whether the payments into or out of the SUB funds were "wages" or otherwise subject to employer tax.

In their opinions on whether SUB payments would be a disqualification of workers from unemployment compensation, most states acknowledged this purpose, applauded it, and pointed out its identity with the purpose of the unemployment insurance law itself. Vermont, for instance, stated:

...supplemental benefits are paid not as a result of services performed, but rather as a result of the joint desire of management and labor to provide a realistic, sufficient income to the employee during his period of unemployment. It is doubtful that state benefits alone, in these times, can be said to meet the needs of our people; but such benefits, taken in conjunction with the contract (supplemental) benefits, do more nearly meet these needs....[48]

The parties were to be commended, as Montana said:

It is gratifying that in this age big business will concern itself with the security of its employees and their families; that it will in proper manner assist workers to insure themselves against hazards of many kinds including a layoff; and that business and labor together can preserve the dignity of the worker in his job.[49]

SUB represented no conflict with public provision of benefits, others said. Illinois observed:

...no provision of the Act can be taken as indicative of any legislative intent or purpose to forbid an employer from gratuitously extending additional aid to personnel in a period of unemployment. That an employer seeks to do so by contract rather than gratuity does not call for a different interpretation.[50]

In fact, SUB furthered this purpose, as New Jersey had found. Mississippi commented that SUB's ultimate objective is "to provide, by private contract, for the implementation" of the public law's objective.[51]

After noting the common purpose of privately negotiated SUB and the unemployment compensation laws, the states then called

[48]Vermont Attorney General Opinion, No. 244. June 4, 1957. CCH, *op. cit.*, vol. 9, Vermont P 8090.
[49]Montana Official Interpretation No. 85, Adopted by the Montana Unemployment Compensation Commission. June 28, 1957. CCH, *op. cit.*, vol. 6, Montana, P 8137.
[50]Illinois Attorney General Opinion, May 17, 1956. *LRRM,* vol. 38, p. 75.
[51]Opinion of General Counsel, Mississippi Employment Security Commission. *SUB,* p. 114.

attention to the fact that both had the same requirements for eligibility. Delaware stated:

It is when, and only when "unemployment" exists and an individual is "unemployed" in any week, as provided in Section 33–2 (15), and the individual is otherwise eligible under the law for the receipt of benefits, that benefits are payable to him.[52]

Oregon, also noting that the recipient must meet the state requirements, commented further:

In this state these requirements include, besides registering for work, that he be able to work, available for work, and actively seeking but unable to obtain suitable work.[53]

It would appear that the states were about to discard the "wages" test of a fringe benefit payment and return to consideration of the individual's availability to determine his eligibility for unemployment compensation. Certainly, it would seem that if he qualified under the state's requirements for eligibility, this should have been sufficient. Yet, even though no individual could receive unemployment compensation without being eligible under the state's own rules, almost every state felt it necessary also to put the payment to the "wages" test—with only Arizona appearing to recognize the sufficiency of the "availability" test of eligibility when it said:

It would indeed require a wild imagination to hold that a beneficiary of a company supplemental benefit plan is *employed* in the face of the requirement that he must first qualify for state unemployment benefits before he can become eligible for supplemental benefits under the company plan.[54]

But imaginations had run wild for so long that the "wages" test of eligibility, after many years' use, was thoroughly accepted. In any case, since most of their decisions relative to other fringe benefits had been based on this test, the administrators could not appear to be making an exception for SUB by using a different

[52]Delaware Unemployment Compensation Commission Ruling. Sept. 13, 1955. *LRRM,* vol. 36, p. 217.
[53]Oregon Attorney General Opinion.
[54]Arizona Attorney General Opinion, p. 30, italics in original. The other states did not consider whether a worker was "employed" but only whether he was "not unemployed."

eligibility standard for it. They did, however, add a new consideration.

Taking a new look at the clause defining the "unemployed" status, they rediscovered the long-neglected first part of the clause, "during which he performs no services." Some states now found that the fact that no service was given after the layoff was sufficient by itself to prove that SUB was not wages. Missouri observed, for instance:

We are unable to see...how the receipt of benefits under the Plan can be called "remuneration" since the recipient of such benefits would be performing no services during the period that such benefits are received.[55]

However, even after they found no service, most states, as noted above, still felt it necessary to go on to the second part of the clause which contained the "wages" test, as they had been doing for other fringe benefit payments. They felt that, as Delaware said, "From an administrative point of view the important question is whether benefits paid out of the trust fund constitute 'wages'....[56] California's Attorney General followed this outline of inquiry:

The language "during which he performs no services" in section 1252 would seem to present no difficulty....The clause "with respect to which no wages are payable to him" contained in section 1252 presents a more troublesome problem....It is necessary, accordingly, to determine whether payments pursuant to the plan are "compensation for personal services."[57]

Almost every state, of course, found that SUB was not "wages," giving a large assortment of reasons, including the fact that the Internal Revenue Service had ruled that SUB was not "wages" for tax purposes.[58]

Yet even a negative answer to the question of whether SUB

---

[55]Missouri Attorney General Opinion. June 21, 1956. *SUB*, p. 119.

[56]Delaware Unemployment Compensation Commission Ruling, p. 217.

[57]California Attorney General Opinion No. 56/38. Feb. 10, 1956. *LRRM*, vol. 37, p. 18.

[58]The Internal Revenue Service ruled that SUB did not constitute "wages" subject to tax for purposes of the Federal Unemployment Tax Act or the Federal Insurance Contributions Act, or "wages" subject to withholding, although taxable as gross income when received. Bureau of Internal Revenue Ruling 56–249, IR–156, May 29, 1956. *LRRM*, vol. 38 pp. 66–67.

was "wages" did not end the matter in some states. Accustomed to taking fringe benefits through the "wages" test to its allocation, a few states considered the question of allocability of SUB even after finding "no service" and that the payment was not "wages." Florida, for instance, found that SUB "...may not be allocated to any particular service or work, and can not, therefore, be treated as wages...."[59] But the payment could not be allocated to past service on the deferred wage theory, either. Although this would have made the employee eligible for unemployment compensation, it would have required the employer to pay taxes into the state unemployment compensation fund on the SUB payments. Only one state, Texas, found SUB to be "wages" and made such an allocation.[60]

SUB Reasoning Applies Equally to Other Fringe Benefits

Although most states found SUB not to be "wages," the many reasons given applied as well to other fringe benefits. In the first place, if a worker receiving SUB was not eligible for unemployment compensation unless he met the law's requirement that he be available for other work, as was so often pointed out, there seemed no reason why such a requirement could not be imposed upon the recipients of other terminal fringe benefit payments. Yet the administrators reasoned that the difference lay in the fact that for SUB the fringe benefit itself required adherence to the law's requirements.

Secondly, the absence of service after layoff quite obviously characterized receipt of other fringe benefits, and some administrators took note of the fact. Although Missouri stated that SUB was not "wages" because no service was given after layoff, it reported that the Missouri law defined vacation and holiday pay as disqualifying "wages." Illinois commented that "the personal services or 'personal efforts' factor was lacking" in the case of paid vacations, but then quoted a court case to explain that "the payment of unemployment compensation to a worker for a period of

[59]Florida General Counsel Memorandum, March 2, 1956. *SUB*, pp. 58–59.
[60]Texas Attorney General Opinion, No. WW–13. Jan 30, 1957. CCH, *op. cit.*, vol. 9, Texas, P 8201.

vacation with pay would not fulfill the purposes of the Act."[61] Wisconsin admitted that its law "includes as wages some payments made for weeks during which an employee performs no wage earning services," naming dismissal wages, vacation pay, and bonuses.[62]

Other reasons given why SUB was not "wages" have been discussed in Chapter 1. We need only note here that they, too, could have been found true of many other fringe benefits. For example, when it was said of SUB that "Wages are remuneration for services; the benefits under discussion are paid because services were lacking and are a form of insurance,"[63] and "...since the benefits are paid to the beneficiary not by the employer but by a trustee, the benefits are not wages,"[64] the non-wage finding could have applied as well to all other fringe benefits paid through trust funds. The argument that SUB payments were not "wages" because they were conditional in nature and were not vested could have been said of almost all fringe benefits.

When the states emphasized the social purpose of SUB, however, they described all fringe benefits the best. Missouri, for instance, said of SUB:

The features of the Plan appear to be quite in keeping with the aforementioned public policy. Certainly such supplemented benefits are no less for the public good and the general welfare of the people of this state when voluntarily provided by contract than when provided by the state....[65]

In saying this, it was suggesting standards by which all fringe benefits might be considered non-wage payments. Health and wel-

[61]Illinois Attorney General Opinion, p. 74. Texas noted that the laid-off employee "manifestly is performing no services. Hence, the applicant meets the first requirement that 'he perform no services'....A more difficult problem arises in determining whether payments under the Plan are 'wages,'..." It resolved the difficulties with the deferred wage theory and the payment was allocated to past services. Texas Attorney General Opinion. *Ibid.*

[62]Wisconsin Industrial Commissioners' Statement. June 1, 1956. *LRRM,* vol. 38, p. 96.

[63]Montana Official Interpretation No. 85.

[64]*Ibid.* Some states also added that the worker receiving SUB performs no services for the trustee. See *SUB,* p. 92 (Louisiana) and p. 197 (Washington).

[65]Missouri Attorney General Opinion, p. 116.

fare plans, paid vacations, and others certainly are "no less for the public good and the general welfare of the people." Paid holidays to free working people to celebrate the American Revolution and other historical and religious days together with the community could be held a laudable purpose. Certainly the various types of dismissal payments, like SUB and unemployment compensation, enable the worker to be more mobile in seeking other employment; and any fringe benefit adds to purchasing power at a time when it is needed. Sick leave and sickness benefits that raise the health level of the country could be found to deserve as much encouragement as private benefits that supplement legislation already in existence. This was especially true if, as was often said in SUB cases, private provision for economic hazards was to be encouraged "to meet the needs of our people." If SUB was non-wages because it voluntarily provided by contract what legislation had determined was public policy, then pensions, too, could be non-wages as they supplement and implement public policy expressed in the Social Security legislation.

Scarcely a fringe benefit exists that could not have been included in Montana's gratification that "big business will concern itself with the security of its employees and their families" and "assist workers to insure themselves against hazards of many kinds" and that "business and labor together can preserve the dignity of the worker in his job."

In the SUB rulings that came so close to discovering the "purpose" criterion which would have distinguished the non-wage social benefits from wage payments, there were also signs that the administrators were occasionally close to seeing a more restricted and more meaningful definition of "wages." Particularly when they noted that the absence of service after layoff suggested a non-wage payment, there seemed hope that the "pay for service" definition might be restored after its years of abuse. But the signs of hope went little further than hints, discussed in Chapter 1, that perhaps there were some payments "for" and some payments "because of" employment. Scarce as such hints were, they bear consideration.

The Wage Purpose as Pay for Service

In their efforts to prove that SUB was not "wages," a number of states found themselves struggling with the definition of "wages." A few states saw the definition as a broad one while at the same time indicating some reliance upon a narrower concept.

Oregon listed the following among its reasons why SUB was not "wages":

These amounts paid by the employer are not deducted from the wage or salary of the employee and they are not a part of his rate of pay.[66]

By this logic, of course, no fringe benefits are "wages,"[67] but more significant in these words was the suggestion, although perhaps not intentional, that *the rate of pay* might be a standard for determining "wages." Illinois noted of SUB:

...independent of such payment the employer's liability to pay the employee for personal services at the agreed wage scale has already been discharged.[68]

If this were so, then other fringe benefit payments were also independent of the wage obligation. Yet, Illinois covered itself by stating that "wages" could be defined broadly, restricted only "when it is necessary to conform to the legislative object and purpose of the unemployment insurance act."[69]

Despite the logic of restricting the broad interpretation of "wages," the trend seemed toward adding new fringe benefit payments to the legal definition of "wages." Idaho, in its SUB opinion in 1957 commented:

The crux of the entire matter under consideration revolves around the statutory definition of the term "wages." We are of the opinion

[66]Oregon Attorney General Opinion.

[67]The question only arises in regard to employer-paid fringe benefits, of course. When money is so deducted, the plan is called a contributory plan and the amount paid by the employee is not considered a payment directly or indirectly by the employer.

[68]Illinois Attorney General Opinion, p. 75. Similarly in a case involving pensions, the Maine Supreme Judicial Court said, "The employee had for many years performed daily assigned tasks which made up the manual routine of his job. For this he had been fully paid week by week the 'wages' which he had earned by his 'personal service.'" Dubois v. Maine Employment Security Commission.

[69]Illinois Attorney General Opinion, p. 74.

that the term "wages" must be restricted to remuneration received by an employee for work actually and directly done by him for an employer.[70]

But four years later, in 1961, the Idaho legislature added to the law the provision that pensions "shall be treated as wages."[71]

Some of the difficulties posed by a definition of "wages" that encompassed social benefits as well as the wage rate were recognized by the Maine Supreme Judicial Court in ruling SUB not to be wages:

If these benefits were in the category of wages then there would be two different wage scales to be determined, not on the basis of labor performed in the same job classification and like work history, but on the number of dependents of each worker. This standard of fixing wages would certainly present an incongruous situation.[72]

So the effort went to discover what "wages" really are in the age of fringe benefits. It would seem that a consideration of the purpose of each fringe benefit might be a quicker way to discover not only what fringe benefits are but also what "wages" are. Judging by the SUB experience, however, the catalyst would appear to be a disposition to find these payments not to be disqualifying "wages."

Even given the necessary disposition, the road back will be long and hard with so many fringe benefits now imbedded in the laws as "wages" or solidified as such in rulings from the highest state courts. The same struggle with meaningless terms goes on with respect to laws other than the one we have used for our example here. Such a struggle is currently going on over the proposed revisions of the Davis Bacon Act to include fringe benefits in its definition of "wages." It may be that the efforts to return to firm definitions must remain largely the result of varying political pressures. But if there is a desire for realism, for rationality to replace rationalizations, as there should be among all third parties, the key to that rationality may be found in a recognition of the importance of consulting fringe benefit purpose. The job of in-

[70]Idaho Attorney General Legal Opinion. August 16, 1957. *SUB*, pp. 64–65.
[71]CCH, *op. cit.*, vol. 4, Idaho, P 4012.
[72]Henry S. Malloch v. Employment Security Commission. Maine Supreme Judicial Court. March 18, 1963. CCH, *op. cit.*, vol. 5, Maine, P 8153.

terpreting and then dealing with fringe benefits realistically lies both with the administrators and courts and with the legislators.

If third parties are not to lose sight of the significance, as well as the purpose, of fringe benefits, the new type of employer obligation they represent must also be considered. Obsession with the "wages" concept of fringe benefits has obscured the fact that employers have assumed more than simply a larger "wage" obligation to pay more for service; they have assumed an additional "social" obligation. If a pension, for instance, is nothing more than the collection of past wages, as the current notion has it, then where is the employer's obligation to provide for his workers in their old age? Are these benefits "social obligations" only at the bargaining table, or, since negotiated benefits are most often called "wages," only when the employer voluntarily grants them? Or is there no such thing as a "social" as well as a "wage" obligation?

Fringe benefits have become the business of everyone. The movement is no longer a matter only of collective bargaining between unions and their employers. The "not legally due" classifications have been outgrown, as many states have recognized, now that these benefits are so widely provided voluntarily by employers as well as in labor agreements. It is important that we return in the final chapter to this two-dimensional nature of the fringe benefit movement, and consider the dynamics of its development and something more of its significance.

We return again to the two parties who created these troublesome fringe benefits.

CHAPTER 10

The Dynamics of Fringe Benefit Development

IN VIEW of the confusion between wages and non-wages described in Chapter 1, and seen again in practical terms in the last chapter, the need to introduce some order in the chaos is apparent. The rationale proposed in Chapter 2 distinguished non-wages from wages on the basis of the purpose for the payment. The non-wage, social nature of fringe benefits was described there, and the two-dimensional character of the fringe benefit movement was suggested.

In Chapters 3 through 7, the historical analysis of paid vacations through fifty years, from 1910 to 1960, traced the development of that fringe benefit in both dimensions. Up to World War II, vacations were a social benefit voluntarily provided by the employer to increase productivity. From World War II on, they were predominantly a social benefit as such, for which the unions took primary responsibility to improve and extend further as an employer obligation. Chapters 8 and 9 described the impact of the wages idea first on vacations and then on all fringe benefits. It is now time again to consider all fringe benefits, not as wages any more, but as the non-wage social benefits they are.

Not all fringe benefits have gone through both management and union phases as vacations did. Some began as employer benefits and are in many firms still in the management phase. Others have made their first appearance in the second phase. Arising from a union demand, they were immediately written into the contract where the employer's responsibility to provide the benefit was established.

In the union phase, fringe benefits follow a three-step pattern of development. The first step is winning recognition of the obligation by securing the benefit in the contract. At this step, the union often takes the benefit however it can be won, with all of the restrictions and qualifications that management feels are necessary to protect its productivity return. As was seen in the case of paid vacations, and as is frequently true in the case of pensions, the first contractual plans may be, word for word, the same as the previous management plans—simply written into the contract.

In the second step, the unions liberalize the benefit provided. In the third step, they work to eliminate the management qualifications and restrictions upon the right to the social benefit. Sometimes these two steps occur simultaneously, but generally the union is concerned first about the size of the benefit. In the case of paid vacations, for example, the desire to increase the length of vacations, a process that began in World War II and continued into the postwar period, preceded the later postwar effort to eliminate the management restrictions—principally the limitation of coverage to employees who could be expected to continue their employment and yield the employer a productivity return. By 1960, the effort to win terminal vacation pay clauses, particularly for those who quit or were discharged for cause, had not yet become a majority practice.

In the case of pensions, the unions usually choose first to put additional money not into vesting provisions but into higher benefits which withdrawals from the pension fund would endanger. Then they turn to elimination of the management restrictions on the right to pension payments, such as the requirement that an employee be still working for the employer at retirement time. In this third-step action, unions are now becoming more interested in provisions of this type and other forms of vesting or partial vesting, and some have already reached the status of majority practice.[1] In negotiating such provisions, the union is telling the

[1]"Pension Plans: Amount of Retirement Benefits," *AFL-CIO Collective Bargaining Report*, vol. 5, December 1960, pp. 73–78. This is a report of two BLS studies found in the *Monthly Labor Review* in October and November of 1960.

employer that the purpose of pensions is to provide for the old age of each individual whose services he has used, in proportion to the amount of service rendered him, and not to increase the employer's productivity through the use of pensions, for example, as an incentive to keep workers with him until retirement time.

Other fringe benefits have followed a similar pattern. For example, workers generally secure additional paid holidays in their contracts before they turn to eliminating the management qualifications upon the right to those holidays, such as the requirement that the day before and the day after a holiday be worked. As the unions turn toward eliminating this qualification, they are telling the employer that he must provide the holiday because it is a day which employees want to spend in patriotic or religious observances with their families and communities, and that it is not to be provided only on condition that continuity of production is maintained.

These are the three steps unions take to establish and extend the employer's obligation to provide social benefit to his workers. But why then, if it is true that all the unions' actions are a steady progression toward the imposition upon employers of a new, social obligation, is it the unions who so persistently call fringe benefits "wages"—which would imply no obligation at all beyond the employer's compensation for their actual service, the same obligation he has always had? The answer lies much deeper than simple expediency in winning arbitration cases, although on the surface this may appear to be the answer.

Unions Seek Equality of Social and Wage Obligations

The very newness of the social obligation the unions were imposing upon management required them, they felt, to call fringe benefits "wages" in order to win an acceptance of the social obligation equal to the acceptance the wage obligation enjoys both legally and in the general public attitude.

Prior to World War II, social benefits provided by employers were considered gratuities. As in the case of paid vacations, em-

---

Vesting in the form of guaranteeing that workers may keep accumulated pension rights even if they leave before retirement age, for instance, is reported as a majority practice. *Ibid.*, pp. 73–74.

ployees knew the social benefits were primarily employer benefits which could be withdrawn at any time. Employees had little or no control over their provision, their terms, or their conditions. This unreliability limited their value as a means of meeting social needs. Pensions were fine in good times, but what assurance had the worker that come hard times, when retirees had the greatest need for a pension, the company would not discontinue the plan? Past experience had seen many of these plans disappear. Those benefits arising before the 1920's (such as savings plans and Mutual Benefit Associations, including a few unemployment compensation plans) and those common in the 1920's (group life insurance and stock purchase plans, for example, as well as many pay-as-you-go pension plans) all were seen to vanish in the depression of the 1930's.[2] Even today there are warnings with respect to unfunded and pay-as-you-go pension plans which may not be able to meet their obligations when, as the plan matures, expenses rise sharply.[3] To protect against the vagaries of the business cycle which endanger their coverage of social needs, the employees have sought permanence and reliability first in making contractual arrangements and then in securing maximum control over the social benefits they have negotiated.

But even when fringe benefits are provided by contract, the employees have found that their claim to these social benefits still suffers from the old attitude toward them as gratuities. The benefits are simply "fringes"—not to be taken as seriously as the wage obligation of the employer. Fringe benefit money may or may not be considered a legal obligation of the employer, as, for instance, in case of bankruptcy. In general attitude, fringe benefits even provided by contract remain partially in the area of management control. The desire to have fringe benefit funds jointly administered is a reflection of the desire to win more control over benefits which are still not wholly accepted as belonging to the employees in the way in which the wages he wins at the bargaining

[2]George K. Barrett, manager, Employee Relations Division of Ohio Oil Company, "Where Are Fringe Benefits Taking Us?" *Addresses on Industrial Relations 1959 Series*, Bulletin No. 27, Bureau of Industrial Relations, University of Michigan, 1959, p. 1.

[3]Rev. Paul P. Harbrecht, *Pension Funds and Economic Power*, (New York: Twentieth Century Fund, 1959), p. 258.

table are. Although the contributory part of fringe benefit funds is irrevocably the employees', no such general attitude exists toward the non-contributory part the employer pays.

Yet the idea of a social obligation is a serious one, equal to the wage obligation in money terms in its origin at the bargaining table. Employees know or believe that they could have taken the fringe benefit cost in a further wage increase, where it would have been fully recognized as theirs and legally due them. But because the social obligation is not yet fully accepted, the employees find they have to call it wages to give it equality with wages. When deciding to put some of the money that is available at the bargaining table into social benefits, they do not altogether willingly give up an additional wage increase for partial ownership and little control over its social benefit alternative. They take the best they can get and then in subsequent negotiations take the next steps toward full recognition of the social obligation, including control over the terms and conditions of the benefits equal to the control they have over wages. It is in these steps that unions use the "wage" argument.

Once a pension plan, for example, is in the contract, the employees do not want its disposition left to the discretion of management. They first want control to assure the permanence of the plan. In order to have the assets permanently out of reach of the employers, the unions must persuade the courts to hold that pension fund assets belong to the employees. The best way to do so, the unions find, is to argue that the pensions are "deferred wages" and not gifts or gratuities from the employers.[4]

The employees also use the "wages" argument to maximize the benefits they will get for "their" money. They are concerned about the level of benefits relative to the cost and seek assurances that administrative costs are low and that over-funding does not tie up "their" money. This attitude, and the use of the "wages" concept to support it, are illustrated by the following fragment from a union report on pension plans:

Are they . . . [the pension plans] "over-funded?" How much money is "too much?" Why should companies put into their pension funds more money than is necessary? Do we care?

[4]*Ibid.*, p. 255.

The last question really comes first, and the answer is: yes, we do care. Money deposited in pension funds by companies (whether or not it passes through the employees' pay checks and gets a tax attached to it on the way) is part of wages—legally, morally and in the opinion of accountants and the Internal Revenue Service. The Unions, speaking for the employees, have consented to this "set-aside" of part of the employees' wages because they want some of their income to come to them in that way. But if twice as much money is being set aside as is required to provide the alternative form of income (in the form of pensions), then each employee (whether a participant or not) has suffered a loss of income.[5]

The "wages" argument to win equal protection for the social obligation has also appeared in support of proposed welfare and pension-plan disclosure legislation. Testifying in favor of federal government supervision over the resources of these funds, requiring detailed financial reports, and bringing all plans including those of doubtful legal status under the protection of the law to prevent embezzlement, kickbacks, and other threats to the funds, the unions argued as follows:

These funds belong to millions of wage and salary earners in the United States. They represent the right to future returns in the form of pensions, health care and other services for which they have given their labor as surely as they have worked for wages. They are, in fact, deferred wages. As such, they should be rigorously protected.[6]

Had the witness stopped after saying that the benefits were as much a right of workers as their right to wages, the union position would have been correctly stated. But it might not have been sufficiently persuasive; the witness felt it necessary to add the next two sentences in order to win for these social benefits some of the legal protection already provided for wages.

The argument, and the reason for it, were the same as in the terminal vacation pay arbitration cases. Believing that all workers are entitled to vacation pay whether they continue with the

[5]Research Department, Pulp, Sulphite and Paper Mill Workers. "Pension Analysis. A Comparative Study of Pension Plans in West Coast Pulp and Paper Companies," May 1, 1959, p. 28.

[6]Legislative Department, AFL-CIO, statement before the Subcommittee of the House Committee on Education and Labor on Welfare and Pension Plan Disclosure Legislation, May 25, 1961, p. 2.

employer or terminate their employment, the unions supported their arguments for terminal vacation pay with almost the very same words: "Workers have earned their vacations as surely as they have earned wages. They are, in fact, deferred wages." Similarly, the worker who seeks holiday pay despite a requirement that he work the day before and the day after a holiday will assert that such pay is "wages" and that, therefore, it is due him with no more restriction upon it than if he had taken it in wages. The basis of the argument, as the unions frequently pointed out, was that since the employees could have taken the money in wages instead of in fringe benefits, they have as much right to the social benefits as they have to their wages.

In some cases, unions saw the use of the word "wages" in a law as requiring that they call fringe benefits "wages" to win equal legal acceptance of the social obligation. The Bankruptcy Act, written long before the day of social obligations, provides priority claim in bankruptcy proceedings to workers' "wages." Legislation introduced in 1962, proposing a revision of that act to give the same priority to certain fringe benefits, did not propose that a social obligation be added to the wage obligation presently given priority, but proposed that these fringe benefit funds themselves be deemed "wages" in the act. The AFL-CIO urged favorable action, citing convention support in a resolution that illustrates the unions' desire for this equal legal recognition of social benefits. After describing the protection against economic hazards that the health and welfare funds give to millions of workers, the resolution finds these fringe benefits not to be "wages" but rather "are equivalent to wages paid in ready cash...." The resolution continues, saying that, to the worker, these payments

represent part of his pay which serve to provide him, and in many instances, his dependents, with insurance protection when confronted with illness, and security in old age, and, as such, these payments are a form of compensation just as real as the monies received in the weekly pay envelopes;...[7]

[7] Thomas E. Harris, AFL-CIO Associate General Counsel, Statement on H.R. 9191 before Subcommittee No. 4 (Bankruptcy) of the House Judiciary Committee, June 7, 1962, pp. 1-2.

Although urging favorable action on the legislation, the AFL-CIO did not directly say that these fringe benefits should be called "wages," but asked that they be accorded "the same priority accorded to direct wage payments made to workers as compensation for services rendered."[8]

The efforts to have fringe benefits included as "wages" in the Davis Bacon Act also represent a desire to have the social responsibilities of employers recognized as fully as the wage obligation. The "prevailing wage," the unions were saying, should include recognition of the employer's social obligations. But rather than changing the name of what was to prevail, it seemed easier simply to call the fringe benefits "wages," the term that has been in use since long before the fringe benefit movement.

Unions were in the anomalous position of calling fringe benefits "wages" precisely because they were not wages. The resulting conflict in the descriptions of the nature and purpose of fringe benefits that we noted in Chapter 1 was inevitable.

Of course, the problem would not have existed if the workers had taken the cost of fringe benefits in higher wage rates and bought their own social benefits. Presumably, they could then buy their own vacations whenever they wanted to, take whatever holidays the employer would allow them off their jobs, stay home when they were sick, pay their own doctor bills, save up for their own old age, buy their own insurance, even feel somewhat richer from their higher wages when they had to work overtime. There would be no employer obligation, but the worker would have had full title and control over the money he used to purchase his social benefits. Even the savings of pooled funds could still be realized by negotiating wholly contributory plans. Such plans would have had full recognition and legal protection, as the contributory part of a fringe benefit plan does now. The Wisconsin unemployment compensation law, for instance, has long provided legal status for contributory SUB plans. Wisconsin noted in its opinion on employer-financed SUB plans:

If the negotiations had resulted in the employee receiving the money directly, namely, 5 cents per hour, and then agreeing to put it into

[8]*Ibid.,* p. 2.

258

a fund to cover supplemental or additional unemployment benefits, it would be exactly the type of plan sanctioned by Section 108.11 (2).[9]

But the trend is not toward contributory plans; it is away from them. In a few cases, in fact, unions have even negotiated provisions under which the employers pay the employees' share of the Social Security tax.[10] The employees see these social costs as properly the costs of industry, of the individual employers who use their services, rather than their own. They decline to increase their employer's wage obligation in payment for their actual service in order to increase his social obligation to them.

But if the unions have been imposing and extending an employer social obligation in the three steps they follow in negotiations on fringe benefits, and if even the unions' "wages" argument is basically an effort to win full and equal acceptance of that new obligation, then what of these same social benefits when they are voluntarily provided by employers in the absence of a contract? What do they represent? It is time to consider the employer dimension of this two-dimensional fringe benefit movement.

Employer-Instituted Fringe Benefits as Social Obligation

Unions led the demand for fringe benefits during World War II because they were organized to petition the War Labor Board for these benefits. After the war, their "package" settlements set a fast pace. But unions alone do not account for the wide extent of fringe benefit coverage. Employers during all these years have been adopting fringe benefits even where no unions threatened. As noted in Chapter 2, employers adopt fringe benefits for the purpose of increasing productivity directly or indirectly and in some cases for certain tax advantages. The employer, however, carefully controls the terms and conditions and keeps the fringe benefit sufficiently qualified to protect the return he expected in initially incurring the cost. Technically, he is free to reduce or eliminate a fringe benefit at any time that he finds its cost not worth the

[9]Wisconsin Industrial Commissioners' Statement, June 1, 1956. Bureau of National Affairs, *Labor Relations Reference Manual* (Washington: BNA, 1935 to date), vol. 38, p. 97.

[10]"Social Security Put on the Bargaining Table," *NAM News,* May 27, 1960, Section 2, p. 1, col. 1.

return; his provision of the social benefit does not represent any assumption on his part of an obligation to provide for his employees' social welfare off the job, as does the contractual provision of a fringe benefit.

In reality, however, the distinction between fringe benefits in the management phase and those in the union phase is not so clear-cut. The fringe benefit movement as a whole, in both its dimensions, quite generally represents an employer responsibility to provide for his workers' social welfare. We may draw several lessons from our vacation study to illustrate why this is true.

First is the difference that employee demand makes to the employer's freedom to withdraw fringe benefits he has voluntarily provided. We may recall from Chapter 3 that the adoption of vacation plans to attract and keep labor during the prosperous 1920's assumed an employee demand for vacations that did not then exist. Employers were able to, and did, drop these plans during the depression without reaction from workers.

In contrast, there is today a sharply different attitude toward all fringes. The present interest in and demand for fringe benefits did not exist for vacation plans, or any fringe benefits, in the 1920's. The effect of this demand alone means that employers who in the past fifteen or twenty years have been providing fringe benefits as a means of attracting and keeping labor may find themselves unable to get rid of them when the labor market is no longer tight.

Second, the extensive coverage itself, whether employer-initiated or union-initiated, creates additional demand. Management created the vacation demand by its voluntary provision of vacation coverage during several decades of employee disinterest in paid vacation plans. But when this management coverage of wage earners approached the 50 percent mark in the late 1930's, employee and union demands for vacation plans appeared. Only a few years later, when the War Labor Board denied further wage increases, paid vacations were one of the first fringe benefits the unions turned to. By the end of the war, with over 90 percent coverage, annual vacations were considered a necessary part of working conditions.

The same result will follow as today's fringe benefits increase their coverage. A demand is created for each benefit on the part of workers not covered, and these fringes, too, will come to be considered an essential part of working conditions, not to be denied by any employer, organized or unorganized. Pensions are already on their way to being so considered, and few unorganized employers can fail to provide some sickness benefits for their workers. Few non-union employers can keep their employees at work on holidays when the majority of other workers are home. Given the demand by workers for social benefits and extensive coverage, employers with or without unions will not be able to withdraw them easily.

Third, provision of social benefits becomes an industry obligation in general conception, whether initiated by union action or by the employer voluntarily. The voluntary provision of paid vacation plans was taken as the employer's recognition of a responsibility to provide each worker with an annual rest period. As Chapter 7 showed, the public came to feel that every worker was owed such a rest by his employer; and arbitrators and courts reflected this attitude in ruling that workers whose employment was terminated also were due vacation pay, even if the vacation plan did not expressly provide it. In fact, third parties did not believe that employers could have intended their plans to exclude these workers, so strong was the feeling about his obligation.

Other fringe benefits will come to be regarded in the same way. It will then be said of them as was said of vacations:

In present day labor relations the granting of a vacation period to workers is so widely accepted that no industry or Company can claim to be exempt from the propriety of this practice. . . . The Company claims that it is not financially able to grant vacations with pay. Today, however, common practice decrees, in general, that those who employ workers assume the general obligation of granting them vacations.[11]

Arbitrators and courts who believe provision of a given social

[11]*In re* J. Zwerdling Bakery, Inc. *and* International Brotherhood of Teamsters, Local 145, AFL. Board of Arbitration: Joseph Donnelly, chairman; Samuel Curry, representing employees; and Warren L. Mottram, representing employers. August 20, 1948, clarification dated Oct. 11, 1948. Bureau of National Affairs, *Labor Arbitration Reports* (hereafter referred to as *LA*) (Washington: BNA, 1946 to date), vol. 11, p. 445.

benefit is management's obligation and part of his proper cost of doing business will rule that other fringe benefits are due, even if not clearly so provided in the contract. And where no contract exists, past practice may come to be taken as the employer's acknowledgment of his obligation to provide the social benefit. The time may come when an unorganized employer who tries to withdraw a benefit the workers have taken as an acknowledged responsibility of the employer may find his workers rising up in righteous wrath. If they do not organize on the spot, they may, collectively or individually, take their case to the courts where they might well expect a favorable ruling. Or the resentment which such a withdrawal of an accustomed social benefit stirs up may simply persuade the employer that it is more to his advantage to restore it.

Employers themselves have been influenced by the extent to which this feeling about their social responsibilities already prevails. At a management conference on fringe benefits, one spokesman observed:

Managements need to ask themselves some rather fundamental questions and try to work out the answers. Some of these questions are:

1. Is the Company obligated...to the employee: To provide income when he is sick or injured? To provide means for paying his medical expenses when he or a member of his family is sick or injured? To provide an income when for reasons of age or disability he can no longer measure up to his job? To help him prepare for a different way of life in "retirement?" To provide income during unemployment which cannot be considered to be his own fault? To encourage him to prepare and save for other emergencies, for the education of his children, for his comfort in his old age? and to his family: To provide income after his death?

2. If the answer to any of the above is "yes," an even more difficult question, perhaps, is "To what extent?"

3. What should the Company receive in return for meeting these obligations, if indeed they are obligations?

4. How well are present benefit plans meeting the needs of employees? What have they achieved for the Company? Where are they weak? Where are they perhaps too liberal?[12]

[12]Victor M. Zink, Personnel Staff, General Motors Corporation, "Where Are Fringe Benefits Taking Us?" *Addresses on Industrial Relations 1959 Series.* p. 9.

Thus, under the dynamics of fringe benefit development, the distinction gradually is being erased between the two dimensions of the movement. It is the employee demand for these benefits that makes the difference; as the demand grows, increased by the very extensiveness of the coverage, the social benefits become an industry obligation in the minds of workers and the public, including third parties in industrial relations, and even to some extent in the minds of the employers.

Fringe benefits become a more or less permanent part of the employer-employee relationship. In a depression, many fringe benefits provided by contract will be negotiated downward or will disappear completely as contracts are lost. But many of the fringe benefits voluntarily provided by employers will not be withdrawn, even though the employer may find no further productivity value in them. Those to go will be those that are least in demand, least broad in their effects, least extensive in their coverage, of least benefit to the employers. But many fringe benefits, beginning with those most in demand and most extensively provided, will be considered a permanent part of the employer-employee relationship and an obligation of the employer equal to his obligation to pay wages for service.

Some Implications—Public and Private

Many years of industrial assistance to employees to meet social needs and to prepare for the economic hazards of illness, layoff, unemployment, and old age create a public belief that these are proper costs of industry and no longer costs exclusively of the individual. But what of those who receive no coverage from industry for these social costs, either voluntarily or by contract? The more extensive the coverage of social needs privately, the more apparent it will become that the most needy groups of workers have the least assistance with social costs. Both parties and the public have a responsibility to those who are left out of the beneficent private provision for social needs.

As the fringe benefit movement began, it reached first those workers, generally speaking, in the high-productivity and highly organized industries already enjoying a relatively high standard of living and relatively better able to take the shocks of unemployment, displacement, and ill health and to prepare themselves for their retirement years. The movement, in its second dimension, extended the fringe benefits more broadly, reaching workers in many industries of low productivity. The public has generally favored this extension of fringe benefits, as it favored the union "package" settlements, in the belief that they were not as inflationary as direct wage increases. Thus broadly sponsored, the fringe benefit movement has gone far in reducing social burdens. But the public and the parties have shown less concern about those who do not have such social assistance from an employer. Legislation to cover them has been as neglected as proposals to provide publicly what has been provided privately.

As noted in Chapter 2, legislation was not really an alternative to private development of the fringe benefit movement for political reasons. It is doubtful that equivalent social legislation would actually have been passed in the last fifteen years. When employers chose to oppose social legislation they knew the greater advantage to themselves of privately assuming these social costs. Besides certain tax advantages, they could realize greater benefit from providing their own workers with social benefits directly, advantages they could not have realized through taxation to provide social gains broadly. Employers are well aware of the value of keeping the cost and the benefit close to the individual worker, as this comment indicates:

I suggest that the sixties must be management's decade so far as employee plans are concerned. The needs for improvement and better design of plans are obvious. We know that our employees want protection against emergencies. It has been stated that they want security, but I do not believe that is a correct statement. They want planned protection against emergencies. The cost of such emergencies has always been paid, in one way or another; the question for us is "How can the burden best be paid by our society?" I believe the best way is to have the cost appear as close as possible to the individual who benefits.

I believe that unless we throw this program back to the individual, unless we let him know what his program is and how it really works, a future speaker looking back over the 1960's may not be able to call that period Management's Decade.[13]

This attitude must be taken into account by those who have argued that management, when "burdened" with enough of these fringe benefit costs, will favor government assumption of some of them. It reflects the employer's traditional reluctance to yield to any enlargement of the government's role in these matters. If, on the other hand, the unions' private successes have blunted their concern for those who have been left out, there is serious question whether the private fringe benefit movement, for all its emphasis on industry's social obligations, will lay the basis for public measures or will present a roadblock to public coverage.

It is obvious that the whole social benefit development has implications beyond the parties immediately involved. Not all of the implications are pleasing to those who would see social benefits carefully planned and broadly distributed. But here it is, and those who deplore our national failure to put more of our wealth into social gains can do better than to ignore this movement, to belittle it, or to see it solely as a substitution for public effort. Rather than blinding themselves to the social nature of the movement by calling it "wages" in payment for actual services rendered, third parties should be adding whatever guidance they can give to its direction. The public should have a larger voice and influence in the fringe benefit movement than it currently chooses to give.

One example of the need for guidance is on the subject of control of medical and hospital costs. These rising costs depreciate not only the benefits of those workers receiving them, but more importantly the ability of those without any health and welfare coverage to meet their health costs so greatly increased as one of the direct results of the extensive fringe benefit coverage of these costs.

Another example is the growth of pension funds and the problems associated with the accumulation and investment of such funds, problems that are beginning to receive attention in some quarters but that need much more. Useful study has also begun, and more should be forthcoming, on the role of government tax

[13]Barrett, *op. cit.,* p. 9.

policies in encouraging one part or another of the fringe benefit movement. New fringe benefits attempting to find solutions to the problems of technological displacement have a special need for direction and guidance. Not yet so important but of growing magnitude is the question of corporate contributions to colleges and to scholarship funds for employees and non-employees alike. As yet this has not become a common subject of bargaining, but perhaps it may, particularly as the need is recognized by organized workers and the federal government fails to provide assistance. There is room to give direction in these and many other ways.

The private social benefit movement is a dynamic and restless development. It will continue to expand its limbs and throw out branches. The form its growth takes can be shaped in socially desirable or socially undesirable ways. It behooves social critics to do more than deplore a force so creative and so typical of the national penchant for private and pluralistic solutions.

The battle between employees, seeking to establish and extend an employer social obligation, and employers, seeking to preserve their qualifications on these fringes for their own benefit, will go on. Each party will continue to call fringe benefits "wages" when its interests are advanced by so doing.

While third parties have called fringe benefits "wages" from much the same motives as the employees or, in other cases, the employers, they cannot be excused as readily since their interest is not so directly involved. Third parties need to keep in mind what one of them has said:

The recorded provisions of Labor Agreements are not merely exercises in semantics subject to abstract interpretation by impartial outsiders whenever the signatories to such Agreements reach an impasse.... Rather, such provisions are expressions of understandings and "meetings-of-the-minds" reached between the parties and recorded to guide their future relationships.[14]

If third parties, arbitrators or administrators, are to make fair and lasting decisions, they need to give more consideration to the

[14]Baugh & Sons Co., Philadelphia Plant, *and* International Chemical Workers Union, Local 128, AFL. Board of Arbitrators: G. Allen Dash, Jr., chairman; J. E. Weer, employer-appointed arbitrator; and G. P. Raber, union-appointed arbitrator. August 16, 1954. *LA*, vol. 23, p. 180.

intentions of the parties in negotiating the fringe benefits and show less concern for expedient arguments. The "great weight of authority" which the third party pronouncements have in the practical world spreads to others who are not in close enough contact with the two parties to be able to discern the truth of the matter. Both courts and legislators must rely to a great extent upon their opinions. There is little hope for improvement in the laws if the terms or intent of the laws are being misunderstood and misinterpreted or if, in reverse, the parties' intentions are being misread and frustrated. Legislators need to know how their laws are working out in actual practice and how they suit reality in order to be able to revise them wisely.

For economists there is a particular challenge. Instead of trying to fit fringe benefits into an outdated framework of wage determination, economists need to develop a wage concept that recognizes the significance of this new form of employee income. They need to find a place for payments made to workers "because of" and not "for" employment, however difficult it makes their job of analyzing "wage" structures. The legislators need their guidance in redefining terms to suit the fringe benefit age in order that the laws may better say what they mean in carrying out public policy, without the confusion and misunderstanding that now exist.

The public has a vague but accurate realization of what the purpose of each of these fringe benefits is, but it is the parties themselves, for all their expedient arguments in one or another case, who know best what they have negotiated. A renewed effort to understand the nature of the fringe benefit movement requires that we keep in close touch with the two parties, always inquiring as to what they are seeking.

Because they have led the fringe benefit movement, the unions are in the best position to say what these fringe benefits intend and what their nature and their significance are. It is time that they acted less as an interested party entitled to use any argument that is successful in the short run and considered the long-run advantages of telling the truth about their fringe benefits. The story needs to be told to their own members, to the public at large, and particularly to the third party representatives of the public with whom they deal. Fringe benefits are not a form of wages in payment for actual personal services but represent a new, non-wage social obligation.

The significant result of twenty years of bargaining has been a transformation of the employer-employee relationship: those who hire the labor of others now have taken on certain social responsibilities pertaining to the needs of the man in his life off the job and in the society of which he is a part. Thus, the employer has two obligations attendant upon his use of his employees' services: the first is to compensate them adequately for the actual service they render and the second is to assume certain obligations of a social nature essentially unrelated to production.

Index

Absenteeism, 61, 64
Accrual principle, *see* Vacations, accrual principle
Accumulated vacations, *see* Vacations, accumulated
Aggregate value concept, *see* Vacations, aggregate value concept
Arbitrability of vacations, *see* Vacations, arbitrability
Area practice, *see* Vacations, prevailing practice
Awards, 37, 41

B

Ball teams, *see* Recreational facilities
Bankruptcy, 7, 11, 195–196, 201, 254, 257–258
Bonuses, 38, 41, 246; *see also* Vacations, as bonus

C

Call-in pay, 41, 155; *see also* Reporting pay
Central vacation funds, *see* Vacation funds, central
Closeness to management, *see* Vacations, closeness to management
Clubrooms, *see* Recreational facilities
Coffee breaks, *see* Time off
Commissions, 41
Company doctor, nurse, 37, 38, 41
Construction industry, 11, 17, 156
Contingent nature of fringes, 16–18, 246
"Continuous service," 59, 81–82, 87–88, 129, 161–164, 168–174, 177, 182
Contributory plans, 258–259; vacation, 57, 207
Counsellors, 37, 38, 41

D

Davis-Bacon Act, 7, 11, 17, 258
Death in family, *see* Time off
Deferred wages, 13, 57, 187, 191–192, 221, 227–229, 245, 256, 257; theory described, 188–217
Discounts, 37, 41
Dismissal payments, 14, 15, 41, 229, 230, 232, 233, 246, 247

E

Earned right, 90, 92, 126, 127, 131–152, 158–187, 190–191, 193; *see also* Vacations, as earned right
Economic hazard protection, 35–37, 263–264

Economic Stabilization, directives, 106, 147
Embassy Restaurant case, 11
Employment costs, 37
Employment stability, 49–50, 60–64, 66, 69, 74, 80–81, 87, 94, 101

F

Fair Labor Standards Act, 7, 31
Forfeiture clauses, *see* Vacations, forfeiture clauses

G

Galbraith, 3
Graduated vacation plans, *see* Vacation plans, graduated
Gratuities, 8, 19, 38, 41, 89, 178n, 205n, 225, 242, 253–254, 255
Green, William, 93

H

Health and welfare plans, 4, 14, 17, 26, 28, 36, 38, 41, 155, 246–247, 256, 265
Holidays, 9, 16, 20, 26, 32, 34, 41, 155, 212, 223, 226, 230, 231, 232, 245, 247, 253, 257, 261

I

Incentive earnings, 41
Industrial psychology, 38
Industry practice, *see* Vacations, prevailing practice
In-lieu-of-notice payments, 20, 33, 40, 41, 233–234
Internal Revenue, 7, 39, 199, 201, 202, 244, 245
Irregular employment, 80, 84, 117–124, 134, 137, 198, 211, 228, 238

J

Jury duty, *see* Time off

L

Labor, attract or keep, 39, 260; *see also* Vacation plans, to attract or keep labor
Labor cost, 5, 37–41
Labor-Management Relations Act, 7
Labor shortage, 39, 60, 65
Legislation, 7, 26–28, 36–37, 217, 246–247
Liberalization, of vacation plans, 113, 114, 155–156, 189; all fringe benefits, 252–253
Life insurance, 41, 254
Little Steel Formula, 104, 105, 110
Loyalty and morale, 61–64

M

Make-whole principle, *see* Vacation pay
Meal periods, *see* Time off
Mutual Benefit Associations, 254

N

National Defense Mediation Board, 99, 124
National health insurance, 4, 26

National Labor Relations Act, 201
Nierotko case, 9, 10, 19
Night-shift differentials, 32, 33, 41; *see also* Shift differentials

O

Office of Production Management, 99
Office workers, 42, 48–55, 71–72, 74, 77; *see also* Salaried workers
"On the payroll," 59, 87, 119–122, 129, 148–152, 161–164, 168–174, 177, 182
Overtime, 30–31, 33, 41, 212

P

Passes, 37, 41
Paternalism, 38, 62, 64
Penalty-premiums, 30–33
Pensions, 3, 4, 36, 41, 233, 252–253, 261; contractual, 26, 252, 254, 255–256;
    earned right, 155, 159; non-contributory, 28; trust funds, 18; wages or
    non-wages, 12, 13, 16, 17, 18, 20, 21, 223, 230, 247, 249
Personal leave, *see* Time off
Personnel administration, 37, 41
Piece rate, 41
Pieceworkers, *see* Vacations, for pieceworkers
Pooled vacation funds, *see* Vacation funds, central
Premiums, 30–33
Prevailing practice, vacations, *see* Vacations, prevailing practice
Prizes, 37, 41
Productivity increase, 26, 37–41, 64, 79, 82, 94, 100–101, 107, 116, 123–124,
    125, 127, 130, 139, 140, 141, 142–143, 151, 166, 181, 183–185, 204, 205,
    259–260; *see also* Work-force efficiency
Psychological gap, *see* Vacations, psychological gap
Purpose criterion (to distinguish non-wages from wages), 18–21, 23, 29–43,
    204–208, 232–235, 240–249

R

Recreational facilities, 37, 38, 41; ball teams, 37, 41; clubrooms, 37
Regular employees, vacations, *see* Vacations, for regular employees
Reporting pay, 32, 33, 40, 41; *see also* Call-in pay
Rest periods, *see* Time off
Rewards, *see* Vacations, as rewards

S

Safety programs, 37, 41
Salaried workers, 68–69, 175; *see also* Office workers
Savings plans, 56, 254
Scheduling of vacations, by employee, 236–239; by employer, 238; by unem-
    ployment agencies, 235–239; by unions, 238
Scholarship funds, 4, 266
Seasonal employment, *see* Irregular employment
Service basis of fringe benefits, 12–13, 30, 33, 34, 35, 36, 173–174, 183, 192,
    208–211; *see also* Wages, as payment attached to service; *see also* Wages,
    defined as pay for service
Severance pay, 12, 13, 14, 16, 20, 40, 41, 132–136, 139, 145, 223, 226, 228,
    234, 235; *see also* Terminal vacation pay

Shift differentials, 212; *see also* Night-shift differentials
Shorter hours, 31, 84
Sick leave, 26, 34, 38, 39, 41, 155, 212, 231, 247
Sickness and accident disability benefits, 17, 19, 247, 261
"Social," defined, 29, 29n
Social obligation, 4, 27–29, 42, 89, 91, 93, 146, 157–158, 172, 189, 207–208, 217, 250, 251–253, 259–263, 268
Social security, 3, 7, 26, 28, 41, 259
Social welfare, 38, 62
Split vacations, *see* Vacations, split
"Standard plan," *see* Vacations, "standard plan"
Standing by, pay for, 230, 232
Stock purchase plans, 254
SUB, *see* Supplementary unemployment benefits
Supplementary unemployment benefits (SUB), 3, 10, 12, 16, 19, 28, 36, 41, 229, 240–249, 252–253, 254, 255–256, 261; Contributory plans, 258–259

T

Technological displacement, 4, 32, 266
Terminal vacation pay, 59, 69, 91–92, 121, 122, 124, 127, 129–152, 158–187, 188–217, 223, 225, 227, 231, 232, 235–240, 247, 252, 256–257, 261; at layoffs, 132–136, 137, 145, 146; at military leave, 130–132, 135, 137, 146, 148; at quits and discharge for cause, 136–145, 149; no fault of employee's, 135, 142–145, 183, 203; prorata, 130, 131, 133, 134, 136, 137, 138, 139, 142–146, 152, 160–161, 173–177, 193, 202; *see also* Severance pay
Time off, 34–35; coffee breaks, 35, 41; death in family, 34; holidays, *see* Holidays; jury duty, 34, 41; meal periods, 35, 41; personal leave, 34; rest periods, 35, 41; vacations, *see* Vacations; voting time, 34, 41; wash-up time, 35, 41
Training programs, 37, 38, 41
Travel time, portal to portal, 35, 41
Trust funds, 16–18, 246, 254–255, 265; *see also* Vacation funds, central
Turnover costs, 39, 60–61

U

Unemployment compensation, 3, 7, 9, 16, 19, 41, 196, 201, 216, 222–249, 254; eligibility to, defined, 222–224, 226, 227, 235, 243–244

V

Vacation funds, central, 92, 119, 121–122, 228, 258
Vacation pay, 59, 146, 190, 198, 211–214, 223; at termination, *see* Terminal vacation pay; calculation of, 176, 189, 198, 211–214; in lieu of vacation clauses, 32, 41, 69, 78, 82, 87, 99, 100, 108–111, 156, 215; make-whole principle, 189, 211–214
Vacation plans, contributory, *see* Contributory plans; coverage, 42–43, 48–49, 68–70, 74–75, 84–88; demand for, 88–92, 101–103, 125–126, 260–263; employee disinterest in, 67–68, 83–84, 93; graduated, 49, 61, 81; instituted by management, 68, 85–88, 128, 150; in union agreements, 14–15, 39,

40, 68–70, 73, 85–88, 128–129, 252–256; liberalization of, *see* Liberalization; to attract or keep labor, 39, 60; union disinterest, 67–71, 73, 83–85; unionism, effect, 39–40, 70–71, 75–76, 95, 103, 125–126, 128–129, 136, 252–258, 260–261; *see also* Vacations

Vacations, 4, 12, 15, 16, 17, 20, 23, 26, 32, 34, 41, 42–43, 47–217, 223, 225–228, 230, 232, 245, 246, 247, 261; absenteeism, *see* Absenteeism; accrual principle, 174–176, 197–198; accumulated, 82, 156, 215; aggregate value concept, 123–124, 137; arbitrability, 195; as bonus, 58, 71, 93, 99, 100, 114, 117, 131–132, 136, 228; as earned right, 90, 92, 126, 127, 131–152, 158–187, 190–191, 193; as gratuities, *see* Gratuities; as rewards, 60, 62, 67, 72, 140; as social obligation, *see* Social obligation; as vested right, *see* Vesting; as wages, 15, 20, 23, 71–73, 104, 105, 106, 133, 145–148, 189–217, 225–227, *see also* Wages; closeness to management, 48–49, 74, 94; "continuous service," *see* "Continuous service"; eligibility, *see* "On the payroll," *see also* "Continuous service," *see also* Work requirements; employment stability, *see* Employment stability; for irregular employees, *see* Irregular employment; for piece workers, 49, 53, 60; for regular employees, 81, 87, 94, 118–120, 121, 150, 174; for seasonal workers, *see* Irregular employment; forfeiture clauses, 87, 163, 177, 179–182, 183, 210–211; in central or pooled funds, *see* Vacation funds, central; in trust funds, *see* Trust funds; liberalization of, 113, 114, 155–156; morale and loyalty, 61–64; office workers, *see* Office workers; "on the payroll," *see* "On the payroll"; prevailing practice, 112–113, 115, 116, 117, 123, 137, 148–149, 152, 159–161, 179; psychological gap, 51–53, 74, 94; purpose of, *see* Purpose criterion; rest purpose, 26, 34, 147, 156, 204–208, 215, 216; salaried workers, *see* Salaried workers; scheduling of, *see* Scheduling of vacations; service basis, 173–174, 183, 192, 208–211; split, 82, 87; "standard plan," 112–113, 116, 156; to increase productivity, *see* Productivity increase; work requirements, *see* Work requirements; work-sharing, 49, 56, 74, 94; *see also* Vacation plans

Vesting, 16–18, 129, 180, 194, 198, 246, 252

Voting time, *see* Time off

W

Wage, guaranteed annual, 230, 241n

Wages, as all income, 9–12, 192n, 200–202; as hourly rate, 8, 12, 13, 23, 29–30, 37, 41, 191–192, 200, 202, 248–249; as pay for service, 8–9, 29–30, 37, 191–192, 200–208, 215, 216, 222, 247–249; as payments attached to service, 12–13, 33, 34, 36, 223–224, 227–232, 244–246; as payments legally due, 12, 13–15, 192–194, 195, 204, 208–209, 216, 250, 254–257

Walsh-Healey Public Contracts Act, 7

War Labor Board, 25, 99–152, 155, 157, 165, 189–190, 236, 259

War Manpower Commission, 107, 145

War Production Board, 107

Wash-up time, *see* Time off

Work-force efficiency, 37–41, 47, 49, 53–57, 59, 60

Workmen's compensation, 28, 41

Work requirements, 82, 119, 120, 121, 162, 183

Work-sharing, *see* Vacations, work-sharing

OTHER SCHOOL PUBLICATIONS

Italy: School for Awakening Countries, by Maurice F. Neufeld. 600 pp. $9.00.

Jobs and Workers in India, by Oscar A. Ornati. 236 pp. $1.50.

Governmental Regulation of Industrial Relations, by Hywell Evans. 128 pp. 75¢.

The Historical Sources of Personnel Work: An Annotated Bibliography, by Frank B. Miller and Mary Ann Coghill. 116 pp. $1.00.

Business Leadership in Air Transportation, by Ralph N. Campbell and Elizabeth Knowlton. Processed. $1.00.

Labor Education Outside the Unions: A Review of Postwar Programs in Western Europe and the U. S., by Alice H. Cook and Agnes M. Douty. 148 pp. 50¢.

American Labor Union Periodicals: A Guide to Their Location, compiled by Bernard G. Naas and Carmelita S. Sakr. 192 pp. $7.00.

Employers' Associations and Collective Bargaining in New York City, by Jesse T. Carpenter. 437 pp. $1.50.

Heritage of Conflict: Labor Relations in the Nonferrous Metals Industry up to 1930, by Vernon H. Jensen. 508 pp. $1.50.

PUBLISHED BY

**THE NEW YORK STATE SCHOOL OF
INDUSTRIAL AND LABOR RELATIONS**

*A Contract College of the State University
Cornell University, Ithaca, New York*